INTERNATIONAL DEVELOPMENT IN FOCUS

Tales of Peasants, Traders, and Officials

Contracting in Rural Andhra Pradesh, 1980-82

CLIVE BELL

WORLD BANK GROUP

Contents

Foreword

I am doubly pleased to write the foreword to this volume by Clive Bell on rural organization in Andhra Pradesh, India, in memory of T. N. Srinivasan. First, T. N. was a cherished and valuable colleague, both at Yale University, where we both taught, and before, as he was one of the pioneers in my field of research, international trade. T. N. combined the highest standards of theoretical and empirical rigor with a deep concern for policy and people, especially in his native India. This volume reflects both those attributes by laying out an analytical framework for contracting in labor, land, and credit markets in a rural setting, followed by interviews and observations of landlords, tenants, laborers, creditors, and borrowers in 14 villages in two districts in Andhra Pradesh. Each component enhances the other. The analytical framework provides a backdrop for understanding and interpreting the narratives of the villagers. Meanwhile, the interviews and anecdotes lead to important nuances and extensions of the analytical framework, so that the research advances.

The second reason I am pleased to be writing this foreword is that this volume represents the type of work I championed while at the World Bank. In academia, we develop theoretical models and then estimate them using some of the most sophisticated techniques. The World Bank engages with policy makers around the world to improve development outcomes. The World Bank's research complex, which I headed, bridges these two cultures. We can bring the best academic tools, insights, and findings to bear on the policy problems of developing countries. At the same time, the engagement with policy makers turns up questions and puzzles that we had not thought of while sitting in our university offices. The interplay enriches both communities.

This monograph builds that bridge in the form of a travelogue—based on trips taken almost 40 years ago—that makes the reader's experience richer and more vivid. When speaking with villagers about their experience with contracts, the interviewers cannot be sure of the information they are getting. In one incident, a villager claimed to have lent money to another person who, when he was interviewed, denied ever taking a loan from the first person. It turns out that the money had been lent to the second person's wife, who had neglected to tell her husband about it. Some marital strife ensued, and the researchers decided to stop cross-checking loan contracts.

The two travelogues from four decades ago also bear witness to the rapid growth and transformation in Andhra Pradesh since that time. For instance, the "farm servant" featured in many of the interviews is hardly an occupation today. In that sense, this monograph, although it describes the complex interactions among labor, land, and credit markets that people living in extreme poverty have to undertake, also offers a hopeful message. Millions of people in Andhra Pradesh have escaped poverty, thanks in part to the rigorous analysis, empirical corroboration, and policy applications described herein—a fitting tribute to the life and career of T. N. Srinivasan.

Pinelopi Goldberg
Former Chief Economist
World Bank Group

Elihu Professor of Economics
Yale University

Preface

The late T. N. Srinivasan was a scholar and economist of the first rank, an esteemed teacher, and a tireless advocate of reforms to improve the common weal. This monograph is dedicated to his memory.

In writing it, I have accumulated various debts, first and foremost to Srinivasan himself, who conceived the project (RPO671-89) that ultimately yielded this monograph, engaged the Indian collaborating institutions, steered the proposal through separate bureaucratic mazes, and harnessed me with him to see it through. T. V. S. Rao, then director of the Agro-Economic Research Centre, Waltair, accompanied me on the two tours described in chapters 2 and 3. His profound knowledge of, and insights into, rural life in Andhra Pradesh were invaluable. I must also mention, though I may not name, the scores of villagers and officials who answered our questions with patience and a fair measure of good humor.

Shortly after Srinivasan's death, I brought this material to the attention of Shantanayan Devarajan, former senior director for Development Economics at the World Bank; he responded by encouraging me to work it into a full monograph. Hans Gersbach, Magnus Hatlebakk, and an anonymous referee read and commented on a draft and responded to revisions. Their constructive suggestions led to great improvements. Penny Goldberg, a longtime colleague of Srinivasan's at Yale, found time from her weighty duties to write a gracious foreword honoring him. To all of them, I express my warm thanks, while absolving them of any responsibility for errors of analysis and opinion. The disclaimer applies to the World Bank itself, as this product of a funding decision taken decades ago comes back to roost.

It is fitting to close with an anecdote from those travels 40 years ago. T.N. and I were returning to Hyderabad at the end of a deep foray into Mahbubnagar District when our taxi spluttered, coughed, died, and resisted the driver's efforts to revive it. At length, we got out. It was pitch black and there was no traffic. A truck, doubtless overloaded like most trucks in India, its motor groaning, lumbered up the slope and passed. A bit later, lights and a strong rattling announced a bus. T. N. was up to the occasion. Stepping almost into its path, he vigorously waved it down with both arms. To my astonishment, it stopped. We climbed aboard, and in the rather dark interior sought to take seats some way back from the engine noise, but the conductor barred our way with a friendly smile. Growing accustomed to the near darkness, I made out numerous pairs of yellow eyes at hip height and then a goat came up to inspect us. T. N. and I were the only human passengers: the driver and conductor were evidently engaged in some private contracting to supplement their incomes. We got out safely in Hyderabad, leaving the poor animals to their fate.

In later years, when chance brought us together or something moved us to correspond, the question, "Do you remember the bus ride with the goats?" was often one of happy reminiscences.

T. N. is sorely missed.

Heidelberg, March 2020

About the Author

Clive Bell read engineering and economics at Cambridge University and received his D.Phil. from the University of Sussex. He held positions as an economist and then senior economist in the World Bank's Development Research Center from 1974 to 1985. Thereafter, he taught at The Johns Hopkins University, Vanderbilt University, and the University of Regensburg in Germany, before his appointment at Heidelberg University in 1995, where he is a professor of economics, emeritus.

Abbreviations

AERC	Agroeconomic Research Centre
AFS	attached farm servant
ARDC	Agricultural Refinance and Development Corporation
BDO	block development officer
CCI	Cotton Corporation of India
CDF	cumulative distribution function
CPIAL	consumer price index for agricultural laborers
CPM	Communist Party of India (Marxist)
DPAP	Drought Prone Areas Programme
f.o.c.	first-order condition
GGS	group guarantee scheme
ICRISAT	International Crops Research Institute for the Semi-Arid Tropics
IDC	Irrigation Development Corporation
i.i.d.	independent and identically distributed
IIM	Indian Institute of Management
IRDP	Intensive Rural Development Programme
ISI	Indian Statistical Institute
kg	kilogram
l.h.s.	left-hand side
LMB	Land Mortgage Bank
LSMS	Living Standards and Measurement Study
MFI	microfinance institution
MP	member of parliament
NSF	Nagarjuna Sagar Farmers
NSS	National Sample Survey
NSSO	National Sample Survey Organisation
RBI	Reserve Bank of India
r.h.s.	right-hand side
SBI	State Bank of India
SFDA	Small Farmers' Development Agency
UNDP	United Nations Development Programme
VLW	village-level worker
w.r.t.	with respect to

Glossary

bandh	general strike
inam	land grant
jaggery	country sugar
khandsari	type of granulated sugar
kharif	monsoon season, July 1–December 31
kurnam	village accountant and land records keeper in Chittoor District
Lok Sabha	India's parliament
panchayat	village council (lowest level of government in India's federal system)
patel	village leader
patwari	village accountant and land records keeper
quintal	100 kilograms
rabi	second season, January 1–June 30
samithi	block-level council
sarpanch	village headman
taluk	subdistrict
tehsildar	tax officer
tonne	1,000 kilograms (10 Indian quintals)

1 Introduction

In 1980, T. N. Srinivasan and I embarked on a study of markets and cultivation in the states of Andhra Pradesh, Bihar, and Punjab. The project really belonged to the broad subfield known as rural economic organization, but we gave it the slightly misleading title, "Impact of Agricultural Development on Employment and Poverty, Phase II," aware as we were of the current concerns of the World Bank, which funded the project as RPO671-89, and the government of India, whose approval for the fieldwork was required. There was, of course, a concern with public policy. We focused on irrigation and institutional credit, which are closely connected, not only as policy domains, but also with the operations of private agents who are active in moneylending and the marketing of crops.

Understanding what motivates agents to contract in a particular way—or not at all—is essential in such an enterprise. Designing samples and formulating questionnaires are unquestionably important to get right, but what they ultimately yield cannot tell the whole story. We did some traveling, therefore, both at the very start to become acquainted with the villages and to persuade the villagers to cooperate with the survey teams, and then 15 months later as the survey drew to a close. In the course of my tour through Andhra Pradesh in September and October of 1980, I wrote fairly extensive notes on these introductory discussions.[1] On my return to Washington, I reflected on them, reworked them into a common format, added some points from memory, and polished them a fair bit. They were circulated among my colleagues in the World Bank's Development Research Center, but not more widely. Although they drew largely favorable comment, they were unsuitable for refereed journals and have since lain in a drawer. They are reproduced here as chapter 2, with some very light copy editing, solely to remove the villages' names, rid the text of some repetition, and correct typos and syntax.

In the second tour, we concentrated on hearing the other side of the story—namely, how the officers of the public institutions in question, especially the branches of the Land Mortgage Bank, the commercial banks, and two sugar mills, saw things. Two private traders engaged in moneylending gave freely of their time to discuss their business and the markets. We also visited eight of the survey villages in order to interview some households, seeking out those that had been drawn in our sample. We managed to have extensive discussions with about a score of them. The aim was to obtain a fuller picture of their dealings and motives than was yielded by the questionnaires, whose rigid format of 80 columns complied with the demands of the punched cards that served as paper currency in those days. The account of this tour forms chapter 3. Based on my handwritten field notes, it is wholly new.

Some remarks on these accounts of the two tours are in order. First, the short-comings of such travelogues in comparison with full-blown studies of villages or public institutions need no emphasis. The discussions with villagers in the first tour were of the focus group kind, but the makeup of the participants, which is described in chapter 2, varied greatly across villages. As groups, they were nei-ther representative nor uniform. Second, my own fieldwork experience in India before that tour had been confined to impoverished northeast Bihar a decade earlier. In that sense, the tour was also one of personal discovery, with some attendant surprises, as the account in chapter 2 occasionally reveals. Third, in writing chapter 3, I have attempted to stick closely to the original field notes in substance and formulation; even so, producing a structured and intelligible account inevitably opens the door to interpretation with the benefit—and pitfalls—of nigh on 40 years of hindsight.

Fourth, general conditions in that period were far from normal. Monsoonal rainfall in 1979–80 fell a little more than 20 percent short of the 100-year average in Coastal Andhra, Rayalaseema, and Telangana; Rayalaseema suffered another, slightly heavier, shortfall in 1980–81 (Kothawale and Rajeevan 2017).[2] A single such shortfall may not seem so out of the ordinary, although it featured strongly in the discussions with respondents. Two consecutive such shortfalls are indis-putably a grave event. Drought was accompanied by brisker inflation: the con-sumer price index for agricultural laborers (CPIAL) in Andhra Pradesh rose from 58.3 in 1978–79, to 63.9 in 1979–80, and then to 72.9 and 84.5 in the following two years (1986–87 = 100), during which the fieldwork was conducted. The sharper increases in the latter years had the effect of further tempering real interest rates, nominal ones remaining rather sticky. The central government also intervened directly in credit markets—by nationalizing the remaining six private commercial banks in 1980. For its part, the state government of Andhra Pradesh passed legislation in June 1980 that verged on an outright prohibition of tenancy. It responded to the drought with an ordinance converting short-term institutional loans into medium-term ones with a three-year maturity, later extended to five. Statements were made suggesting the possibility of forgiving some debts—private as well as public. Nothing came of these statements at the time, but they weighed on some lenders' minds, including those of bank officials. All in all, the drought and its consequences featured prominently in discussions during both tours.

So much for the immediate setting. Yet a broader account of developments in Andhra Pradesh is needed to place the study in context. Some momentous events and profound changes have occurred in the four decades since then, and these elements of the big picture are sketched in the section entitled "Andhra Pradesh: Formation, Development, and Dissolution." The subsequent rise of microfinance institutions (MFIs) demands specific attention, not only because credit had such a prominent place in the study, but also because two MFI crises played out in Andhra Pradesh, first in 2006 and again in 2010, the latter on such a scale that it reverberated globally. They are described briefly and discussed in the section entitled "The MFI Crises." Crises of a different kind have stemmed from the exploitation of groundwater to extend irrigation and the vagaries of the rains.

Wells featured prominently in the study: the section entitled "Wells and Groundwater" gives an account of subsequent developments. The chapter closes with the section entitled "Methods of Inquiry," which discusses the methods of inquiry in empirical investigations of rural life, the choices we made, and how the tours and the resulting travelogues contributed to our findings, followed by some remarks on theory.

ANDHRA PRADESH: FORMATION, DEVELOPMENT, AND DISSOLUTION

In 1956, there was a wholesale reorganization of the states of the Indian union, with language as the guiding principle for the redrawing of state boundaries. Andhra Pradesh arose as the union of the Telugu-speaking parts of the former Madras Presidency, known as Coastal Andhra and Rayalaseema, and the greater part of the Hyderabad Nizamate, known as Telangana (see map 1.1). The reorganization was concluded not without misgivings among the Telangana party, which was concerned about the sharing of revenues and river waters, as well as competition from their better-educated and, perhaps, more enterprising cousins from the coastal districts, especially for government jobs in the designated capital city of Hyderabad. Certain legal safeguards were provided at the time, although some were subsequently challenged in the courts, with rulings that brought one or the other party onto the streets.

After one ruling in 1969, simmering tensions erupted into violent protests in Telangana, with loss of life and much damage to property. When another ruling was overturned by the Supreme Court in 1972, there was a replay, now in Coastal Andhra, followed by the imposition of President's Rule in January 1973. Two years later, the central government introduced a set of measures known as the "Six Point Formula," which helped to maintain relative quiet until 2000. The agitation for a separate Telangana, now promoted by several political parties, then resumed once more. In December 2009 it culminated in a rerun of the events of 40 years earlier, with violent disturbances, first in Telangana and then in Coastal Andhra and Rayalaseema. The central government responded by appointing a special committee, chaired by a retired Supreme Court judge, B. N. Srikrishna, to look into the matter and make recommendations. The committee submitted its report in December 2010 (Government of India 2010), coming down on the side of preserving Andhra Pradesh as constituted in 1956, with further measures to assuage the grievances of the Telangana party. It was to no avail: what the Lok Sabha (India's parliament) had joined together in 1956, it now put asunder, taking effect on June 2, 2014.

One of the minor consequences of that separation was to complicate the task of providing an account of changes in the state's salient economic indicators over the whole historical period up to the present, a task to which the chapter now turns, concentrating on the period up to that recent event.

Beginning, conventionally enough, with the growth of per capita net state domestic product, Andhra Pradesh performed worse than the union as a whole over the period from 1960 to 2000. For the subperiods 1960–61 to 1969–70, 1970–71 to 1979–80, 1980–81 to 1990–91, and 1993–94 to 1998–99, the annual rates of growth of that measure of output for Andhra Pradesh were –0.4, 1.1, 2.1, and 3.5 percent, respectively; nationally, they were 0.8, 1.2, 3.3, and 4.8 percent (Government of India 2002, 34–35). What they had in common was a clear

MAP 1.1

The regions of Andhra Pradesh, as constituted between 1956 and 2014

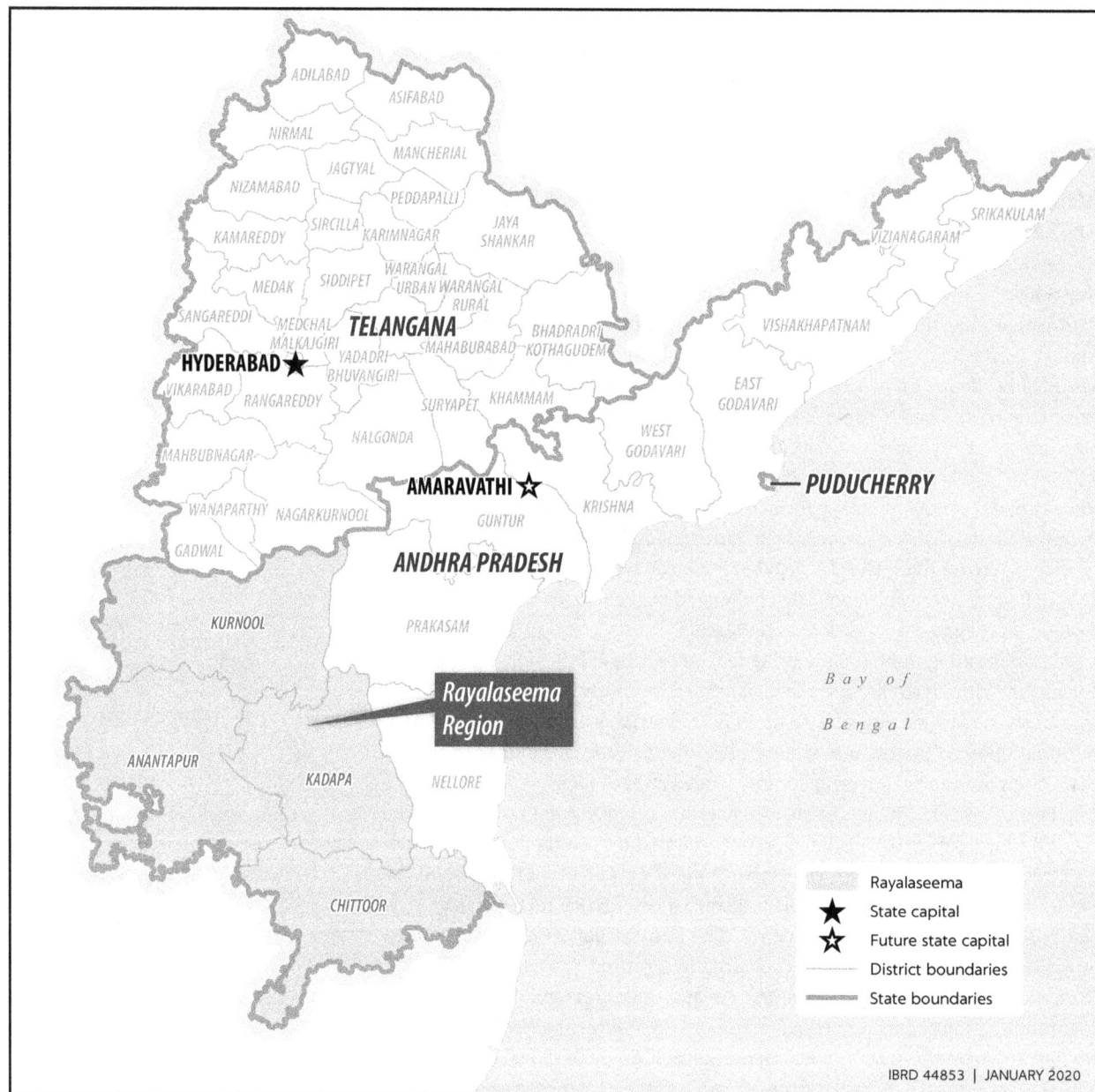

Source: World Bank.

acceleration after 1980. The level in Andhra Pradesh on that starting date was Rs 1,380 in 1980–81 prices; it rose 62 percent to Rs 2,232 in 1993–94 (Government of India 2008), when there was a change in the basis of the price index. With that year as base, the level was Rs 7,416, rising to Rs 9,445 in 1999–2000 (RBI 2019, table 16). Another change in base occurred in 1999–2000, with the level rising from Rs 15,427 to Rs 19,963 in 2004–05. Deflating and splicing these series together yield the level in 2004–05 of Rs 3,678 at 1980–81 constant prices.

Not only was the base changed once more in 2004–05, but the aggregate series was also replaced by separate ones for (the rump of) Andhra Pradesh and Telangana. Their levels were Rs 25,959 and Rs 24,409, respectively—measurement errors aside, hardly a difference to warrant censure—rising to Rs 44,831 and

Rs 51,017, respectively, in 2014–15. This striking reversal in the course of a mere decade was doubtless due largely to the dynamism of Hyderabad, which had become a real metropolis. On the eve of divorce, therefore, certain sections of society in Telangana had much to be happy about. At all events, real net output per head in undivided Andhra Pradesh at that juncture was about fivefold its level in 1980–81. Growth in both parts continued apace thereafter, the levels rising a further 34 and 33 percent, respectively, up to 2017–18.

This long-term increase in aggregate productivity was accompanied by largely predictable changes in economic structure. The share of agriculture in net state domestic product fell from 40.7 percent in 1980–81 to 26 percent in 2007–08 (Government of India 2008, 2010). The shares of the workforce engaged in the primary, secondary, and tertiary sectors shifted from 67.4, 10.3, and 22.3 percent, respectively, in 1987–88 to 60.6, 9.3, and 30.1 percent in 1999–2000 (Government of India 2002, 75). The population grew from 36.0 million in 1961 to 53.5 million in 1981 and then to 76.2 million in 2001, becoming more urban in the process. The associated urbanization rates were 17.4, 23.3, and 27.3 percent, respectively (Government of India 2010, 199).

How did all of these developments affect poverty? In volume III of the *Tenth Five-Year Plan* (Government of India 2002), the Planning Commission gives estimates of the headcount ratio, apparently yielded by applying the Lakdawala method to the National Sample Survey (NSS) rounds: 0.489 in 1973–74, 0.289 in 1983, 0.222 in 1993–94, and 0.158 in 1999–2000. The later switch to the Tendulkar method resulted in a sharp shift upward thereafter: 0.299 in 2004–05 and 0.211 in 2009–10, with a precipitous fall to 0.092 in 2011–12 (Government of India 2014, tables B2–B4). In a further revision, the expert group chaired by C. Rangarajan proposed changes in method that yielded another shift upward: 0.281 in 2009–10 and 0.137 in 2011–12 (Government of India 2014, tables 4.6 and 4.4, respectively). There appears to have been progress on this front, albeit rather jerky in nature.

A related key indicator is the agricultural wage. To summarize the findings reported in chapter 5 (see table 5.2), the daily wage for casual male laborers in 1980 varied strongly over villages and somewhat over seasons, ranging between Rs 2 and Rs 5 (sometimes supplemented with a meal or two) when paid in cash and between 2 and 6 kilograms of grain when paid wholly in kind. Females were often paid a bit less, but the tasks were not always the same. Grain prices were about Re 1 per kilogram. Current levels are far higher. The average daily rate for male workers in Andhra Pradesh had risen to Rs 295 in 2015–16 (Government of India 2017), whereas the associated CPIAL had increased only about 15-fold between 1980–81 and 2015–16 (Government of India 2018). Rapid economic growth and structural change in the national and state economies had brought about a remarkable increase in real agricultural wages in all states of the union (Lanjouw and Murgai 2009). Invoking the common yardstick of a dollar a day, at the official exchange rate, the dollar was worth just over Rs 8 in 1980, rising toward Rs 9 at the end of 1981. It fluctuated between Rs 64 and Rs 68 during 2015–16.

THE MFI CRISES

In 1980, the Grameen Bank was still in the project stage in a few districts of Bangladesh; in Andhra Pradesh, villagers as a group were engaged, to varying degrees, in borrowing from the banks, cooperatives, professional moneylenders, landlords, merchants, commission agents, and one another, as described in later chapters. About one-third of the households surveyed had borrowed in the kharif season, and 60 percent had outstanding debt at its close. Doubtless many of those who wanted loans were unable to obtain one: in current parlance, they were excluded.

MFIs in India started up as not-for-profit entities on a small scale in the late 1990s. Two based in Hyderabad went on to become among India's largest, changing their charters to for-profit status (nonbank financial companies) along the way, with an explosive growth of operations from 2005 onward, presumably heavily concentrated in their regional backyard. The results were not long in coming. Early in 2006, a demonstration in Krishna District by borrowers demanding the return of their title deeds turned violent. There were allegations that up to 200 borrowers, unable to repay, had been driven to suicide. The chief minister leveled grave charges at the MFIs: as he put it, they were "worse than moneylenders by charging interest rates in excess of 20 percent" (*The Hindu*, March 18, 2006) and used unethical means to recover loans. The authorities proceeded to shut down 50 branches of two leading MFIs. Shylendra (2006) gives a sharp account of the affair, viewing it as a conflict between the state and civil society organizations, complicated by the structural problems of the MFIs.

The MFIs promised to mend their ways by adopting a Voluntary Code of Conduct. After a short hiatus, operations went full-steam ahead once more, ultimately leading to a replay of the earlier crisis on a vastly larger scale in 2010. Overall indebtedness had become extremely high (Johnson and Meka 2010; Nair 2011, 25). As related by Mader (2013, 55), once again there were reports of rising rates of default, coercion, and suicide. The Andhra Pradesh government passed an ordinance granting borrowers various forms of protection on October 15, and the industry responded by attacking the government for attempting to shield its own pro-poor lending programs by limiting competition.

The ordinance delivered a thunderous shock to the whole system in India, with global reverberations, as foreign equity capital had been drawn in. It also divided scholarly opinion. In what might be called a statement of the received view of the merits of MFIs as intermediaries promoting inclusion, a group of very distinguished economists (Banerjee et al. 2010) published a piece in the *Financial Times* entitled, "Microcredit Is Not the Enemy." Others like Mader (2013) and Nair (2011) argued, on the contrary, that credit is not a substitute for productive livelihoods and that the origins of the indebtedness of Andhra Pradesh's rural households lay in an unfolding agrarian crisis partly brought on by economic liberalization.

There is no space here to try to resolve the matter definitively, but some remarks are warranted. First, there is a long history of attempts to deal with rural indebtedness and thus, indirectly, to improve rural welfare. The authors of the first All-India Rural Credit Survey advocated a system of cooperatives covering all villages to remedy "a twofold [credit] problem of inadequacy and unsuitability" (RBI 1954, vol. 2, 151). They concluded, "The moneylender can be allotted no part in the scheme, ... [which] is to provide a positive alternative to the moneylender himself, something which will compete with him, remove him from the forefront and put him in his place" (RBI 1954, 481–82). It is fair to say that the cooperative movement failed to meet their hopes. The stories in chapters 2 and 3 join legions of others that relate how the movement foundered.

In the next act, the banks were nationalized in 1969 and forced by decree to open branches in rural areas, which they had largely avoided previously. There is evidence of some success, but far short of completely remedying the twofold problem of inadequacy and unsuitability. The promotion of self-help groups and MFIs should be viewed as the latest attempts to deal with it, ideally once and for all. History is against them; for the fundamental underlying problem remains. The traditional lender, whether in the guise of landlord, employer, commission agent, trader, friend, or relative, has a decisive advantage in the information that matters. "There is little that escapes his eye. ... [H]e actually possesses ... knowledge of the 'character and repaying capacity' of those he has to deal with" (RBI 1954, vol. 2, 171). This is not to say that measures to put him in his place are necessarily doomed to failure, but expectations of success must be tempered in the light of past experience.

Second, there is the structure of lenders' costs. Their main "input" is funds, and here MFIs enjoy the advantage of access to the banks and equity capital. As for-profit entities that also aim for substantial size in order to spread their overhead and retain and reward staff who have good alternative employment opportunities, the advantage of size is surely needed if they are to put traditional lenders under strong competitive pressure. Nair (2011, 24), for example, gives the following cost structure for a typical debt-funded MFI: operational expenses account for about half, funds for nearly 40 percent, and loan loss provision and margins for the rest. If this is indeed typical—no source is given—traditional lenders are unlikely to go out of business.

Third, the contrary claim that these financial crises have their roots in a general agrarian crisis is very hard to square with the almost fivefold increase in per capita net output between 1980 and 2010; for it was accompanied by a proportional rise in real agricultural wage rates at least as large and a very substantial reduction in rural poverty. In 2010, Andhra's villagers as a whole were unquestionably materially much better off, and far fewer of them were in acute need, than a generation earlier. If they had gone headlong into debt, it was not a desperate attempt to make ends meet in the face of declining income; for their capacity to service debt had improved immensely. It is much more plausible that, on observing the sort of consumption that accompanied growing affluence in India's cities, they desired to follow suit. The chief motive for going into debt, therefore, was not want, but aspiration, which the MFIs were well placed to exploit. In this connection, it should be recalled that, in his classic study, *The Punjab Peasant in Prosperity and Debt*, Darling (1925) emphasized that indebtedness rose in good times, followed by retrenchment in bad ones.

After a retrenchment of its own in the wake of the crisis of 2010, the MFI industry resumed growth in 2012. The gross loan portfolio increased by about 160 percent in the following four years; about half of it was concentrated in just 50 districts. The number of active borrowers rose by a much more modest 30 percent, thus barely regaining its level in 2010 (Sinha and Navin 2018). What can be said in closing, then, is that, in this new, much more heavily regulated environment, the industry is still passing a market test.

WELLS AND GROUNDWATER

The report of the Srikrishna Committee (Government of India 2010, ch. 4.1) provides a compact account of the development of, and problems with, irrigation over the period 1955–56 to 2007–08. In the latter year, the possible cultivable area was 15.78 million hectares, the net area sown was 10.69 million hectares, and the net and gross areas irrigated were 4.45 million hectares and 6.07 million hectares, respectively. The ratio of the net area irrigated to the net area sown differed sharply across the three regions: 55.4 percent in Coastal Andhra, 42.1 percent in Telangana, and 20.5 percent in Rayalaseema. The gross cropped area fluctuated somewhat over this period, but without any evident trend. The gross irrigated area, in contrast, had a clear and strong upward trend, albeit with substantial fluctuations; but whereas the said two areas increased substantially in Coastal Andhra and Telangana, they simply fluctuated in Rayalaseema.

The importance of the various sources of irrigation water underwent big changes, both relatively and absolutely. The net area under tanks declined strongly in all three regions and the net area under canals rose modestly up to about 1980–81, but very little thereafter. Wells, from decidedly modest beginnings in 1955–56, had become the overwhelmingly dominant source of irrigation water in Rayalaseema and Telangana by 2007–08 and second after canals in Coastal Andhra. The area under well irrigation in Telangana then accounted for almost 60 percent of the state total. These developments, moreover, had gained increasing strength after about 1980–81. The Srikrishna Committee noted them with concern. It cited official estimates that in 2007, one-third of all watersheds in Rayalaseema were either overexploited or critically exploited (in the range of 90–100 percent of availability), one-fifth in Telangana, and a mere 4 percent in Coastal Andhra (Government of India 2010, 184). Well densities were 13.7 per square kilometer in Telangana and 7.0 per square kilometer in the other regions.

Excessive exploitation of a common property resource should occasion no great surprise. The total draw on an aquifer depends on the density of wells and how hard their owners pump. Easily available credit without regulation of well spacing promotes density, and subsidies on diesel fuel and electricity encourage harder pumping. Whether the aquifer can be replenished sufficiently to meet these demands without a fall in the water table depends on geology, rainfall, and surface irrigation.

An interesting study of three contiguous districts in Telangana—Nalgonda among them—by a team of hydrologists and agronomists (Sishodia et al. 2016) sheds much light on what happened over the period from 1989 to 2012 and the underlying causes. They preface their analysis by emphasizing that the crystalline aquifers of central and southern India are rather shallow and have limited storage capacity, so that the water table is seasonally strongly volatile. In contrast, the deep alluvial aquifers of Haryana and Punjab have substantial storage and are fed by the plentiful surface waters of the Himalayas' rivers.

The authors employed bimonthly data on the water table (meters below ground level) provided by 194 open observation wells, which are 10–20 meters deep and not used for irrigation. The Mann-Kendall test yielded the following results: 34 percent of the wells exhibited a statistically significant (at the 5 percent level) declining trend in groundwater level, and 9 percent exhibited an increasing one, whereby the trend rates also varied significantly. Of the group of 64 wells for which a complete series was available, only 14 (that is, 22 percent) exhibited a statistically significant declining trend. They conclude that the common perception that falling groundwater levels are a widespread phenomenon is unwarranted.

Public policies were, all the same, still at work. In 2004, the state government absolved farmers from electricity charges, a generous addition to the raft of subsidies that this politically powerful group already enjoyed. A Mann-Whitney test on groundwater levels before the monsoon season revealed that about two-thirds of the wells exhibiting a significant declining trend over the whole period also exhibited a step-up change from 2005 onward. After an adjustment for rainfall, the proportion was still almost 60 percent (Sishodia et al. 2016, 52). As for the regulation of well spacing, under the Andhra Pradesh Water, Land and Trees Act of 2002, farmers were required to register existing bore wells and obtain a permit to drill new ones. The latter requirement appeared, unsurprisingly, to be honored almost wholly in the breach: 2,500 permits were granted in 2005, but the Transmission Corporation of Andhra Pradesh Limited reported an increase of 66,000 individual agricultural electrical service connections during that period (Sishodia et al. 2016, 54–55).

The great expansion of the area under well irrigation was accompanied by a remarkable switch in the type of wells. Open, dug wells, which feature prominently in the chapters that follow, depend directly on monsoonal recharge. In 1990–91 they commanded about half of the net irrigated area of some 400,000 hectares in the three districts studied; tube wells, some more than 70 meters deep, accounted for just 12,000 hectares. In 2011–12 the position was the reverse: tube wells commanded 374,000 hectares, and dug wells commanded just 36,000 hectares, with the total net irrigated area having risen to 532,000 hectares (Sishodia et al. 2016, 46). This switch had an important effect on cultivation. It is clear from chapters 2 and 3 that dug wells essentially supplement monsoonal rains, thus enabling, in particular, the cultivation of paddy when the rains are good. Tube wells, in contrast, also enable the irrigation of crops in the postmonsoon months from November onward and into the following rabi season, and so they make correspondingly heavier draws on the aquifer. The reader should bear these points in mind when wells are discussed in the earlier setting of 1980–82.

METHODS OF INQUIRY

It is a truism, perhaps, that the method to be employed depends on what is to be investigated. Nationwide and regional surveys are designed to yield aggregate measures of the state of affairs in some sphere or other. Thus informed, policy makers should be able to formulate better policies. When repeated, such surveys provide not only a series of snapshots of changes in those measures, but also a basis for evaluating how policies may have influenced them. India's National Sample Survey Organisation (NSSO), established in 1950, has an enviable reputation and record. The Living Standards and Measurement Studies (LSMSs), promoted vigorously by the World Bank since 1979, have come to enjoy a similar status.

Some scholars are ill-satisfied with pictures on such a large canvas. Those who undertake intensive village studies seek not only to compile detailed accounts of individual actors' dealings with one another in a whole variety of spheres, but also to understand what motivates them to do so in that particular setting. If the villages are resurveyed, these studies can yield histories with a wealth of insights into the mechanisms of change—or of stasis. In what is now a classic longitudinal study, Bliss and Stern (1982), later joined by Drèze, Himanshu, Lanjouw, and others, have told the story of Palanpur in Uttar Pradesh (Himanshu, Lanjouw, and Stern 2018; Lanjouw and Stern 1998). The surveys of the six International Crops Research Institute for the Semi-Arid Tropics (ICRISAT) villages in the Deccan plateau between 1976 and 1980 have spawned enough literature to fill a small library. Binswanger and Rosenzweig (1984) contains several important, early contributions. Of older vintage, Slater (1918) and his students surveyed five villages in Tamil Nadu in 1916. At intervals of several decades, other scholars followed up, most recently Harriss, Jeyaranjan, and Nagaraj (2010), who chose a polarized community. A valuable study of two Bihari villages over the period 1981–2009 (Datta et al. 2014) pays particular attention to agrarian structure.

It might be said that economists who proceed in this way have fallen under the influence of social anthropologists, although it is debatable whether what they produce is economic anthropology. Suffice it to say that Bliss and Stern, both outstanding theorists, remarked in their conclusions that they had not expected their findings to conform to economic theory in any simple way.

The study on which this monograph is based, RPO671-89, lies somewhat uneasily between these two extremes. Srinivasan, a statistician by training and erstwhile leading figure in the Indian Statistical Institute (ISI), viewed single-village studies rather skeptically, largely, I suspect, because of his profound concern with drawing firm conclusions for policy. Limited resources forced compromises in the project's sample design: three states, a total of 34 villages, and 40 households per village, as described in some detail in chapter 4. A salient feature of the design was dictated by the need to identify a sample household's transacting partners. This information was desired not only to investigate in what respects the transacting parties were matched from a contracting point of view, but also to check whether their answers to questions about the terms of the transaction were in agreement. The discrepancies that emerged were not infrequently dismayingly large.[3] In some cases, one party—usually a landlord or lender—effectively denied that there had been a transaction. Given the sensitivity of some of these dealings, the blame should not be laid at the field investigators' door. The following instance is revealing in several ways. A respondent—almost all were male—claimed to have lent money to a fellow villager, identified by name and hence with a household serial number. When the enumerator went to the house of the alleged borrower, the latter denied all knowledge of the loan; whereupon the enumerator returned to the lender, who adamantly insisted that he had indeed advanced a loan to the household in question. Upon further inquiry, it transpired that the "borrower's" spouse had obtained the loan without telling him; this discovery led to severe marital strife. Our principal collaborator prohibited any double checking of transacting partners' answers from that point on.

The difficulties confronting the reliable collection of a wide variety of data are well known, and they need to be confronted. Scholars who pursue village studies can hardly avoid them and must make hard choices.[4] Those who analyze large-scale surveys, however well designed, may have to resort, to some degree, to a willing suspension of disbelief. Deaton (1993, 22–32), for example, gives a cogent summary of the problems encountered in using survey data to investigate living standards.

There remains the question of what place, if any, travelogues—even those arising from standard surveys—have in scholarly inquiry. A flying tour of villages out of the blue, involving discussions with groups of varying sizes and makeup, cannot yield findings that bear comparison with those arising from patient observation during a long-term stay in, or continuous visits to, a single village. Yet such a tour may still yield something more than first-hand experience of conditions in the field, to be used in assessing how to treat the subsequent survey data and in judging the results of ensuing analysis. The participants in such discussions have interests of their own, as is clear from chapter 2. (Two chance encounters with politicians, in Chittoor and Nalgonda Districts, were especially revealing.) How participants express their interests may give the investigator useful hints about lines of research that could be especially fruitful. That is to say, a tour preceding the survey may have inductive value, even if the questionnaire is already largely fixed.

A tour toward the end of the survey, especially if the latter has run for some considerable period, holds more promise. The survey will have become part of village life, and if it has been conducted competently and sensitively, respondents will be attuned to its topics and to talking about them. Faced with the scholar once more rather than the field enumerator, they may well engage seriously in a more open-ended discussion of their dealings—the sort of discussion that even a competent enumerator is unable to conduct satisfactorily. Whole passages of chapter 3 exemplify what can emerge from such discussions. The findings in that second tour also prompted us to supplement the survey with an additional set of questions on the transaction costs of getting loans. There was still time to fit them in, and they yielded some valuable results (see chapter 4).

Most important, the two travelogues, though generally interesting in their own right, also led to specific lines of inquiry that might well have escaped notice otherwise or, if seen, could not have been pursued on the basis of the survey data alone. As noted at the outset, research on the topic of rural economic organization had become quite active when the project was launched, and it grew in importance in the decade that followed, before petering out in the course of the 1990s. The tales related by villagers, traders, and officials reveal some promising lines of theoretical inquiry, pointing as they do to a few twists, misplaced emphases, or unresolved puzzles in that literature, even as it now stands. Chapters 5, 6, and 7 pursue certain of these possibilities. Each combines a synthesis of the relevant empirical findings in the travelogues and the survey data with formal economic analyses of agents' contractual decisions.

In closing, something should be said about the discourse between the investigating scholar and the respondent, whether it be during a flying tour or a long-term stay in a village. If, as is almost invariably the case, they do not speak the same tongue, an interpreter must be involved, which erects a sort of barrier and is a source of potential distortion. Yet there is another, perhaps more troubling, source of distortion: the fact that the scholar, in virtue of his or her training, possesses a certain way of looking at things, which the respondent does not share—in the present case, that afforded by economic theory, quite conceivably in a largely intuitive form. In order to avoid what would be called "leading the witness" in a court of law, scholars with great field experience argue that questions should be posed in a simple and neutral way: for example, how do you get paid, do you get any meals, when do you start working in the morning, do you own any animals, do you work on other people's land? Yet it is doubtful whether this approach solves the problem; for on receiving such answers as, in cash, breakfast only, sunrise, no, and yes, the scholar can hardly leave matters at that. These answers will naturally lead to other questions, some of them increasingly less simple and more marked by the scholar's mental apparatus and interests: leading the witness, however unwittingly, tends to get under way.

Now, it is obvious that respondents should not be interviewed in a way that keeps them in a straitjacket of the scholar's preconceptions, which would greatly reduce the chances that they will reveal something of real surprise and interest, and so defeat the very purpose of the interviews. Yet the dilemma remains. To illustrate, suppose a farmer reports that he got a bag of fertilizer from a trader, to be repaid on delivering the crop to that trader. He may not see this transaction as a loan, for there may have been no explicit interest charge. Only after a detailed discussion of the whole contractual relationship does it emerge that the parties had entered into what is called an interlinked contract under whose terms the farmer must sell to the trader at a discount on the ruling spot price. Payment for the services of capital in the form of funds is shifted to another part of the accounts. Or consider a peasant who seeks a loan from a known lender, not because he really needs one at that particular time, but because he wants to establish a relationship with that lender, so that he has a better chance of getting a loan when his situation demands one. In effect, he has bought an insurance policy, one whose premium stems from the interest charges on the loan he does not really need and whose coverage is a random variable about which he has some set of beliefs. These interpretations of the transactions are suffused with theory, and it is hard to see how any interpretation aimed at gaining an understanding of them could be otherwise. The sequence of questions, however simply posed, that uncovers what underlies the transactions is inevitably influenced by some prior notions of what factors are at work.

There are dangers in trying to draw parallels between the natural and social sciences, but Toulmin's (1953, 50–55) distinction between physics and natural history is relevant here: "Natural historians, then, look for regularities in given forms; but physicists seek the form of given regularities." The accumulation of observations has a value in itself for natural historians. Thus, the specialist in lepidoptera, armed only with a butterfly net and possessing a keen eye, can go into the countryside on the lookout for new species from the start. It is otherwise with social scientists who attempt to understand contractual relations. They might be mildly surprised on discovering a moneylender in a hitherto unknown guise, but what would command all of their attention would be to ascertain the exact terms of the associated contracts and the parties' circumstances and motives. However carefully and neutrally they would frame their questions, each and every one of them would still be guided by a mental apparatus that owes much to theory of some kind.

THEORY

The last third or so of this monograph is devoted largely to theory, but although Srinivasan and I certainly had some prior notions, it cannot be said that we embarked on the project with a precisely formulated picture of the questions addressed in chapters 5, 6, and 7 and still less of how, exactly, to tackle them. Our efforts subsequently yielded the theory in a paper on the choice of labor contracts (Bell and Srinivasan 1985) and in another on credit and marketing in the Punjab (Bell, Srinivasan, and Udry 1997). The passage of time has made chapters 5, 6, and 7, in substantial measure, inductive. They have grown out of my reflection on the travelogues and the survey data in light of the literature, some of it quite recent. It is improbable that all the years in the interim will have left my mental apparatus—intuitive and otherwise—largely unchanged.

NOTES

1. Two villages were selected, purposively, in each of the following seven taluks (subdistricts): Tanuku, West Godavari District; Miryalaguda and Devarakonda, Nalgonda District; Kalvakurthy, Mahbubnagar District; Adoni, Kurnool District; and Vyalpad and Chittoor, Chittoor District. They are labeled village 1 though village 14, in that sequence. For the details of the sampling scheme, see Srinivasan and Sussangkarn (1984). A brief summary is provided in the section entitled "The Surveys and Background" in chapter 4.
2. The agricultural year runs from July 1 in one calendar year to June 30 in the next. The kharif season runs from July 1 to December 31, while the rabi season runs from January 1 to June 30.
3. I had encountered similarly discordant accounts in my study of two Bihari villages in 1970; see Bell (2018, 284).
4. Nicholas Stern told me long ago that he and Christopher Bliss had been led on a dance by one respondent, and, after reviewing things, they decided to drop that household from parts of the analysis.

REFERENCES

Banerjee, A., P. Bardhan, E. Duflo, E. Field, D. Karlan, A. Khwaja, D. Mookherjee, R. Pande, and R. Rajan 2010. "Microcredit Is Not the Enemy." *Financial Times*, December 13, 2010.

Bell, C. 2018. "Labour and Tenancy in Retrospect: Two Bihari Villages in 1970." In *Markets, Governance, and Institutions in the Process of Economic Development*, edited by A. Mishra and T. Ray. Oxford: Oxford University Press.

Bell, C., and T. N. Srinivasan. 1985. "The Demand for Attached Farm Servants in Andhra Pradesh, Bihar, and Punjab." RPO671-89 Working Paper 11, Development Research Center, World Bank, Washington, DC.

Bell, C., T. N. Srinivasan, and C. Udry. 1997. "Rationing, Spillover, and Interlinking in Credit Markets: The Case of Rural Punjab." *Oxford Economic Papers* 49 (October): 557–85.

Binswanger, H. P., and M. R. Rosenzweig, eds. 1984. *Contractual Arrangements, Employment, and Wages in Rural Labor Markets in Asia*. New Haven: Yale University Press.

Bliss, C. J., and N. H. Stern. 1982. *Palanpur: The Economy of an Indian Village*. Oxford: Oxford University Press.

Darling, M. L. 1925. *The Punjab Peasant in Prosperity and Debt*. Oxford: Oxford University Press.

Datta, A., G. Rodgers, J. Rodgers, and B. Singh. 2014. "Contrasts in Development in Bihar: A Tale of Two Villages." *Journal of Development Studies* 50 (9): 1197–208.

Deaton, A. 1993. *The Analysis of Household Surveys*. Baltimore, MD: Johns Hopkins University Press.

Government of India. 2002. *The Tenth Five Year Plan*. Vol. III, *State Plans—Trends, Concerns, and Strategies*. New Delhi: Planning Commission.

Government of India. 2008. "State Domestic Product: State Series, 1980–81." Ministry of Statistics and Programme Implementation, New Delhi, June.

Government of India. 2010. "Report of the Committee for Consultations on the Situation in Andhra Pradesh." New Delhi, December.

Government of India. 2014. "Report of the Expert Group to Review the Methodology for Measurement of Poverty." Planning Commission, New Delhi.

Government of India. 2017. "Agricultural Wages in India, 2015–16." Directorate of Economics and Statistics, Department of Agriculture, Cooperation, and Farmers' Welfare, New Delhi, November.

Government of India. 2018. "Consumer Price Index Numbers." Labour Bureau, Ministry of Labour, New Delhi. https://www.indiastat.com.

Harriss, J., J. Jeyaranjan, and K. Nagaraj. 2010. "Labour and Caste Politics in Rural Tamil Nadu in the 20th Century: Iruvelpattu (1916–2008)." *Economic and Political Weekly* 45 (July 31): 47–61.

Himanshu, P. Lanjouw, and N. Stern. 2018. *How Lives Change: Palanpur, India, and Development Economics.* Oxford: Oxford University Press.

Johnson, D., and S. Meka. 2010. "Access to Finance in Andhra Pradesh." Centre for Micro Finance, Jaipur; Institute for Financial Management and Research, Centre for Microfinance Research, Chennai; and Bankers' Institute of Rural Development, Lucknow. https://ssrn.com/abstract=1874597.

Kothawale, D. R., and M. Rajeevan. 2017. *Monthly, Seasonal, and Annual Time Series for All-India, Homogeneous Regions, and Meteorological Subdivisions: 1871–2016.* Research Report RR-138. Pune: Indian Institute of Tropical Meteorology, Earth System Science Organization, and Ministry of Earth Sciences.

Lanjouw, P. F., and R. Murgai. 2009. "Poverty Decline, Agricultural Wages, and Nonfarm Employment in Rural India: 1983–2004." *Agricultural Economics* 40 (2): 243–63.

Lanjouw, P. F., and N. Stern. 1998. *Economic Development in Palanpur over Five Decades.* Oxford: Oxford University Press.

Mader, P. 2013. "Rise and Fall of Microfinance in India: The Andhra Pradesh Crisis in Perspective." *Strategic Change* 22 (1-2): 47–66.

Nair, T. 2011. "Microfinance: Lessons from a Crisis." *Economic and Political Weekly* 46 (6): 23–26.

RBI (Reserve Bank of India). 1954. *All-India Rural Credit Survey.* Vol. 2, *The General Report.* Bombay: RBI.

RBI (Reserve Bank of India). 2019. *Handbook of Statistics on Indian States: State Domestic Product.* New Delhi: RBI, March.

Shylendra, H. S. 2006. "Microfinance Institutions in Andhra Pradesh: Crisis and Diagnosis." *Economic and Political Weekly* 41 (20): 1959–63.

Sinha, N., and N. Navin. 2018. "Indian Microfinance Sector: An Overview." MPRA Paper 90478, Munich Personal RePEc Archive, December.

Sishodia, R. P., S. Shukla, W. D. Graham, S. P. Wani, and K. K. Garg. 2016. "Bidecadal Groundwater Level Trends in a Semi-Arid South Indian Region: Declines, Causes, and Management." *Journal of Hydrology: Regional Studies* 8 (December): 43–58.

Slater, G. 1918. *Some South Indian Villages.* Oxford: Oxford University Press.

Srinivasan, T. N., and C. Sussangkarn. 1984. "Sampling Scheme and Estimation." RPO671-89 Working Paper 4, Development Research Center, World Bank, Washington, DC.

Toulmin, S. 1953. *The Philosophy of Science.* London: Hutchinson.

2 Notes on 14 Villages, 1980

During the fall of 1980, I went to India in order to help our colleagues to establish the fieldwork for the research project "Impact of Agricultural Development on Employment and Poverty, Phase II," which was a joint venture of the World Bank, the Indian Institute of Management (IIM), Ahmedabad, and the Agroeconomic Research Centre (AERC), Waltair. Among other things, I spent two weeks traveling widely in Andhra Pradesh, in the course of visiting 13 of the 14 villages to be surveyed in that state. (A little later, I was able to visit Aurepalle, a village that the International Crops Research Institute for the Semi-Arid Tropics [ICRISAT] had been studying for the past five years.) Dr. T. V. S. Rao, director of the AERC, was my companion throughout. His main concern was to explain the purpose of our research to the villagers and to persuade them to cooperate with the enumerators who would carry out the survey work. He also proved to be a most patient interpreter when I wanted to pursue certain discussions with the villagers. Without his knowledge, stamina, and kindness, the following notes on those discussions would not have been possible.

The notes on each village, which I wrote up in December 1980, follow the same format, each concluding with a commentary on things that I found interesting, did not see clearly at that time, or consider unresolved. Elsewhere, shorter comments are entered in brackets, to alert the reader to the fact that I am no longer reporting what our respondents said.[1]

VILLAGE 1, WEST GODAVARI DISTRICT

Respondent

A farmer of some means, who is trustee of the local temple and secretary of the cooperative. When Dr. Rao and Mr. Prasad had visited the village some weeks earlier in order to persuade the villagers to cooperate with us in carrying out the study, this man was their principal contact. In keeping with his social position, he made the arrangements for hospitality on that occasion. He struck me as a sober, serious individual. No doubt his economic and social position influenced his responses to certain questions, but overall I would rate him as a reliable respondent. The interview took place on September 23, 1980, in the relative privacy of the verandah of his house.

General features

The villages in West Godavari are served by an old canal system. The main crop is paddy, which is grown in both seasons, there being a wide range of planting dates in each. The only other crop of any significance is sugarcane. Throughout the area, crop stands appeared to be uniformly good, and the harvesting of the kharif crop was well under way.

This village is about 2 kilometers from the nearest surfaced road, which leads to the local market town 7 kilometers away. The houses are clean and well kept. The surrounding fields of ripening paddy and the stands of palm and coconut trees make the atmosphere gently bucolic.

Labor and wages

About 80 percent of households depend mostly on agricultural labor for their livelihood. Some of this work is done outside the village.

About 50 people work as attached farm servants—that is, they have continuous and exclusive employment with one landlord for a season or more. They have many duties, including the supervision of casual laborers. Their main wages are paid monthly in kind, but they also receive clothes and other sundry items once or twice a year. Some attached laborers get a small plot of land to cultivate. It appears that most of these laborers want consumption loans and enter into such labor contracts in order to obtain them, in the form of an advance of salary. In the event of a dispute, the laborer may be reassigned to another landlord.

There are also 250 casual laborers, some of whom are attached to landlords on a first-call basis at a fixed wage rate. These semiattached workers commonly take loans from their principal employer. Wage rates for casual workers are flexible, varying with seasonal demand. There is no trade union.

Land and tenancy

About one-sixth of the land is leased out, although many tenancies are being resumed following the passage of legislation in June 1980. Tenants may lease land from more than one landlord and may sell their output to anyone they please. However, tenants must normally work for their landlords on a first-call basis. [There was a suggestion that they get less than the going casual wage rate when doing so, but this was accompanied by a remark to the effect that the fixed rent is also lower, so perhaps this is simply a variation in the terms of rental-cum-wage contracts.] Tenants also commonly take loans from their landlords, although they are rarely prohibited from borrowing from other sources. Rental contracts take the form of fixed rents in kind in kharif (July 1–December 31) and sharecropping in rabi (January 1–June 30). In the former season, the landlord has the option to reduce the rent if the crop is insufficient to pay off the rent in full, and in this village, he often does so. In the latter season, both output and certain expenses are shared 50:50. The tenant pays for all inputs of labor and draft power and decides on the quantities of those inputs whose costs are shared. However, the choice of crop and the particular variety are negotiated. Special arrangements are made in the case of banana cultivation: the tenant pays a fixed annual rent in cash (in advance or arrears), the reason being that most landlords do not want to get involved in marketing the crop. It is claimed that more land is leased out in rabi because the requirements for working capital, especially for

outlays on labor, are much greater in that season and tenants have ample supplies of family labor. [However, this is hardly convincing if the principal crop in
both seasons is paddy, as is surely the case.]

Landlords look for the following qualities in would-be tenants. First, the
tenant should have a good reputation both as a cultivator and as a person, for
under the prevailing leasing arrangements, the landlord's rental income depends
on both. Second, the tenant must possess draft animals and a good supply of
family labor, there being little hiring of draft animals. Third, the tenant should
have access to a line of credit and must be able to finance his working capital
requirements.

In the event of a dispute, a mediator living in the village is appointed to
resolve it.

Credit and other inputs

The cooperative was founded 23 years ago and serves two villages. At present,
there are about 300 members, one-third of whom have no land of their own.
Membership has grown slowly over the past decade. In the nearby marketplace
are a branch of the State Bank of India (SBI) and a group of moneylenders. A few
moneylenders reside in the village, but their operations are very small [presum-
ably because moneylending is not their principal occupation]. It is just possible
that the local, privately owned sugar mill also advances loans to cultivators, but
all other lenders insist on a statement of the borrower's current position with the
cooperative. Our respondent reckons that the cooperative provides about
three-quarters of the finance needed for working capital in these two villages.

Output

Commission agents are active at harvest time, mainly to determine the quality of
the crop. Forward sales of paddy are very rare. In the case of bananas, buyers
come before harvesting to assess the crop and make an advance payment. In
effect, the standing crop is sold, and harvesting costs are borne by the buyer.

Commentary

The apparent emphasis on resolving disputes through local mediation and the
general cleanliness of the village's public places suggest that there is a significant
degree of collective action to produce local public goods. Certain aspects of tenancy are unclear. If the tenant has access to a good line of credit, his endowments
of family labor and draft animals do not matter to the landlord, since laborers
and tractors can be hired easily. (There are four tractors in the village, the current rental rate being Rs 65–Rs 70 per acre for plowing and puddling.) Of course,
if the tenant cannot get finance, his endowments matter a great deal. In this
sense, a tenant ought to be qualified by either suitable endowments or credit-
worthiness. The claim that tenants often borrow from their landlords is also at
variance with the requirement that tenants be able to provide their own working
capital, whether in the form of endowments or loans from other sources. Perhaps
such borrowing takes the form of modest consumption loans secured by the
tenant's share of output. As indicated above, the reason given for the switch from
fixed rents in kind to sharecropping between kharif and rabi is not convincing if

irrigated paddy is grown in both seasons. This question needs to be investigated more closely.

VILLAGE 2, WEST GODAVARI DISTRICT

No meeting took place. A general strike (bandh) had been called for the following day, so we decided to travel on to village 3 in Nalgonda District immediately after our discussion in village 1. The strike confined us to our quarters on September 24, 1980. [This explanatory remark was added on December 8, 2018.]

VILLAGE 3, NALGONDA DISTRICT

Respondents

The patwari (village accountant and land records keeper) and a few farmers, who were young and quite well educated. Their answers to questions seemed to be serious and careful. The meeting took place on the verandah of the patwari's house, which opens onto the village street. (Date: September 23, 1980.)

General features

This village lies within the command area of the Nagarjunasagar Scheme, a few kilometers from the Block headquarters, which is also the market center. Irrigation began in 1969. The soils are red and somewhat gravelly; the terrain is slightly undulating. The subtropical climate is much harsher than the humid one of the Godavari coastal valley, and there are no coconut or palm trees to relieve a rather unforgiving landscape. As only to be expected, the village is slightly dusty, but most of the houses are whitewashed and fairly neat—unquestionably a more pleasant place than any village in Bihar that I have seen. Many of the houses are daubed with the CPM (Communist Party of India [Marxist]) emblem, a reminder that radical sentiments have survived the quelling of the Telangana uprising in the late 1940s. This is hardly an area in which one would emphasize one's establishment connections.

Labor and wages

There are about 200 attached laborers and about 400 cultivating households. Very few of these laborers are members of households possessing land. Indeed, many of the households came from taluks (subdistricts) outside the command area and established houses on sites provided by their employers. While they undertake a wide range of tasks, the work of transplanting, harvesting, and threshing of the paddy crop is done by large gangs of seasonal migrant workers. The attached workers are paid twice a year, the first payment being made at the start of the year. The wage is 24 bags of paddy a year, the value of which is about Rs 1,750 at current support prices (Rs 105 per quintal, a measure equal to 100 kilograms). Seasonal migrants are recruited through negotiations with the leader of each gang. Farmers pay a one-way fare for each laborer and provide the gangs with fuel and kerosene for cooking. The piece rates for harvesting and threshing are 1 quintal and 1.35 quintals per acre, respectively. Wages for weeding are paid solely in cash.

Land and tenancy

There is little tenancy: perhaps 15 households are presently leasing in land. Rents are fixed in kind, with no sharing of costs. Normally, there is no reduction in rent, even if total output is less than the rent. The only qualification to be a tenant is to have the reputation of being a capable cultivator. Since title to the land is needed to obtain credit from institutions, tenants have to approach moneylenders for finance, but there is no obligation to sell output or the services of family labor to such lenders, nor was there any in the past. [The detail in which all of these arrangements are described suggests that tenancy is much more extensive than the respondents were prepared to admit. In view of recent legislation, that is not too surprising. However, it is also possible that tenancy was more prevalent in the past and that they were simply reporting what was then common practice.]

Land itself is not frequently sold nowadays. Soon after the arrival of irrigation, however, several big farmers sold off some of their land.

Credit and other inputs

About 50 to 60 cultivators are members of the cooperative. In addition, the village has been adopted by Syndicate Bank, which advances short-term loans at the highly subsidized rate of 4 percent per year. These two institutions, it is claimed, finance virtually all working capital requirements. Before the bank adopted the village some four years back, cultivators had depended heavily on moneylenders, who charged 2 percent a month (simple) on the security of a promissory note. The bank also makes loans to landless persons for the purchase of milch animals on the condition that a third party stand guarantee for the loan. In the event of a default, the guarantor is obliged to pay off the loan and take possession of the livestock. [Remarks made during other interviews suggest that defaults on this kind of loan are common.]

Long-term loans are taken from the Land Mortgage Bank (LMB). Private sources are important only for "consumption loans"—to the extent that the distinction is tenable. Households generally obtain consumption loans from fellow villagers.

It seems that there are always ample supplies of fertilizers and certified seeds. It is also easy to hire tractors from the state corporation that organizes custom services. Such hiring accounts for about one-quarter of the cultivators' requirements for draft power.

Output

Paddy is sold in the market by auction; the crop is transported by cart. It is claimed that the Food Corporation of India does not support the price as it should when the crop is good, although it is certainly an active buyer in times of scarcity. Forward sales are rare.

Groundnut is grown in rabi. The marketing arrangements are the same as those for paddy, the village lying within the local system of regulated markets.

Commentary

The most striking feature of this village is the strong and pervasive support it gets from public institutions. It gets irrigation from a public canal; most of its credit is provided by institutional sources; inputs are in ample supply; and it is close to a regulated market (even if the farm roads are excruciatingly bumpy). Our respondents were keenly aware of all this, and I gained the impression that the villagers may engage in some form of collective action to secure this access to quasi-administered resources. At present, they are pressing for a metaled or surfaced feeder road.

The village economy is probably highly commercialized, and agricultural practice is correspondingly intensive, requiring careful and constant management. This may explain the prevalence of annual contracts for village laborers charged with general duties, for if migrants stream in from the fringe areas during the peak seasons, employers will enjoy a flexible supply of labor without having to establish a pool of casual laborers within the village itself. It may well be that public policy is nurturing a strong group of petty capitalist farmers from the ranks of the village's middle peasantry.

The recent arrival of canal irrigation makes for an interesting contrast with the century-old system in the Godavari delta. In this connection, many people apparently sold land in the delta, where prices were always relatively high, and purchased larger holdings in Nagarjunasagar at modest prices just before, or soon after, irrigation came on stream. There was a suggestion that much of this land was bought from small and marginal farmers, who then became landless laborers. If there were significant numbers of such settlers, it would be interesting to compare their performance as farmers with that of the locals and to explore the extent to which they transplanted the institutions of the delta to the "frontier" areas of the plateau.

Another question that arises is, why did land prices remain relatively low when irrigation was introduced a decade ago? Even if those who sold up lacked the husbandry skills needed to exploit the possibilities introduced by irrigation or were simply myopic, strong bidding by settlers from the delta would have been enough to raise prices. Perhaps, after all, the settlers were not so numerous, and little land was sold off, either to settlers or to other locals.

The highly developed system of markets for inputs and credit is consistent with the claim that the only qualification that would-be tenants need is the reputation of being a good cultivator, although if the rent is not reduced in a bad year, that qualification appears to be redundant. As indicated above, I am not wholly persuaded that there is so little leasing of land.

The other matter that deserves some attention is whether the commission agents who purchase on behalf of the Food Corporation of India, which does not purchase directly, also extend finance for cultivation. Implicitly, our respondents claimed that they do not. Yet these agents are very active in financing agriculture, not only elsewhere in Andhra, but also in Punjab, which is highly commercialized. If they have been confined to marketing activities alone by the operations of the cooperative and the local branch of the Syndicate Bank, that would be an interesting finding indeed.

VILLAGE 4, NALGONDA DISTRICT

Respondents

A petty revenue official, who happened to be paying a visit to his home village, and a few farmers. The interview took place in a farmer's house. The official did much of the talking, although he was obviously speaking as a private individual.

All of them conveyed a strong sense of being deprived, if not as individuals, then certainly as members of this village. There were good grounds for their despondency if casual observation is a trustworthy guide, and if they exaggerated their woes, there was nothing evidently outrageous in their general account. (Date: September 25, 1980.)

General features

This "tail-end" village is about 20 kilometers from the Block headquarters, a journey that takes about one hour over what was once a surfaced road. The fields are rocky, and the village itself stands on a low rise in the terrain. It has a despondent air about it, reminiscent of many villages in Bihar. A cement factory and a railway spur to serve it are under construction close by.

Labor and wages

About 60 percent of the households are landless. Before the arrival of irrigation, attached laborers and their families were given one-quarter of the output realized by their employers. This practice has since given way to fixed rates, paid partly in cash and partly in kind. Since the laborer works from 4 a.m. to 10 p.m., his contract is exclusive in a very complete sense. For all this, such contracts are desired for security of employment. Before construction work on the cement factory began, there was little employment for casual laborers. At present, the daily wage is Rs 1.50 in the slack season and somewhat higher in the peak. A lot of work is done under contract, the rate being 60 kilograms per acre for paddy transplanting and 2 kilograms of grain for an eight-hour stint of threshing the crop. These rates are about half of those prevailing in village 3 just 25 kilometers away and far below those paid to unskilled labor employed on government projects. Factor price equalization is long in coming.

Land and tenancy

About 50 households are leasing in land. If a tenant is known to be a good cultivator, he can obtain a sharecropping contract, the terms being a 50:50 division of both output and (usually) the costs of fertilizers and pesticides. Otherwise, there are fixed-rent contracts in cash, the rate being Rs 300–Rs 400 per acre, half of which is payable in advance. Land leased on a fixed-rent basis may be subleased to a third party on a sharecropping basis. Tenants do not have to work for their landlords, nor are they obliged to sell their output to them. Tenants can also lease from several landlords if they wish. Many small farmers have sold off their land since the arrival of irrigation.

Credit and other inputs

The cooperative has been defunct since 1978, when there were 200 members. While it was functioning, the society advanced loans only for the purchase of fertilizers. There are moneylenders in this village and those nearby. Together with the traders who purchase commercial crops, they finance all cultivation. Moneylenders charge 6 percent a month (simple) on the security of a promissory note. [This rate seems rather high on the evidence from the other villages visited in the unirrigated tracts of Mahbubnagar and Nalgonda Districts.] Credit contracts are exclusive in the sense that other lenders will not advance a loan if the would-be borrower has an outstanding debt, but at least borrowers are free to sell their output to third parties. Loans of seed in kind carry an own rate of interest of 100 percent.

Moneylenders are also the main source of long-term loans, although "long-term" is never more than three years. A moneylender might advance as much as Rs 5,000 to a client.

Fertilizers are purchased at the Block headquarters.

Output

The main crops are paddy and commercial crops: chilies, groundnut, cotton, and tobacco. One indication that this tail-end village is ill-served is that paddy is grown purely for home consumption. One farmer went so far as to claim that irrigation had made matters worse: fields that once yielded good crops of chilies were now too moist for chilies, but not sufficiently well irrigated to grow paddy.

The commercial crops are normally sold to middlemen, who purchase in the village itself. About 10 traders are active in the village and nearby. Forward sales are rare.

Commentary

The contrast with village 3 is striking, not merely in the matter of irrigation, but also in the virtually complete absence of support from public institutions. The repair of the road, for example, would certainly improve the prices that farmers receive in this tract. Were it not for employment in constructing the cement factory, the condition of the landless might well be even more miserable than it is now, although it is puzzling why there has apparently been little migration, either seasonal or permanent.

The sense that the village lies on a neglected periphery is perhaps brought home most vividly by a remark made by the official:

> There is no well in this village, so the women must walk 3 kilometers to draw drinking water from the river Krishna. This is such a burden for them that families in other villages are unwilling to marry their daughters into our households.

The remark made the cup of tea I was given seem more like a precious offering than an ordinary courtesy.

For a few thousand dollars, the women could be spared this unspeakable drudgery and released to do other things. (Less important, our respondent's fears for the marriage prospects of the village's young men in an exogamous society would also be stilled.) Here, indeed, is a cheap way for the government, the World Bank, the United Nations Development Programme (UNDP), or some such agency to increase the sum of human happiness. Yet if it is so cheap, even relative to the income of the village as a whole, why has there been no collective action by the villagers themselves to undertake the investment? It is also worth reflecting on the fact that the cost of conducting a full appraisal of the net social benefit of such a well by a member of the World Bank's staff would handsomely exceed the cost of constructing the well itself.

VILLAGE 5, NALGONDA DISTRICT

Respondents

A dozen or so farmers and the local member of parliament (MP), who accompanied us in order to visit his constituents. His presence made me somewhat apprehensive about the reliability of the farmers' responses; but as it turned out, there was a very revealing altercation between them, which is described in the commentary. Besides this, the interview was a bit short, so the account that follows is rather sketchy. (Date: September 26, 1980.)

General features

The village is upstream of the dam, which is clearly visible. The soils are the same as those in the command area, but the terrain is more rugged, being frequently interrupted by spectacular outcrops weathered into fantastic shapes.

Most of the fields are unirrigated. Altogether, there are 50 percolation wells, each commanding, on average, 1.0–1.5 acres. Most of the wells were dug in the past 10 years under the Drought Prone Areas Programme (DPAP). Most of the villagers are tribal people, so the general cleanliness of the village and its splendidly maintained houses came as no surprise, even though the village is far from affluent. The village is about 30 kilometers from the Block headquarters, 20 kilometers of which are over village roads.

Labor and wages

About 100 of the village's 300 households depend mainly on agricultural labor for their livelihood. There are roughly 100 attached farm servants, who are paid Rs 400 a year plus 25 kilograms of grain each month—that is, a cash equivalent of about Rs 700 a year. All the cash is paid in advance, serving, in effect, as a loan. [However, payment in advance may be the only means whereby laborers can be sure of enforcing the terms of the contract.] The workers desire these contracts because they provide security of employment and income. There are some casual workers, who migrate to other villages in the command area outside the peak season in this village.

Land and tenancy

Some land is leased out under sharecropping arrangements, and about 10 farmers are leasing in land under fixed rent in kind. Under the former, the output and certain costs (fertilizers and pesticides) are split equally, except in the case of plots that lie far off, for which the rental share is 40 percent. The quantities of those inputs subject to cost sharing are negotiated. To qualify for a lease, would-be tenants must possess draft animals and a good reputation.

Credit and other inputs

There is no cooperative. All short-term crop finance is obtained from moneylenders; apparently, commission agents do not get involved in financing cultivation. Some long-term loans for digging wells have been obtained from the LMB, which is discussed in the commentary.

It costs, on average, about Rs 6,000 to dig a well. Pumping is done by draft animals, since finance for pump sets has been difficult to get and diesel fuel is very expensive in this inaccessible village. Some of the finance for the wells was obtained by selling off assets. The rest was advanced by moneylenders at an interest rate of 18–24 percent a year. While there was no explicit demand for collateral, many cultivators fear that they will have to sell animals and other assets to pay off these loans.

Output

The main crops are millets and castor, with paddy grown on irrigated plots. The nearest market is 9 kilometers away. About 80 percent of the cultivators sell their crops directly in auctions, using bullock carts for transport. The sale of small lots is organized by commission agents.

Commentary

The capital costs of irrigating an acre are rather high in this tract, with the hazard that the diggers are not invariably successful in finding water. (The LMB writes off 50 percent of the costs in such cases.) Under the DPAP, cultivators are eligible for a subsidy of 25 percent of the total outlay, rising to 33 percent if they are members of scheduled castes or scheduled tribes. The discussion of this subsidy led to a heated exchange between the farmers and the MP, although my colleagues did not translate the proceedings until much later that day.

It appears that when these farmers applied for a loan and the associated subsidy from the LMB, the bank's officers demanded a bribe of at least half of the subsidy before processing the application. Moreover, the patwari demanded Rs 200 or more for making out the certificate of ownership for the land pledged as security. What with the numerous trips needed to complete the deal, it was claimed that, when all transaction costs had been totted up, the real subsidy was negligible.

Until this point, the MP had taken little interest in the discussion, preferring, naturally enough, to chat with his constituents; but now he strolled over to join us. The farmers who were relating their dealings with the LMB continued by asserting that, if farmers attempted to enlist the help of politicians to speed up their applications and, presumably, reduce or eliminate the bribe demanded by the officials, the politicians themselves insisted on a fee for their services.

"Not so," countered the MP. "It is the farmers who are corrupting the politicians by offering them money." Charge and countercharge were exchanged at some length, with one farmer claiming that the MP himself would demand such a payment. Finally, the MP conceded the case: "All this is true, but you shouldn't say such things in front of these people from the World Bank, because then they won't give us any money."

An obvious conclusion is that we must pay close attention to the allocative decisions of public institutions and how they are influenced by the structure of private supply for the same resources. Why, for example, were there no complaints of this sort from the farmers of village 3? True, this question was not put to them, and their experience may have been the same. But if it is not, I suspect that collective action may have curbed the demand for bribes in their dealings with public institutions.

VILLAGE 6, NALGONDA DISTRICT

Respondents

The patwari, the village development officer, and three landless laborers. Coming at the end of the day, the discussion was rather brief. However, this was the only occasion during our travels in Andhra when landless laborers were our principal respondents on questions concerning the labor market. The discussion took place inside the patwari's house. (Date: September 26, 1980.)

General features

The village lies in the same tract as village 5, but it is closer to Hyderabad. It is a much larger village, having about 500 households (300 of which are engaged in cultivation) and covering 1,600 acres. Its economic structure is more diversified than most, with a good number of shops and other small businesses. Many of the houses are quite substantial, and the main street gives it the air of a small town. It lies about 15 kilometers from the nearest surfaced road.

One salient feature is a dense cluster of about 100 wells, all of them energized, which command an area of more than 200 acres. In kharif, virtually all of this area seems to be sown to paddy. It was rather startling to come upon a wide area of green paddies after passing by patchy crops of castor, some of which were clearly wilting.

Labor and wages

About half the households depend mainly on earnings from agricultural labor. Attached laborers receive 48 kilograms of grain a month, whose cash equivalent is about Rs 600 a year. The possibility of getting a loan from the employer is an important reason for entering into such a contract. If cash is borrowed at the beginning of the year, the employer will make deductions from the laborer's monthly wages in kind. Laborers usually stay with the same employer for several years [perhaps because indebtedness keeps them effectively tied].

The daily wage rate for planting and other casual work is 4 kilograms of grain, except weeding, which is paid in cash. Casual laborers also work outside the village to a significant extent, much of this work being done in gangs. It is usual for the gang leader, who does the negotiating with employers, to receive a lump-sum fee from the gang members: one figure mentioned was 160 kilograms of grain, presumably for a whole season's work.

Land and tenancy

There is little tenancy, so it is claimed, and what there is takes the form of share-cropping arrangements in which the landlord takes 50 percent of the crop and meets 50 percent of the outlays on fertilizers and pesticides. If the tenant is unable to finance his share of these outlays, the landlord will do so. In such cases, the landlord decides how much of these inputs to use and deducts the tenant's share of the costs from his share of output. Would-be tenants must possess draft animals (tractors are not available in the village) and access to a line of credit. They may sell their output to third parties if they wish.

Credit and other inputs

The village is served by a cooperative, but there are only 20 members. The other source of institutional credit is a branch of a bank in the marketing center 14 kilometers away. The bank advances crop loans of up to Rs 500 per acre on submission of a certificate of title and the signature of two guarantors. It is common for villagers to borrow from big landlords and merchants, with the loan to be repaid after the harvest. However, it is claimed that there are no specialist moneylenders and that traders do not advance finance to the cultivators from whom they buy.

About 15 of the wells in the village have been constructed since 1976, and all of them have been financed under DPAP, with a 25 percent subsidy. (In one or two cases out of 10, the diggers fail to find water.) There have been many defaults on these loans, in part, it is claimed, because farmers have not been able to obtain sufficient working capital to exploit all of the opportunities offered by irrigation. After three years, legal proceedings are started against the borrowers and those who stood guarantee for them.

Seed is generally available from the Block office. There are also two fertilizer dealers, but supplies are often scarce.

Output

The main crops are paddy, red gram, bajra, and jowar, the pulse being frequently intercropped with one of the millets. The nearest marketplace, where a number of private traders are active, is 14 kilometers away. Three or four traders come to the village to purchase there. Payment is usually made on delivery, and there are no forward sales.

Commentary

From its appearance, I suspect that there is a fair amount of wealth in this village, although it is almost certainly concentrated in the hands of a few. With relatively poor transportation links and weak public infrastructure, the big landlords and merchants have ample opportunity to exercise market power, and there is much scope for collusion among the leading families. At any rate, I offer this as a hypothesis to be followed up.

The village also provides a vivid example of the effects of irrigation on the kharif cropping pattern in this tract: castor, an important commercial crop, and millets give way to paddy. Whether this shift reduces the degree of commercialization is unclear, since irrigated paddy goes with much larger inputs of nonfarm goods—pumps, electricity, diesel, fertilizers, pesticides—and the income elasticity of demand for food grains is less than unity. (Both total output and value added must rise if the wells are to be privately profitable.)

VILLAGE 7, MAHBUBNAGAR DISTRICT

Respondents

The patwari, the schoolteacher, and a score of farmers (mostly affluent ones, I suspect). We were accompanied by the village development officer and an extension worker, who introduced us to the villagers. The respondents were rather guarded at first, but their replies struck me as being serious. The meeting took place in the village school. (Date: September 27, 1980.)

General features

The village lies in the same general tract as villages 3 and 4, but being on the plateau, the terrain is slightly less rugged. There are 450 households, 10 of which own more than 50 acres, with another 50 holding between 20 and 50 acres. The village is 2 kilometers from the nearest surfaced road. Irrigation facilities are comparatively good, there being two tanks, three ponds, and about 100 wells, all of them energized. Approximately 40 wells have been sunk in the past five years.

Labor and wages

There are about 100 landless households and another 150 who supplement their earnings from cultivation with agricultural labor. There are more than 70 attached laborers, who receive 48 kilograms of grain (paddy or jowar) monthly and a blanket and 40 kilograms of grain at harvest time (the cash equivalent of about Rs 700 a year). Employers seek attached workers who are strongly motivated and trustworthy, since the worker's duties are general and wide-ranging. Although the contracts are annual, the relationship usually endures for a good run of years. The laborers find the contracts attractive because they receive a secure income and can take cash advances from their employers. It is not uncommon for employers to give their employees loans to finance marriages and other important ceremonies. Such loans carry the comparatively modest interest rate of 1.5 percent a month. The casual laborers engaged in agriculture do not appear to work outside the village. Most operations are paid on a contract (piece-rate) basis. The principal rates are 120 kilograms of grain per acre for both planting and harvesting. Wages for threshing are paid individually. (If the crop is threshed by tractor, the rate is 3 parts in 80 of the gross yield.)

There are also some nonagricultural laborers, who are engaged mainly in construction. Apparently, construction workers in this locality have a reputation that extends throughout the state, and much of their work is done outside their home villages.

Land and tenancy

It is claimed that land is no longer leased out, with the exception of perhaps 15 sharecropping leases. The tenants seem to get two-thirds of the crop, with the usual costs shared in the same proportions. Both the cropping pattern and the level of purchased inputs subject to cost sharing are negotiated. If the landlord has to provide these inputs, he deducts the tenant's share of the cost before the rest of the output is shared. Would-be tenants must possess draft animals and be of good character.

Credit and other inputs

About 100 villagers are members of the cooperative, but the society has been "dormant" for about four years. It seems that, at one stage, there was little pressure on borrowers to repay their loans. Following recent legal proceedings, however, it is possible that enough loans have been paid off to warrant an application for the society to be resuscitated. So far, no bank has adopted the village, although the SBI may do so in the near future. This prospect is somewhat clouded by the poor repayment record of nearby villages, which are sponsored by the Bank of Hyderabad. In recent years, therefore, the farmers have had to rely on private sources to finance cultivation, the usual rate being 2.5 percent a month (simple). If the borrower has an established relationship with the lender, no security is demanded; otherwise, the borrower must pledge gold, animals, or land. Commission agents sometimes arrange credit for cultivators from merchants and traders, usually in the form of fertilizers. About 15 to 20 percent of the cultivators use this facility, with the understanding that the crop will be marketed solely through the agent who arranged the credit.

The new wells were financed partly by the LMB and partly by private sources. More wells could be sunk, but small farmers are not eligible for sufficient credit under the present rules, since the LMB values the land before it is improved, not afterward.

Indeed, the respondents went on to claim that shortage of finance is their main problem. The supply of purchased inputs is also somewhat precarious. There are four tractors in the village, which are hired out both in the village itself and elsewhere. The current rates are Rs 80 an acre for plowing (puddling) wetland and Rs 55 for plowing dryland.

Output

The main crops are paddy, millets, and castor, with small acreages of red gram and groundnut. The crops are sold in a regulated market some 30 kilometers away, and farmers arrange their own transport, using both trucks and tractors. There are no forward sales, and in the market itself, sale is by auction. As noted, commission agents are active.

Commentary

As in village 3, there is evidence that some people in the village are making a fair living, although here the only source of income is agriculture. A number of houses are under construction or being improved; the material is granite, which is in ample supply. There appears to be a substantial group of middle peasants as well as a narrow circle of big cultivators, so it is plausible that the recent investment in wells has not been undertaken only by the well-to-do. Nevertheless, the distribution of income within the village is almost certainly rather unequal. That would-be tenants must have draft animals is difficult to square with the village stock of four tractors and an active rental market for their services. If, however, credit is as tight as our respondents claim, the requirement that tenants possess draft animals makes good sense. In view of the skewed distribution of landownership and shortage of finance for working capital, I am not persuaded that tenancy is as limited as was claimed. Once again, the relatively detailed account of tenancy arrangements suggests that tenancies are common, although it is possible, as in village 3, that our respondents were referring to a fairly recent past before tenancies were resumed on a large scale.

It is interesting that efforts are under way to revive the cooperative, for they must be collective. It is possible, therefore, that the repayment of outstanding loans owes something to group pressure as well as the threat of legal penalties. Moreover, to the extent that a revived cooperative would improve the chances of getting sponsored by the SBI, the payoff to collective action against current defaulters would be all the greater. I gained the impression during the interview that the respondents share a feeling of community, which might make the costs of such collective action individually tolerable. Of course, collective action normally involves some measure of coercion. The distribution of land being what it is, I have little doubt that collective action in this village would be attended by coercion.

VILLAGE 8, MAHBUBNAGAR DISTRICT

Respondents

A score of farmers, including a man who had left his post as a village-level worker (VLW) to manage the family's holding of 100 acres. Two extension workers accompanied us to the village. The meeting took place in the panchayat (village council) meeting house and was rather brief, having started late in the afternoon. It also became rather chaotic: farmers came and went, and by dusk most were milling around outside—time to drink country liquor, we were told. I place less confidence in the replies to our questions here than to those in village 7, but I think they are still worth reporting. In particular, the ex-VLW struck me as being a fairly reliable and serious informant. Telling us that he was formerly a VLW was in itself an attempt to establish credentials with outsiders, and admitting to a family holding of 100 acres is rather unusual. (Date: September 27, 1980.)

General features

The village has about 350 households, including a new hamlet established by settlers from the coastal areas. Its total area is about 3,000 acres, some of which are black soils suitable for growing cotton. The sole source of irrigation comprises 40 wells, which command about 50 acres. About 20 of the wells were constructed during the past five years. The village is more than 20 kilometers from the nearest surfaced road and market, at Amangal.

Labor and wages

Almost a third of the households depend on agricultural labor for their livelihood. There are about 50 attached farm servants. Some are paid Rs 300–Rs 600 a year (depending on their age and duties) plus daily meals. Others choose to be paid only in kind at a rate of 72 kilograms of grain a month (the cash equivalent of about Rs 900 a year). These attached servants usually have quite general duties. The contracts are desired because they offer security of income and employment. They also open a line of credit, and advances of salary are frequently taken. The qualities desired by employers are obedience and trustworthiness. In contrast to other villages, these relationships do not last for long periods. [I am skeptical about this claim in light of the responses to this question in other villages.]

Casual laborers do not seem to be attached to particular employers on a first-call basis. Such laborers are in ample supply and work in gangs, most operations being paid in kind on a contract (piece-rate) basis. The prevailing rates are 5 kilograms of grain a day for plowing and 75 kilograms per acre for both planting and harvesting; threshing wages are paid on a daily basis.

There is some seasonal migration out of the village, perhaps 25 households in all.

Land and tenancy

There is some tenancy, most of it under sharecropping arrangements, with output and the costs of the usual subset of inputs being shared equally. Both the cropping pattern and the levels of inputs are negotiated. The tenant must finance his share of all costs, borrowing from third parties if necessary. He is free to sell to whomsoever he pleases. Land is occasionally rented out for a fixed sum in kind. One figure quoted was 240 kilograms an acre, the "landlord" in question being a laborer who was a beneficiary of a redistribution of surplus lands under the Land Ceilings Act. Apparently, after cultivating the land himself for a while, he found it better to receive rents and hire out his labor to others [perhaps he lacked finance or husbandry skills]. Under both systems, would-be tenants must have draft animals and be of good character.

Some farmers have sold land in order to finance the construction of wells.

Credit and other inputs

The cooperative is effectively defunct owing to widespread default on loans for the purchase of bullocks and other inputs. The village has not been adopted by a bank, although a neighboring village has a branch of the SBI. Some of the newer wells were financed by the LMB. At one point, it was claimed that farmers finance their own working capital requirements, but later remarks suggest that traders and commission agents do advance short-term loans against future deliveries of crops. The loans from private sources for the construction of wells carry an interest rate of 2.5 percent a month (simple), with gold, animals, or land pledged as collateral.

Getting sufficient finance (at modest rates) appears to be a pervasive and serious problem. Our respondents had particularly strong feelings about the corruption they encountered when seeking institutional credit. One of them claimed that, in order to obtain a loan of Rs 1,000, a farmer must give a bribe of Rs 500; no one dissented. [If finance from private sources is readily available at 2.5 percent a month, this claim is surely exaggerated.]

There are also certain technical difficulties in sinking wells. First, the water table is usually deeper than 40 feet, so that wells must be lined with masonry, adding greatly to their cost. If the figure of Rs 30,000 a well that was cited to us is reliable, it is hard to see how the investment could be profitable, even with the 25 percent subsidy under the DPAP, for these wells command only 1.5 acres at best. Second, the water tends to be saline.

The alternative is to sink tube wells. One experimental boring has been made in the area of black soils, but the results are still awaited. If they are promising, the Irrigation Development Corporation (IDC) might install some public tube wells. Currently, IDC charges Rs 200 an acre for the service. There are no tractors in the village.

Output

The main crops are millets and castor on red soils and chilies, tobacco, and cotton on black soils. For the most part, crops are sold to agents who live in the village.

[It is not clear whether these people are big cultivators or specialist traders.] However, big cultivators sometimes take tobacco and chilies to Amangal for direct sale (see also Aurepalle).

Commentary

It would be interesting to see whether there are any differences in economic organization and performance between the group of settlers from the coast and the locals (a question arising in village 3).

In general, the village has a rather weak infrastructure. It is inaccessible; transport costs are high; irrigation is limited and faces very high development costs; and institutional credit appears to be limited to long-term loans from the LMB. However, as in other villages in this tract, house construction and improvement were very much in evidence, and the villagers we saw did not appear to be utterly impoverished. Perhaps the rather gloomy account of the farmers' economic condition that emerged from the discussion is heavily colored by recent experience. After all, the monsoon in 1979 was poorer than usual, and 1980 is almost certain to be much worse (October signals the start of the dry winter season.) The former VLW told us, rather mournfully, that he would have been better off staying in government service, modest though the salary is. This must be a statement of his present woes rather than an assessment of the long-term net advantage of cultivating a large farm, but it does convey the stresses to which the villagers in this semiarid tract are subjected when the rains are meager.

VILLAGE AUREPALLE, MAHBUBNAGAR DISTRICT

Respondents

Two enumerators employed by ICRISAT. I was accompanied by Dr. Singh and a senior investigator, who used the occasion to check on the enumerators' work. The discussion took place in the house where the enumerators live. (Date: October 16, 1980.)

General features

A detailed description can be found in the many research papers produced by ICRISAT's research team over the past few years (see Jodha, Asokan, and Ryan 1977). The dirt road that connects Amangal with village 8 passes through the village. In physical appearance, the two villages are much alike. This proximity to village 8 and the opportunity to talk with enumerators who knew the village intimately persuaded me to make this additional trip into the field.

Labor and wages

About half the households depend mainly on agricultural labor for their livelihood, and there are more than 50 attached farm servants (Binswanger et al. 1984). The latter are paid 54 kilograms a month, a pinch of tobacco daily, and a blanket once a year, yielding a total cash equivalent of about Rs 700—somewhat lower than the Rs 900 in village 8. (Binswanger et al. [1984, 151] give the lower figure of 44.5 kilograms a month.) It is common for laborers who are indebted to work for their creditors as attached servants. [Here the direction of causation is unclear. Perhaps the indebtedness is no more than a simple consequence of the laborers taking an advance of salary. Binswanger et al. (1984) make the stronger suggestion that laborers seek annual contracts because they can then obtain credit from their employers. There is corroborating evidence for this viewpoint from our discussions in other villages.] The rate of interest on such loans is 1.5 percent a month (simple), a common use of the funds being the financing of marriage; the typical outlay is Rs 1,000. As these debts exceed the laborer's annual wages, the relationship usually continues for a number of years.

Land and tenancy

About 250 acres are owned by a single family. The eldest brother lives in Hyderabad, where he manages other branches of the family's business. Another brother lives in the village to oversee the day-to-day operations of the farm. A third brother lives in Canada. Perhaps 15 percent of the cultivated area is leased out under one arrangement or another. The predominant form is sharecropping, with output and the costs of the usual subset of inputs being shared equally. No one uses fertilizers on unirrigated land. Moreover, irrigated land is not normally leased out, and if it is, the rent usually takes the form of a fixed payment in kind.

Households that have no bullocks often lease out part or all of their holdings. Tenants are occasionally indebted to their landlords; small farmers and laborers owning small plots usually lease out their land to other small farmers, so the question of indebtedness does not arise.

Credit and other inputs

Half a dozen of the largest farmers are active moneylenders.

The prevailing rates charged on loans in kind are 100 percent a season for seed and 50 percent a season for consumption (these are own rates of interest). The rate on cash loans is 2.0–2.5 percent a month (simple). No collateral is demanded if the loan is relatively modest. The traders in Amangal seem to be engaged in financing cultivation.

There is a tank, which commands about 50 acres in a normal year, but it has been empty for the past two years.

Output

The main crops are sorghum, castor, and pigeon pea. Paddy is grown on irrigated land. In rabi, safflower is grown on black soils.

It is quite common for small farmers to sell their crops to big cultivators, who then resell in the regulated market in Amangal. [It is not clear whether these sales are tied up with indebtedness or tenancy, for transport costs are high and small farmers normally sell in small lots.]

There are only five or six registered traders in Amangal, and there is some evidence that they collude quite effectively.

Commentary

Wealth and power in Aurepalle are highly unequally distributed, and there appear to be numerous opportunities for the leading families to exercise market power. After studying the village for five years, ICRISAT's researchers have arrived at this conclusion with some confidence, even though their treatment of it is rather sotto voce. Leaving aside the pathological detail of the leading family's males who live in Hyderabad and Canada, the four villages in this tract—villages 6, 7, and 8 and Aurepalle—merit the same label.

Our respondents' estimate that about 15 percent of the cultivated area is leased out strikes me as being of the right order. (Recall the denials that there is any tenancy to speak of in villages 6 and 7.)

VILLAGE 9, KURNOOL DISTRICT

Respondents

The patwari, an extension worker, and two farmers. Much later, we were joined by one of the richest farmers in the village, who had just suffered a large loss in the cultivation of cotton for certified seed. His gloomy presence cramped what had been a free and interesting discussion. The meeting took place in the extension worker's office. (Date: September 30, 1980.)

General features

The village is high up on the Deccan plateau, about 15 kilometers from Adoni, the subdivisional town and close to the border with Karnataka. The terrain is somewhat less rugged than that of Mahbubnagar and Nalgonda Districts, with occasional rocky outcrops. For the most part, this is a tract of black soils suitable for growing cotton, the principal crop, changing to red gravelly soils near the outcrops and rising ground.

The village has a slightly grubby appearance and, with the exception of villages 4 and 5, is outwardly less prosperous than those we visited in Nalgonda and Mahbubnagar. The grubbiness is due to the villagers' practice of stabling their livestock in a yard or room in front of the house. [It is hard to believe that this practice reduces the chances of theft; perhaps it is simply to deter squeamish visitors from calling too often.]

There are 540 households, 350 of which are engaged in cultivation. The area of the village is about 6,600 acres, about 5,500 of which are cultivable. Four hundred and fifty acres are irrigated by public canal. Groundwater is scarce, and what there is tends to be saline, so there is little or no investment in wells.

The main crop is cotton, none of which is irrigated. About 1,000 acres are planted with sorghum and millets, and the irrigated area is entirely under paddy. In rabi, groundnut is grown on 250–300 acres.

Labor and wages

There are 30–40 attached farm servants, who are paid between Rs 800 and Rs 1,200 a year, usually wholly in cash. Wages are paid every six months, but advances can be taken at any time. Requests for advances are usually granted and carry no interest. As in other villages, these laborers have general duties, so employers look for workers who are trustworthy. For their part, the laborers desire continuity of employment and the opportunity to obtain loans over and above advances of salary (such loans carry an interest rate of 2 percent a month). Once established, these relationships tend to endure for a run of years.

All of the important operations—planting and harvesting—are done under contract, in which the rate is negotiated either in cash or kind. It seems that there are no established gang leaders. [Perhaps an employer asks a worker to organize a group to do a particular piece of work, but approaches different individuals at different times.] Although in the past laborers were often attached to an employer on a first-call basis, this practice has now ceased. There is seasonal migration of laborers both into and out of the village. Whatever the pattern of this migration, there is no real shortage of labor. The wage rate for casual work is Rs 1.50 a day for women and Rs 2.50 a day for men, although their tasks are different.

Land and tenancy

Although land is leased out under both share and fixed-rent arrangements, the former predominates. The landlord's share is 50 percent of the crop on land of average quality and 60 percent on fertile plots. It is claimed that all costs, including outlays on labor and draft power, are shared between landlord and tenant in the same proportion as output; the cropping pattern and the level of inputs are set by negotiation. With all input costs shared, the landlord must trust the tenant in all things if the costs of monitoring the contract are to be kept within reasonable bounds. As well as being trustworthy, tenants must own draft animals.

Since the banks will not lend to persons without land, the landlord plays an important part in financing cultivation on each tenancy, either directly by providing inputs and subsequently deducting the tenant's share of the costs at harvest time or indirectly by introducing the tenant to a commission agent and standing security for the loan that the agent advances.

Rents in cash are usually paid in arrears. The rent may be rolled over if the crop is poor and the landlord has no grounds for charging the tenant with negligence.

There seems to be no bar to tenants leasing land from more than one landlord. Tenants are obliged neither to provide labor nor to sell their output to their landlords.

Credit and other inputs

The village's cooperative has been defunct for 10 years, so the farmers go to a cooperative in a village some 5 kilometers away. The latter also enjoys the luxury of having the branches of two banks [surely, a very large village or an uncommonly well-connected one]. These banks are the main sources of institutional credit for working capital.

Commission agents in Adoni are also highly active in financing cultivation, and because they are more flexible in their dealings and are prepared to advance larger sums, the farmers take more finance from the agents than they do from the banks. These loans carry an interest rate of 2 percent a month. Such a loan is given in cash, kind, or both, with all accounts settled after the crop is sold—solely through the commission agent who advanced the loan, this being an implicit condition attached to it. The relationship between an agent and a farmer is usually built up over several years, and if they know one another well, current debts will be rolled over if the crop turns out to be poor.

While big farmers are financed by commission agents, small farmers take loans from local traders, who charge a slightly higher rate, 2.5 percent being usual.

Long-term loans are taken almost exclusively from the LMB and SBI.

Adoni is the main market center. Big farmers sell directly to traders there, using the services of commission agents to place the lots for tender. The agents will store the crop for an additional fee if the farmer is not satisfied with the highest bid received. Small farmers sell to three or four traders who live in the village itself. These traders do some cultivation on the side, but trading is their main source of livelihood.

There are half a dozen tractors in the village, which are extensively hired out for marketing cotton and groundnut in Adoni.

Commentary

The provisions for sharing costs in the sharecropping contracts are intriguing. It is well known that when (a) all costs are shared in the same proportion as output, (b) all markets are perfect, and (c) the costs of monitoring the tenant's doings are negligible (as would be the case if he were completely trustworthy), then production will be efficient. Why, then, is it necessary for the landlord and tenant to negotiate how much of each input is used? If negotiation does accompany an efficient lease, the reason probably lies in the presence of credit rationing. For whether the landlord himself extends credit or stands surety for credit advanced by a commission agent, the possibility that the tenant may default will lead to credit rationing, even if there is free entry into moneylending (Bell and Zusman 1980).

The account of how markets function suggests that the village conforms fairly closely to a classic pattern. A few farmers own tractors; wage rates for casual laborers are very low; big farmers sell their output in the regulated market, while small farmers sell to local traders; and credit and tenancy are intimately linked, as are credit and marketing.

VILLAGE 10, KURNOOL DISTRICT

Respondents

The patwari, the patel (village leader), and perhaps a score of farmers. The patwari is a spry, meticulous old man, who obviously takes his records very seriously. He did much of the talking, occasionally breaking into English, as if to emphasize the veracity of his responses, most of which I have little reason to doubt. As the meeting took place on the verandah of the patel's house—hardly the best place for a discussion of wages, tenancy, and moneylending—the patwari's dominant role was somewhat reassuring. (Date: September 30, 1980.)

General features

The village lies astride a surfaced road, which connects it with Adoni, some 40 kilometers away. Like village 9, it has a rather grubby appearance, the casual visitor's first impressions being formed by the numerous huts of the landless that line the road.

There are about 400 households altogether, 350 of which are engaged in some form of cultivation. The average holding is about 5 acres. There are roughly 200 small holdings in the 2- to 3-acre range, so the distribution of land must be quite unequal. A public canal commands 300 acres, and another 110 acres are irrigated by 30 percolation wells, all of which are energized and 20 of which were constructed in the past two years.

Labor and wages

About 100 households depend wholly or mainly on agricultural labor as a source of livelihood. There are attached farm servants, but they are paid daily and are called, confusingly, "daily laborers." [Perhaps most of them are indebted to their employers, and the adjective "daily" is a thin disguise to evade the provisions of the laws prohibiting debt bondage.] The wage rate is Rs 3 to Rs 5 in cash or kind. As in other villages, these laborers do all sorts of work. They seek continuity of employment and access to credit, while employers look for able-bodied and trustworthy workers. The relationship usually endures for a run of years [probably because past debts and the need for future credit maintain the tie.] Other members of the household are also available to the worker's employer as casual laborers on a first-call basis.

Planting and harvesting, the main operations, are paid on a contract basis. The laborers form themselves into gangs, each of which has a de facto leader, who negotiates the rate for the job and works alongside the rest. The daily wage in the main season is Rs 2.5 a day for women and Rs 3 to Rs 4 a day for men, dropping to Rs 2 and between Rs 2.5 and Rs 3.0, respectively, in the off-season. These wages are paid wholly in cash, in accordance with the laborers' preferences.

There is some seasonal migration, both into and out of the village at planting time.

Land and tenancy

It is claimed that there is no tenancy [a claim that I find implausible—consider village 9 just 30 kilometers away].

Credit and other inputs

There is a functioning cooperative in a village 8 kilometers away, to which about 50 farmers in village 10 belong. However, about 90 percent of all finance for working capital is provided by commission agents in Adoni, on the same terms as those described by our respondents in village 9, with the additional condition that land may be required as collateral if the loan exceeds Rs 1,000. As in other places, the farmers complained about the banks' cumbersome procedures when sanctioning loans. The fact that defaulters are not eligible was also mentioned, which suggests that default on institutional loans may be widespread in this village.

Most of the new wells were financed with loans from the LMB. A well and pump set can be had for about Rs 5,000, which is well within the limit of Rs 10,000 set by the LMB. Moreover, the prospects for sinking new wells are good, there being fairly abundant groundwater. Yet investment in wells is hampered by two factors. First, the LMB's procedures are lengthy, and much land is encumbered with debt. Second, the LMB values land in its undeveloped state, so small farmers are unable to raise enough finance.

There are no tractors, but there is some hiring in from nearby villages.

Output

The main crops are cotton and groundnut, which are marketed in Adoni under the tender system described above.

Commentary

At our prompting, the respondents offered to introduce us to a commission agent in Adoni with whom several of them have been dealing for several years. The patwari accompanied us to the agent's business premises (a general store) and made the necessary introductions. What follows is a rather condensed account of the interview, many details being left out to preserve the agent's anonymity.

Before 1974, crops were sold by auction, with both sides paying a commission. This system was replaced by the present tender system, in which the farmers' produce is graded and displayed by staff of the marketing yard ("commercial" grading) and would-be buyers make sealed bids. If a farmer sells through a commission agent, he pays a fee of 1.5 percent ad valorem on unginned cotton and 2 percent on groundnut. In exchange, the farmer gets paid on the spot by the commission agent, who is paid, eventually, by the buyer. Buyers typically take 20–30 days to settle accounts; for example, the Cotton Corporation of India (CCI) takes a month. In effect, the commission agent provides the farmer with insurance against late payment. [Since commission agents charge their clients 2 percent a month on outstanding loans, the commission fee is roughly equal to the interest charged on a loan equal to the value of the sale and held for one month.] Farmers can sell directly to traders or the CCI if they wish, but most choose to sell through commission agents. One further advantage of selling through an agent is that if the farmer is dissatisfied with the highest bid and wishes to offer his lot for tender at a later date, the agent will arrange for the crop to be stored until that time (for an additional fee). In the case of an unsuccessful attempt at a direct sale, the farmer either would have to make these arrangements himself, which is not always possible, or would have to transport the crop back to his village.

Where the financing of cultivation is concerned, this agent has about 2,000 clients, three-quarters of whom have been dealing with him for 10 years or more. New clients are not taken on without an introduction from someone of good standing, preferably an established client. Debts have to be rolled over due to adverse growing conditions. There are also some bad debts, which often result in forced sales of land, although recovery is becoming more difficult. In the past 10 years, there have been about 50 cases of bad debts among his clients. The default rate has increased in recent years because there is less integrity now. In the long term, this development will diminish his moneylending activities, as will the steady penetration of the organized banking system into rural areas.

When advancing credit to cultivators, he employs a simple rule of thumb to determine the size of the loan: Rs 150 per Rs 1,000 of expected output in kharif and between Rs 250 and Rs 300 in rabi. The ratio for rabi is more generous because the crop is more assured. [As the rabi crop is normally unirrigated, this reason is rather puzzling, unless the covariance of yields and prices is such as to make the expected value of revenue relatively stable.] The purpose for which the loan is taken does not affect its terms; only the client's reputation matters. [As clients will normally take loans in kind from his general store, he can keep a rough check on how they are allocating their loans between current consumption and investment in working capital.] He also employs a group of subagents who move about the countryside, keeping a close eye on how his clients' crops are progressing, especially at harvest time.

His own land is leased out. To avoid the provisions of tenancy legislation, his tenants pay no rent directly; rather a special fee is deducted from the proceeds of sale when the crop is marketed (all of it through our respondent). All decisions concerning inputs are left to the tenants' discretion.

VILLAGE 11, CHITTOOR DISTRICT

Respondents

The patwari and a score of farmers. They were serious in their replies and occasionally rather preoccupied with their present difficulties. While they may have exaggerated the burdensome terms of their market dealings, casual observation of the fields and the village sufficed to confirm that their present condition is lamentable. The meeting took place in the schoolroom. (Date: October 2, 1980.)

General features

The village lies high up on the plateau, with terrain and soils similar to those of Mahbubnagar and Nalgonda Districts. It is about 40 kilometers from the Block headquarters, the last 10 kilometers over a metaled road in poor repair. There are about 400 households, 350 of which are engaged partly or wholly in cultivation. The rest depend exclusively on agricultural labor, but many cultivators exchange labor. Irrigation is provided by six ponds, a tank, and about 150 wells. In a normal year, the surface irrigation works and the wells command 500 and 300 acres, respectively, but now, after a second year of poor rains, the big tank is irrigating only 15 acres.

The main unirrigated crop is groundnut, about 800–900 acres all told. Irrigated plots are sown wholly to paddy—when water is available. [Casual observation of this and other areas of Andhra suggest that the paddy terraces have been left fallow. Presumably, farmers wait for so long in the hope that there will be enough water for paddy that it becomes impossible to plant sorghum or other dryland crops.]

Labor and wages

There is no contract system for the main operations. Employers simply go in search of laborers the evening before the work is to be done. The daily wage rate is Rs 3 and two meals; work begins at 8 a.m. and ends at 4.30 p.m. During the harvest season, the cash component of the wage rises somewhat, since there are spot shortages of labor. Between 100 and 150 households work outside the village, so many households have to supplement their income from cultivation with wages. Laborers from other villages do not work here.

Land and tenancy

Dryland is not leased out because farmers' holdings are very small. Half of the irrigated land is owned by absentee landlords, and this is leased out. [This is probably the area commanded by the big tank.] Tenants prefer fixed-rent contracts if irrigation is assured. The current rate is 300 kilograms of paddy per acre. If the total yield is insufficient to pay the rent in full because of drought, the rental contract is converted into sharecropping, with half the crop going to the landlord. Otherwise, the rent is payable in full. Those landlords who can monitor their tenants' doings offer sharecropping contracts (50:50 shares), but they neither share in any costs nor provide any finance. Would-be tenants must possess draft animals and access to a line of credit. They are obliged neither to provide labor to their landlords nor to sell their output to them.

Credit and other inputs

The cooperative has about 200 members, but after 30–60 people had defaulted, it became dormant. In any event, the procedures for obtaining loans are very cumbersome, so many farmers have resorted to private sources of finance. At present, all cultivation is financed by moneylenders who live in two nearby villages. They are also active in trading. Indeed, marketing and finance are tied together in the usual way. Lenders usually advance loans up to 50 percent of the expected value of the crops to be grown, with interest charges of 30–35 percent a season (that is, 5–6 percent a month). The own rate of interest on groundnut seed is 50–100 percent a season, while cash loans to finance wage payments bear a rate of 5 percent a month. No security is required for such loans: the reputation of the borrower suffices. Debts are commonly rolled over.

About a score of wells have been dug over the past five years, all of them financed by private sources (at 24 percent a year) and savings. Land must be pledged as collateral in these cases, and about a dozen households have lost their land as a result of unsuccessful investments in wells. Since the sums involved are quite large, borrowers approach only those lenders with whom they have a long-standing relationship.

The main difficulty with long-term loans from the LMB—aside from cumbersome and corrupt procedures—is that land is valued (as collateral) at the rate of Rs 600 an acre, whereas it fetches Rs 10,000 an acre once the well has been constructed. Since a well costs at least Rs 7,000, most farmers do not have enough land to finance a well. The water table is about 35–40 feet deep, and wells are normally profitable investments on the terms offered by the LMB. [The presence of a large tank and several ponds probably ensures ample water through percolation in most years.]

There are no tractors in the village, nor are any hired in from other villages.

Output

About a quarter of the groundnut produced is sold in a nearby market. The rest is purchased in the village by traders who deal with oil mills elsewhere. It appears that they, too, are active in financing cultivation.

Commentary

The thin and wilting crops of groundnut everywhere in this tract tell a simple story lucidly. Yet these villagers are weighed down by more grievous burdens than the certainty of a second poor crop in a row. Much of the irrigated land is held by absentees, who take little interest in cultivation, and the terms of credit from the nearby moneylenders who finance all cultivation smack of usury.

As one farmer put it, "They finance everything, from seed to seed, and leave us nothing." Like village 4 in Nalgonda District, the village lies in a neglected, even more remote, periphery; although it has a well for drinking water, this, too, is drying up.

Most of the complaints against the LMB and the cooperative followed what was by now a familiar refrain, but a new charge was also leveled at the institutions providing credit. It seems that each district has a sort of cooperative bank or banking committee. Although the district collector is ex officio chairman, most of the members are local politicians or party workers drawn from the dominant party. [In light of the treatment meted out to civil servants in Andhra Pradesh, I have little doubt that the district collector does the politicians' bidding in such matters.] When this committee meets, so the farmers claim, it decides on the allocation of funds and other resources among the district's cooperatives, granting ample amounts to those localities where the members enjoy strong support and starving those who voted for the opposition. It is possible to construe this as just one more instance of competition for resources that are allocated by administrative fiat rather than the market, and in a sense that is so. However, when the goal is no more than the short-term expedient of shoring up the local political base and the means involve wholesale distortions in the allocation of resources in production, I would call this simply "the politics of spoils."

VILLAGE 12, CHITTOOR DISTRICT

Respondents

About 30 farmers and three or four young men who had college degrees but no jobs. The proceedings were not very satisfactory and, at times, bordered on the chaotic. The plight of the young men was brought up on several occasions, and they too had plenty to say for themselves as the meeting drew to a close. We were accompanied by an important man of the village, the vice president of the Block samithi (Block-level council), who turned out to have a son in Canada. His presence may have been at the root of a certain tension that persisted throughout the discussion, and, on reflection, our insistence on holding the discussion in the panchayat meeting house and accepting hospitality there rather than in his house was surely wise. The notes that follow are brief, and some of the information therein is of dubious reliability. The commentary deals at some length with a subsequent incident. (Date: October 2, 1980.)

General features

The terrain and soils are similar to those of village 11, but the village is better placed, its several hamlets lying athwart the surfaced road that connects it to the Block headquarters 12 kilometers distant.

There are about 300 households, 250 of which are engaged in cultivation. Irrigation is provided by some 60 wells, all of them energized. The main crop is groundnut.

Labor and wages

About 100 households depend mainly on agricultural labor for their livelihood. There are 20 or 30 attached farm servants, who receive three meals a day and

450 kilograms of grain and three sets of cloth annually (the cash equivalent lies between Rs 800 and Rs 1,000 a year). As elsewhere, these servants tackle all sorts of work. They seek the continuous employment offered by such contracts and the opportunity to take advances of salary, which carry no interest. For their part, employers want, above all else, workers who are trustworthy.

Casual laborers are hired in the evening for work to be done the next day. The wage rate is Rs 2 and two meals for a day of six hours; it does not fluctuate during the course of the year. These laborers also work in gangs outside the village. [If the numbers of cultivating and laboring households are both correct, many of the cultivating households must have very small farms.]

Land and tenancy

It is claimed that there is no tenancy, holdings being very small. [I do not believe this claim. Our companion almost certainly possesses a large holding, as do the fathers of the young men with degrees but no (salaried) jobs. With the technology available to them, it is unlikely that they could manage cultivation on the whole area I suspect them of owning. Moreover, there was a curious remark to the effect that dryland is not leased. Is there a tract of irrigated land owned by absentees, as in village 11?]

Apparently, land sales are quite frequent, but they never involve people who live outside the village.

Credit and other inputs

There are 195 members of the cooperative, which has been dormant for six years, following a wave of defaults similar to that which overwhelmed the cooperative in village 11. Nowadays small farmers [and perhaps others] are financed by the traders who purchase their crops of groundnut, the two transactions being contractually linked. The relationship between cultivator and trader usually lasts for a good many years, but even then traders will not advance large sums unless the cultivator pledges land as collateral. Farmers need about Rs 300 to finance an acre of groundnut; the interest rate is between 2 and 3 percent a month.

About a dozen wells were sunk in the past five years. They were usually financed as follows: a loan of Rs 4,000 to Rs 5,000 from the LMB was combined with a slightly smaller sum from private sources outside the village, the latter bearing the familiar interest rate of 2 percent a month (simple). More wells could be sunk, but financing them remains a serious problem. Dealing with the LMB always involves lengthy and corruption-ridden procedures. More recently, the LMB has pursued defaulters with vigor: five defaulters had their bullocks seized and then auctioned off. Moneylenders usually offer a more flexible schedule of repayments, but even here, farmers who fell behind had to sell off some assets to settle their debts.

Output

A dozen big cultivators sell their groundnut directly to millers, using bullock carts for transport. Small farmers sell to traders, who buy the crop in the village itself.

Commentary

Such comments as I wish to make on village 12 itself have been made in passing above. On our return to the Block headquarters in the evening, another incident occurred that is so revealing of the relationship between the local political structure and the administration that it is worth setting down here.

In choosing villages 11 and 12 that morning, we had rejected a suggestion by the block development officer (BDO) that we replace one of them with another, particular village. The latter had been designated as a "focal point." It had been adopted by a German voluntary agency, and it just happened to be the home village of a minister of the state government. We explained our (evident) reasons for rejecting this suggestion courteously but firmly; this was not enough—interested parties wanted to hear it all from our own mouths. So when the BDO greeted us on our return with the news that the president of the samithi, who was none other than the minister's brother, had telephoned and asked that we go and visit him, we had little choice but to agree. After all, we would need the support of the administration in carrying out our survey, and now there was compelling evidence that the BDO was at the beck and call of powerful local politicians. (He, poor fellow, was visibly agitated; it was plain that he had telephoned the minister's brother, rather than the other way around, in order to cover himself.) If the fieldwork was to go ahead, we would have to convince the minister's brother that we possessed no resources worthy of his attention.

At length, we drew up outside a magnificent and spotless building, which would not have disgraced the more affluent sections of Southern California. This was the panchayat meeting house, doubtless paid for—in part, at least—with contributions in deutschmarks. As we ascended the wide flight of steps leading up to the terrace on the second story, a figure in an impeccably laundered dhoti and kurta waited to receive us: the minister's brother. We introduced ourselves, while the BDO hovered nervously in the background. Chairs were drawn up, tea was brought, and, for the sake of form I suppose, a small group of farmers was ushered up the steps and thence to one side, where they squatted down (without mats) as instructed.

The minister's brother began by addressing me in English: "I hear that you have come to help us."

We had prepared for this. As agreed, Dr. Rao did all the talking, emphasizing the primacy of research in our study and the tenuous connection between it and the practical operations of the World Bank in the near future. After Rao had finished, there was a brief exchange, and then I restated what Rao had said. But just when we had persuaded him that we disposed of nothing of any value and were preparing to depart, an ancient American car arrived and the minister himself got out, accompanied by a few robust-looking young men.

The play was enacted once more, with baroque variations. The minister held forth at some length on what he had said in a recent cabinet meeting that had considered the drought now afflicting agriculture. If I understood the general thrust of what he said, there was no need for research: it would suffice to control the weather. At length, he too decided that we had nothing to offer. He then turned upon the unfortunate BDO, who had sat silently, bent forward in his chair, and addressed him sharply in Telegu, whereupon the BDO stood up.

Even afterward, my colleagues did not translate what was said, and I spared their blushes by not pressing the matter. It was clear enough that the BDO was being severely reprimanded by the minister: why had his time been wasted on these people who controlled no resources to speak of? (What is more, the cowed farmers huddled to one side were being treated to a demonstration, not of his ability as a successful leader of a cargo cult, but quite the reverse.) And it was done in a manner that reeked of contempt and arrogance. (My colleagues later told me that the minister had used the second person singular, an insulting form of address usually reserved for recalcitrant, disobedient children and social inferiors of the lowest rank, a form of address they themselves would never use, even toward their office peons and sweepers.) Eventually, we managed to make our farewells, but the wretched BDO was detained for a few minutes longer, as if the previous upbraiding was not enough.

As the rules of the game now stand, the BDO had done everything he could; for after failing to "deliver" us himself, he had placed the matter—and us—before his political masters. When it turned out that we had nothing of value to offer them, he was subjected to public humiliation. Even if we had had real resources to dispose of, his task as a civil servant was to advise us in the light of his own understanding of the aims of public policy. Instead, his first reaction was to try to bolster the power base of those who, for the present, hold sway over this locality.

It is hard to know what is meant by public policy, as the term is usually understood, when the administration has been demoralized and undermined as it has been here. How can there be any public policy when civil servants are, in effect, merely the functionaries of local political bosses? In such cases, discussions of public policy are simply surreal.

VILLAGE 13, CHITTOOR DISTRICT

Respondents

A score of farmers, some of whom had much to say for themselves. This meeting in the schoolroom was one of the most interesting of our tour of Andhra. Our respondents were open and lively, with a curiosity that extended to such embarrassing subjects as the salaries paid by the World Bank. (They were the only villagers to raise this question.) (Date: October 3, 1980.)

General features

At this lower elevation, the climate is tropical once more. Palm and coconut trees grace the villages and soften the landscape, which is interrupted only occasionally by rocky outcrops. Much of the land is irrigated, but here, unlike the areas of the plateau, sugarcane competes with paddy for land having assured supplies of water. Village 13 itself is quite pleasant in appearance, with well-maintained houses and people who look both fairly well fed and dressed. It lies about 40 kilometers from Chittoor Town, the first 23 kilometers of the journey over a dirt track.

There are 170 households, about half of which supplement their income from cultivation with earnings from casual labor. Irrigation is provided by two tanks, which command about 60 acres in a normal year, and 140 wells, half of which are energized. The main crops are sugarcane (130 acres) and groundnut (150 acres). This year, owing to drought, the area under paddy is only 15 acres.

Labor and wages

There are only 10 or so attached farm servants, and these are children who tend the employer's livestock and are paid Rs 30 a year and three meals a day. In recent years, adults have avoided annual contracts, preferring instead to work as casual laborers.

With the exception of cane harvesting, which is done under a piece-rate contract, casual laborers are paid on a daily basis. With year-round employment, there is a uniform rate for the five-hour working day: Rs 3.0 and a meal for women and Rs 4.5 and a meal for men. [Is this simply discrimination, or do the sexes in fact perform different tasks?] Laborers are hired through a "contact" person. Although each farmer has his own particular contact, these individuals apparently do not receive a special fee for their services. There is no seasonal migration, except when the cane crop is harvested, when laborers are brought in. Cutters receive between Rs 13 and Rs 15 a tonne.

Land and tenancy

It is claimed that there is no tenancy in the village, nor has there been any in recent memory. Farms are small—95 percent are smaller than 5 acres—so there is no reason to lease. There has, however, been a substantial change in land rights. About a year ago, 185 acres of surplus lands were distributed among 72 households, and another 40 acres are to be parceled out in the near future. Apparently, this distribution of land simply conferred legal title on those households that had been occupying and cultivating the land in question for a good many years. [It is possible that the land was owned by an absentee who could see no way of collecting rents without falling foul of legal action by his tenants. The passage of time would have weakened his claim on ownership, and if rents could not be collected or the tenants evicted, the land would have had no value to third parties. The tenants would cease to regard themselves as such, and ceding legal title to them would cause the absentee no further loss.]

Every year, there are four or five sales of land, as farmers attempt to improve the location of their various plots.

Credit and other inputs

About 90 percent of all cultivators finance their working capital needs for sugarcane cultivation by taking loans from the banks in Chittoor. These loans bear an interest rate of 9–11 percent a year and must be accompanied by the deposit of the title to the borrower's land. Credit is advanced up to a total of between Rs 1,000 and Rs 1,200 per acre, some of it in the form of fertilizer supplied by the cooperative sugar mill. This is not enough for many farmers. A few seek additional loans (at 3 percent a month) from private bankers in Bangalore and Madras, pledging gold as security. Others resort to the ubiquitous commission agents, who charge 2 percent, with the usual tying clause on the marketing of the crop. [This apparently more favorable rate may stem from the long-standing nature of the relationship between farmer and agent, as emphasized in the notes on other villages.] The commercial banks are not involved in the financing of groundnut cultivation, so here the commission agents have the field to themselves.

Only one well has been sunk since 1973. There is a stratum of rock at 30 feet, so tube wells are the only feasible means of tapping groundwater. [Presumably, the area that can be commanded by percolation wells has been exploited to the full.]

There are two tractors in the village, but little in the way of custom hiring.

The marketing of the sugarcane crop is especially revealing. Virtually all of the villagers who grow cane are shareholders in the local cooperative mill. All members are under contract to deliver 8 tonnes of cane for each share they own, for which the cooperative pays Rs 1,040. There is a scale of penalties for failing to deliver at least 85 percent of the contracted quantity: Rs 5 a tonne on the first offense, Rs 10 a tonne on the second, and Rs 20 a tonne and up to six months in prison on the third.

The alternative is to risk fines and imprisonment by selling some or all of the contracted quantity to commission agents, who are currently offering Rs 3,200 a share, with the additional condition that the cultivators transform the cane into jaggery (country sugar), an operation that costs about Rs 200 for every 8 tonnes of cane. Faced with the choice of realizing Rs 3,000 a share from commission agents and Rs 1,040 (less Rs 120 in transport charges) from the mill, it comes as no surprise that many farmers have chosen the former, the penalties for first and second offenses against the mill being so paltry. Only half of the cane produced last year went to the mill; the proportion should have been much higher, and several people were prosecuted (see below). [Thus are the pressures exerted by high world prices for sugar felt in this small village. The government was considering increasing the official price by 10 to 20 percent, but unless world prices collapse, this step would hardly affect farmers' marketing decisions.]

Groundnut is marketed entirely through commission agents at auction sales. The standard commission fee is 4 percent ad valorem, but it may be lower if the cultivator is not indebted to the agent [a hidden cost of tying?] or the lot to be sold is large. The agents keep a close eye on the progress of the crop, as well as keeping one another meticulously informed of their clients' doings. For example, if a farmer is indebted to agent A but sells through agent B, the latter will deduct any principal and interest owed to A from the proceeds of sale and then pass on the repayment to A. [What striking evidence of collusion to achieve contractual enforcement! While this does not necessarily imply that there are barriers to entry in this activity, the existence of such barriers—with all they entail—strikes me as being quite probable.]

Commentary

The remark that adult laborers are no longer interested in annual contracts is rather puzzling. Only one new well has been sunk in the past seven years, so if casual laborers are now fairly certain of getting employment all year round, whereas before they faced lean periods, the causes must lie in changes either in the cropping pattern or in the availability of jobs outside the village. The former seems implausible, for there is little room to stray outside the seasonal rhythm of cultivation imposed on dryland by the pattern of rainfall, and if, as our respondents claimed, laborers do not work outside the village, the latter is irrelevant.

Once more, there was a revealing tale, this time concerning the arbitrary and predatory behavior of certain officials who oversee the marketing of sugarcane. When the farmers complained about being sent to jail, I remarked that they knew what risks they were taking. "That is not the reason for our complaint," they replied. "Two farmers who have never grown sugarcane have been summonsed for not delivering cane to the mill. While you have traveled to this village from America, we have never seen the official who filed these charges."

VILLAGE 14, CHITTOOR DISTRICT

Respondents

A score or more of farmers, including the patel. Those few who did most of the talking were clearly among the powerful section of the community. The meeting took place in the schoolroom; it was rather brief, so the notes that follow are somewhat sketchy. (Date: October 3, 1980.)

General features

The village lies on the meter-gauge railway, about 8 kilometers south of Chittoor Town. Physically, both the village and its lands resemble village 13.

There are about 250 households, more than half of which depend mostly on earnings from agricultural labor. Irrigation is provided by 150 wells and two tanks. The wells normally command 1.5 to 2.0 acres each and about 90 of them are energized. In a normal year, the tanks command about 90 acres. After two poor monsoons, the tanks and all but 20 wells are dry. The main crops are sugarcane, paddy, groundnut, and ragi (finger millet).

Labor and wages

There are no attached farm servants, for there are plenty of jobs close by in Chittoor and workers can easily secure a steady income. About 50 people are doing nonagricultural work outside the village at present; some of them have been driven to it by the lack of agricultural jobs caused by poor rains.

The daily rate for casual work over an eight-hour day is Rs 5 and two meals, with the exception of paddy harvesting, for which the rate is 6 kilograms of paddy. Cane cutters are paid at the standard rate because local supplies of labor are sufficient and there is no rush to get the cane to the mill, since virtually all cane is processed into jaggery by family labor. Seasonal migrant workers come to the village for harvesting the groundnut crop.

Land and tenancy

It is claimed that there is no tenancy [which I find implausible].

However, land is sold occasionally—perhaps a dozen transactions a year, some of which are forced by the need to pay off debts to merchants and others. Surplus lands have also been distributed to 30 or 40 agricultural labor households.

Credit and Other Inputs

Only 10 cultivators are shareholders in the cooperative sugar mill; the rest depend on commission agents for finance, as in village 13. If a farmer sells 7.5 tonnes of jaggery (the equivalent of about 75 tonnes of cane), he can expect to raise a loan of between Rs 4,000 and Rs 5,000 from that agent for cultivation in the following season. [This ratio of the size of the loan to the expected value of gross output is roughly the same as that quoted by the agent we interviewed in Adoni.]

Just recently, the village was adopted by Andhra Bank. About a score of farmers were able to get loans for cultivation in the present season, the terms being an interest rate of 11 percent a year and the deposit of a legal certificate of ownership of the borrower's land. Although there was a slight delay in the disbursement of these loans, demand will be heavy next year. The bank's rule of thumb for the financing of cane cultivation is Rs 1,500 an acre. [This may be high enough to squeeze out the commission agents. Also, the respondents' claim that the demand for loans from Andhra Bank will be heavy next year suggests that its effective terms are competitive with those offered by the agents. Presumably, there is enough competition among them that they are unable to insist on a contract that attaches finance to marketing.]

Only 10 wells were sunk during the past five years, but 50 older ones were deepened. These investments were financed mainly by private sources at the rather modest rate of 12–18 percent a year, backed by a promissory note specifying delivery of jaggery. [So the agents were actively securing long-term supplies, too.] Another 40 or 50 wells could be sunk, and although they must be 50 feet deep, there are no rocky strata with which to contend. It is claimed that Andhra Bank will extend loans for the purchase of pumps, but not for the construction of wells. [This sounds like a rather odd practice in the light of public policy, but it makes sense inasmuch as pumps can be repossessed easily, whereas repossession of the well would require that the land it commands be sold, a step that may involve more costly and lengthy legal proceedings. I wonder whether the agents are no longer prepared to finance new wells.]

There are two tractors in the village, which are hired out quite frequently.

Output

The marketing arrangements have been described at some length in the notes on village 13.

Commentary

I have a strong suspicion that this village is much more stratified than village 13. Yet there are compensating advantages for the laborers in the form of proximity to Chittoor Town and apparently ready job opportunities there. Indeed, on a daily basis, the wage rate is higher than in village 13, although the working day there is somewhat shorter.

Another interesting difference between them is in the proportion of farmers who are shareholders in the cooperative sugar mill. It appears that the commission agents dealing in jaggery have had a deeper involvement in financing the farmers of village 14. If this is indeed the case, they would have had greater power to prevent farmers from becoming shareholders, and it would certainly have been in their interest to use it. For the present, of course, the gap between the regulated price of cane and the open market price of jaggery has sent the cooperative shareholders of village 13 off in search of agents; time may change all that.

NOTE

1. Parentheses in the original serve as normal syntax and are retained as such.

REFERENCES

Bell, C., and P. Zusman. 1980. "On the Interrelationship of Tenancy and Credit Contracts." World Bank, Washington, DC.

Binswanger, H. P., V. S. Doherty, T. Balaramaiah, M. J. Bhende, V. B. Kshirsagar, V. B. Rao, and P. S. S. Raju. 1984. "Common Features and Contrasts in Labor Relations in the Semiarid Tropics of India." In *Contractual Arrangements, Employment, and Wages in Rural Labor Markets in Asia*, edited by H. P. Binswanger and M. R. Rosenzweig. New Haven, CT: Yale University Press.

Jodha, N. S., M. Asokan, and J. G. Ryan. 1977. *Village Study Methodology and Resource Endowments of the Selected Villages in ICRISAT's Village-Level Studies*. Occasional Paper 16. Hyderabad: ICRISAT, Economics Program.

3 Following Up, 1982

The tour covered Miryalaguda and Devarakonda Taluks in Nalgonda District, Kalvakurthy Taluk in Mahbubnagar District, and Vyalpad and Chittoor Taluks in Chittoor District. With time rather short, we chose not to visit Tanuku Taluk in West Godavari District and Adoni Taluk in Kurnool District, largely for logistical reasons. Srinivasan's tight schedule restricted him to the two days in Kalvakurthy Taluk. For the remainder of the time, my companion once more was the indefatigable Dr. T. V. S. Rao, who translated, prompted, and probed our respondents as he had during the first tour. I am much indebted to him, but the responsibility for the account that follows is wholly mine.

In chapter 2, the text's progress through the calendar, like the tour's, runs from north to south. The text in this chapter also runs from north to south, in the same order; the second tour's chronology is far less tidy, so readers will occasionally find it useful to go back and forth, certain details appearing later in the text than in the tour. Although the text is already quite long, I have repeated certain procedural details common to discussions in different places, because the prime purpose of the interviews was to allow the individuals to speak for themselves. The dates are also given, so that those readers who prefer chronology to geography can leaf back and forth accordingly, starting on January 4, 1982, in village 8 in Kalvakurthy Taluk, thence to January 7 in Chittoor and Vyalpad Taluks, and finally to Nalgonda District on January 27.

A PRELIMINARY REMARK

All institutions—especially financial ones—have procedures; the following account sets out some of them in considerable detail. The aim is to convey an idea not only of how the institution in question functioned, but also, more particularly, of how the procedures' complexity created difficulties for loan applicants and officials alike, while also providing the latter with some privately profitable opportunities. The procedures varied a bit from place to place, but some repetition is unavoidable in a travelogue of this kind. To give a fuller picture, the account also includes various quantitative details of the loan programs, so as to put the individual transactions into a larger context.

MIRYALAGUDA TALUK

Land Mortgage Bank (January 29–30, 1982)

Established in 1960, this branch of the Land Mortgage Bank (LMB) serves more than 150 villages in the taluk, about half of them within the command area of the Nagarjuna Sagar canal system.

As of June 30, 1981, the loans outstanding (including interest) amounted to Rs 20.6 million, of which Rs 6.2 million was formally classified as overdue and another Rs 9.2 million was subject to demands for immediate repayment. The branch's status is partly restricted, based on the average performance over the past three years. At present, new loans are restricted to collections on a one-to-one basis.

The chief components of the outstanding loan portfolio by purpose are as follows:

- Rs 1.6 million for land grading and construction of field channels in connection with irrigation by the Nagarjuna Sagar canal system. These loans were advanced between 1962 and 1966, with a maturity of 15 years.

- Rs 0.9 million for tractors under the Agricultural Refinance and Development Corporation (ARDC) and Rs 0.5 million under a World Bank scheme, both with a maturity of seven years.

- Rs 12.2 million, mostly for minor irrigation, under the LMB's normal lending program (Rs 2.5 million), ARDC (Rs 7.6 million), and Small Farmers' Development Agency (SFDA) (Rs 2.1 million).

The target for disbursement in the previous financial year, 1980–81 (April 1–March 31), was Rs 3.51 million, of which Rs 3.36 million was under the ARDC. Again, this disbursement was mostly for minor irrigation. The target was met. In the current year, only Rs 1.08 million had been disbursed up to December 31, against a target of Rs 3.3 million for the whole year.

The stages of application for a loan are as follows:

1. The applicant approaches the patwari (village accountant and land records keeper) for the certificates of ownership and no dues owing of institutional loans. The registrar then produces the encumbrance certificate. The latter step normally takes 10 days, but perhaps as long as a month.

2. Field inspection follows in a week or so. The cooperative's subregistrar does this for loans up to Rs 15,000. For larger loans, he is accompanied by the deputy registrar.

3. The bank's supervisor fills in the application form. The administrative (evaluation) fee is 50 paise per Rs 1,000 of the estimated loan amount (minimum fee, Rs 5; maximum fee, Rs 45). Legal scrutiny follows, usually taking 15 days.

4. The file goes before the board or, if there is no meeting, the chairman.

5. If the loan is sanctioned, the bond is executed. The applicant must purchase shares in the value of 6 percent of the sanctioned amount up to Rs 7,500 and 7.5 percent on any excess. He must make these purchases out of his own funds, not out of the loan itself. Big farmers—that is, those owning more than 5 acres of wetland—must also remit 3 percent of the loan in stamp duties in order to register the bond.

6. The branch seeks funds for the loan from headquarters. This takes another week or so.

7. Disbursement follows at once.

The tortuous course of one application is revealing where departures from "normality" are concerned. The application was filed on February 16, 1981, followed by a field inspection on February 27. The encumbrance certificate was issued on March 5, with initial legal clearance on March 16, followed by initial sanction on March 24. So far, so good, but then the officer had second thoughts, which brought the process to a halt. He did not give the final go ahead until January 8, 1982. The president signed once more on January 16, and the loan was registered on January 22. [We did not probe into what might have induced the officer to ponder on the matter for almost 10 months.]

The main program is for minor irrigation. A well normally has the dimensions 18' × 24' × 20'–30' (length × width × depth in feet), and costs about Rs 7,000. The normal amount sanctioned for a new well is between Rs 5,000 and Rs 6,000. The farmer must find the rest, so moneylenders may get involved. Disbursement and work on the well are linked as follows:

1. Big farmers must dig the trial pit at their own expense. Small farmers get a disbursement of Rs 1,000 for this purpose. Water is normally struck at 15 to 20 feet; in the event of failure, the whole of the Rs 1,000 is due, unless the applicant is certified under the SFDA. At 1 or 2 percent, the failure rate is very low.

2. The manager, the cooperative subregistrar, or the assistant development officer inspect the trial pit.

3. Half of the remaining amount sanctioned is then released. An inspection of the work follows, but a receipt for it is not required.

4. The regional officer allocates responsibility for the final inspection, after which the final installment is paid.

The scale of overdue payments burdens current operations. Three lift irrigation schemes have failed entirely; these account for one-third of the total. The government has ordered the bank not to collect penal interest until July 1, 1982. Its public statements—as distinct from its ordinances suspending payments of interest and principal—have also encouraged farmers to default on their payments in the past year. Except for about 100 applications for sheep loans that were approved in September 1981, no new applications have been accepted since April 1981. There are now 200 pending applications, most of them gathering dust for eight months or more. Many of these applications have been filed by applicants from villages where the overdues rate exceeds 50 percent. New applications may be taken up after the forthcoming collection drive is over.

Nizam sugar factory (January 29, 1982)

This is an undertaking of the government of Andhra Pradesh. Commissioned in 1976–77, a trial year in which just 3,500 tonnes were crushed, the unit has a rated capacity of 1,250 tonnes a day. It is the only major processing unit on the left bank of the canal system.

Although the unit's rated annual capacity is 1.6 million tonnes, the current crushing will not exceed 1.3 million tonnes. The recovery rate is also unsatisfactory. The accumulated losses to date are Rs 25 million.

This unhappy start has several causes. First, the crushing period is just 140 days, due to the prevailing agroeconomic conditions. If this period were extended, the recovery rate would fall further still. (In 1979–80, the heavy use of immature cane reduced the rate to just 6.3 percent.) Second, there are problems with the irrigation system. The Irrigation Department is under a contractual obligation to supply adequate water to one block of 5,000 acres, in which yields are normally very good (38–40 tonnes an acre).

The distributory was closed on December 15, 1981, but it should be opened again on February 1, 1982. This hiatus will seriously affect the recovery rate. The canal in question was not, moreover, always fully charged before its closure. Third, transportation is a serious bottleneck, and skilled labor has to be brought in from outside the command area. Then there are the farmers, who, having no previous experience with sugarcane cultivation, are more inclined to grow paddy, and their cattle go on the loose and do severe damage to the cane crop when the canal is closed. Finally, a fundamental problem cannot be remedied: the location is not suitable for sugarcane, because there is no real "winter season." The temperature never falls below 18°C, whereas a minimum of 16°C–17°C is necessary for proper sucrose formation. In short, the plant should never have been established.

Syndicate Bank, which is also the designated Nagarjuna Sagar Farmers' (NSF) bank, is the captive credit institution. It has set financing limits of Rs 2,500 an acre for fresh plantings and Rs 1,500 an acre for ratoon crops, up to a maximum total loan of Rs 40,000. The average cost of cultivation is Rs 3,500 an acre. Farmers must find the difference, which gives them an incentive to take cultivation of the crop seriously. There was some diversion of funds during the first two seasons, but not now. Farmers receive payment for their deliveries of cane through the bank to ensure collection of dues. The crop itself is security for the loan. This mode of enforcement is effective because the farmers are not yet familiar with the processing of cane into country sugar. [Such diversion is a central problem for the cooperative mill in Chittoor Taluk.] In this connection, the NSF has recently proposed that two units be established to produce khandsari (a type of granulated sugar). In that event, their operations would have to be coordinated with those of the Syndicate Bank.

Complementing the financing of cultivation is an excellent network for the supply of fertilizers; pesticides and implements are also made available, sprayers at no charge. Payment for all of these inputs is made through the farmers' accounts with the bank. Seven agricultural graduates have been employed as extension agents.

In the current season, 914 farmers are under contract to deliver cane. Since the factory is a government undertaking, the government sets the price, which is Rs 185 a tonne. There have been no contractual defaults—on either side. Three purchasing centers are located at 26, 45, and 53 kilometers, respectively, from the mill, with associated transport costs of Rs 24, Rs 36, and Rs 40 a tonne, respectively, which farmers must pay.

The catalog of errors made at the start is not complete. The efforts to transfer knowledge about cultivating cane were not timely. As a result, perhaps 45 percent of the land is under lease, often in huge blocks, and rented to big cultivators. In the course of time, however, the owners may master the techniques involved and cultivate themselves. In the initial stages, the poor performance of the canal system induced some farmers to take out loans for wells and pumps. Most of these borrowers have defaulted on the loans and given up cultivating sugarcane.

When the Irrigation Department failed to supply irrigation in 1979–80, cultivators received compensation, at a total cost of Rs 0.16 million.

Further measures to improve operations are needed. Farmers continue to rely on chemical fertilizers, when they should also apply farmyard manure in bulk. The correct annual crop rotation—namely, planting, then ratoon, then paddy, which deters the buildup of pests—has yet to be widely followed. In the coming year, an in-kind subsidy of Rs 400 an acre will be granted for the planting of early varieties. Proposals for the "localization" of 10,000 acres have also been submitted, thus doubling capacity. The latter may be throwing away good money after bad.

DEVARAKONDA TALUK

Land Mortgage Bank (January 27, 1982)

This LMB branch was established in 1965. In addition to normal lending, its current programs include those connected with the Agricultural Refinance Corporation, ARDC, and Drought Prone Areas Programme (DPAP). Total lending in 1980–81 amounted to Rs 1.05 million: Rs 0.36 million for new wells, Rs 0.3 million for repair and deepening of wells, Rs 0.2 million for pump sets, Rs 0.12 million for tractors, and Rs 60,000 for citrus orchards.

The stages of application for a loan are as follows:

1. The supervisor fills in the application form, which costs Rs 3; there is also an entry fee of Rs 10.5. Only then does the applicant go to the patwari to obtain the certificates of ownership and no dues owing. Upon presentation, the application is filed in the office, following which the applicant must approach the branch's subregistrar for an encumbrance certificate (Rs 16 for applicants owning 10 or more acres of dryland or 5 or more acres of wetland; otherwise, there is no fee). The forms are collected and attested to at the time of field inspection.

2. The field inspection takes place 10 days after the application has been filed. The spacing and performance of neighboring wells are checked. (Our respondent inspected about 70 proposed sites in 1981. About 35 of the 50 applications for new wells have been approved for loans and 14 of those were for well deepening.) Three days later, the report is sent to the assistant development officer for legal scrutiny. Since he is presently dealing with two branches, this takes some 20 days. In the course of such scrutiny, it may emerge that the certificate of the tehsildar (tax officer) does not square with that of the patwari, in which event, the application is rejected at once. It can also happen that a family partition has occurred, but not been recorded. Either all of those whose names appear in the record must execute the bond or those not borrowing must provide a disclaimer. The files that pass scrutiny are placed before the management committee, which sits in Devarakonda every 15 days.

3. Approval follows submission after a few days. After approval, the bond is executed and the agreement is registered. Disbursement of the loan is made from Nalgonda, with a lag of about five days. On average, the elapsed time between filling in the application form and disbursement of funds is about 50 days.

On March 31, 1981, 31 cases were pending. In the current financial year, 600 applications have been received, 112 of which are pending.

The lending target for 1981–82 is Rs 0.75 million. The level of overdues at the start of the financial year was such that no new lending was sanctioned until December 1981, when a special provision was introduced. Disbursements of funds under existing commitments were honored. The scale of overdues was the result of the severe drought in 1979–80, reinforced by rather poor rains in 1980–81. That 20 percent of all the trial pits dug in 1980–81 were unsuccessful is evidence of the severity of the droughts.

The cost of a well measuring 18' ×24' × 36' is about Rs 8,000. In most cases, as assessed by the farmer in question, a depth of 36 feet is enough. The loans sanctioned will not suffice to cover the whole cost, so farmers will have to find a source of additional finance, for which the level of current income is usually enough.

Under the DPAP scheme, the village development officer draws up a list of eligible applicants and forwards it to the extension officer, who returns to the village for verification and comment. The amended list then goes to the block development officer and then to the DPAP officer. The latter submits the lists, which are made up irregularly, to the bank branches that are named as first choices. This process takes about 10 days. The process described for a formal loan can then begin. In 1980–81, there were about 800 applicants, 500 of whom were eligible. Residents of villages with more than 50 percent overdues are excluded, and some eligible applicants may have decided to borrow from other branches of the LMB. Funds sufficed for 400 applicants. The rest were left pending on a first-come, first-served basis from the date of a normal application, as defined above.

Central Bank of India (January 28, 1982)

This branch was established in November 1974 and now covers 60 villages. The village in which it is situated has many of the facilities of a taluk township, an advantage that weighed heavily in the location decision. Earlier, the area had been served by the main branch in Hyderabad itself. The lead bank is the State Bank of Hyderabad. There is only one officer to deal with all of the branch's operations.

Currently, the branch has 2,170 accounts and deposits of about Rs 1 million. There are 1,300 borrowers, with a total outstanding amount of Rs 3.2 million. Table 3.1 presents details of the loan portfolio, as of September 1981. The terms and conditions are set by the Reserve Bank of India (RBI), most recently in April 1981.

A client with an existing crop loan must first settle the whole outstanding amount before applying for a new loan. Only then, about a week later, will his fields be inspected. The applicant then returns to the office with all of the relevant certificates and signs the necessary documents; the signatures of two guarantors are also needed. Disbursement follows in a couple of days.

A new client must reside in the branch's "command area." His reputation is the subject of inquiry; if judged satisfactory, he is given the application forms, which cost Rs 15. In about half of all cases, the bank requires that 10 percent of the loan amount be placed in a one-year deposit account; such accounts now yield 7.5 percent annually.

TABLE 3.1 **Loan portfolio of the Central Bank of India branch in Devarakonda taluk, as of September 1981**

PURPOSE OF LOAN	TOTAL AMOUNT (RS 10,000)	NUMBER OF LOANS	TERM	RATE (%)
Crop	200	800	6 months	12.50[a]
Well deepening	65	278	3 years	10.25
Pump sets	8	25	5 years	10.25
Tractors	20		7 years	12.50
Buffaloes	19	105	3 years	12.50[b]
Bullocks	2	13	3 years	12.50[b]
Citrus orchards	2	2	5 years	12.50

Source: Information provided by the bank's officer.
a. 15% on loans of Rs 5,000 to Rs 10,000; 17.5% on loans over Rs 10,000.
b. 10.25% for small farmers.

Loans for well deepening are subject to the following procedure:

1. The well is inspected about one week after the application has been made. The agricultural assistant assesses its dimensions and the water table and proposes digging to a particular depth. The maximum amount sanctioned is Rs 5,000.

2. The applicant then proceeds through the steps described for crop loans, which takes about 20 days.

3. One-third of the loan is disbursed.

4. Inspection of the work follows completion of that stage. A certificate (receipt) from the contractor is required.

5. Two like stages follow.

Misuse of loans (for other purposes) is not common. When it does occur, the diversion of funds is about 20–30 percent of the loan.

The program for the purchase of milch animals started in 1976–77. This was an SFDA scheme, with a subsidy of 25 percent. A milk cooperative society was formed to supply the local Dairy Corporation. The society was supposed to deduct the dues on these loans from the farmers' revenues at source, but the farmers sold to private parties instead, and the society failed. Recovery of these loans fell off accordingly, with the drought exacerbating matters. Insurance fees are imposed to cover the death of animals, with a veterinarian certifying the value of the animal at death. The officer reckons that about 15 percent of reported deaths are bogus.

There are two special loan schemes, evidence of eligibility for which is to be provided by village officials. The first is for scheduled castes who own at most 2 acres or have an annual income not exceeding Rs 2,500. The applicable annual rate of interest for those thus eligible is 4 percent. The second is for artisans, forestry workers, students in higher education, and the handicapped, but not persons engaged in agriculture. The current target for lending under the latter scheme is 1 percent of all outstanding advances. There are currently 10 such accounts, and the officer had to go in search of clients.

On the branch's lending operations more generally, the credit squeeze has restricted new loans to existing clients. Shortage of staff at this branch rules out lending secured by gold. Restrictions apply here anyway. Other banks have entered the area recently, which is something of a relief. Those clients living in the villages adopted by these entrants must close their accounts with the Central Bank of India before they are permitted to open an account with the entrant in question.

The present level of overdues is Rs 1.2 million. Clients are sometimes reluctant to repay, despite pressure on them to do so. If a person makes no repayments at all on a loan taken five years earlier, legal proceedings may be launched against him. These cases are referred to the legal officer in the bank headquarters, who makes the decision once the file is placed before him. Four years ago, the bank proceeded against four people, who then repaid part of what was due.

Households: Village 5 (January 27, 1982)

Both respondents belong to households in the sample.

Respondent A's dealings in connection with wells have the qualities of a saga. He is able to irrigate 3.5 acres with two wells, which were constructed in the late 1950s. He obtained a loan to purchase an oil engine in 1957; the samithi (Block-level council) informed him that he would receive a subsidy of 25 percent, and he paid off the loan in two years. About 10 years later, he received word from the tehsildar that he had not, in fact, obtained a subsidy, and even now he does not know whether the deed has been registered. In any event, he pledged other plots when applying for a loan from the LMB in 1971. [It would appear, therefore, that the deed had been registered and that this fact emerged in the course of legal scrutiny of his application in 1971. The source of the earlier loan is unclear.]

The purpose of the loan from the LMB was for well deepening, for which he requested Rs 5,000. The samithi officials inspected the wells and recommended a subsidy. On this occasion, too, he did not actually receive a subsidy, but at least he came to know as much before disbursement. It appears that a priority list had been drawn up—by whom is not clear—and his name was not on it. In any event, he went to the branch office at least a dozen times in the course of the application, spending about Rs 300 on bribes and transportation. The amount sanctioned was Rs 2,000, against a pledge of 15 acres of land (valued at Rs 400 an acre). The first disbursement followed more than one year after his application had been filed. He repaid the loan installments on time.

He spent another Rs 8,000 over the past 10 years in order to deepen the wells to 36 feet. He raised this sum in loans from various parties in and outside the village and from his own resources. (He made further inquiries at the LMB— most recently about five years ago—but nothing seems to have come of them.) In order to repay these private loans, he sold off about Rs 4,000 of dryland to scheduled tribe households, which seem to have the cash on hand to make such purchases. Scheduled tribes prefer dryland; they do not have access to finance for fertilizers [yet they paid cash for land], and local wells are not reliable sources of irrigation.

A large tank irrigates a fairly substantial part of the village's cultivable land. When the tank is full, following good monsoonal rains, the wells below it recharge completely. Dryland fetches Rs 500 to Rs 1,000 an acre; wetland fetches only Rs 1,500. This small premium reflects the fact that irrigation is not secure. With adequate rainfall, he can irrigate a total of 15 acres from the tank and his wells. The land commanded by the latter is sown to irrigated dryland crops such as castor and hybrid jowar. He grows traditional varieties of jowar for fodder on unirrigated plots; these varieties yield more bulk than hybrids. He sprayed his castor crop once this year, following a pest attack.

The discussion returned to credit institutions. A facility (acronym AWARE) to serve scheduled tribes opened a couple of years back. The only other agencies are the samithi and the LMB. There is a commercial bank in Devarakonda, but it has adopted only villages in its neighborhood.

In the past year, 80–100 villagers submitted applications to these institutions, most of them to AWARE. Respondent A filled in the forms for the applicants, most of whom sought a subsidy of one kind or another. (He recommends everyone for a loan, so as to displease nobody.)

The samithi draws up the list of eligible applicants, which it forwards to the DPAP officer for scrutiny, who then sends the amended list back to the village for renewal of the applications. The officers of the bank concerned came to the village to find the most promising clients, whereby there appeared to be some reluctance to advance loans if a subsidy had not been granted. Due to a shortage of funds, only 20 or so applicants obtained loans; the remainder are pending.

Finance for the sinking of 20–25 wells was received under the DPAP. The sum of Rs 6,000 normally sanctioned is sufficient to dig a successful well, but only 15 trial pits were actually dug, all of them unsuccessful. Borrowers often bribe the inspectors and put the funds to other uses. About 15 applications to sink wells are currently pending. Loans for sheep are also at hazard. If the animals die, the loan is written off. The reported mortality rate is correspondingly high.

As for legal proceedings in connection with defaults, there are currently five cases in which the threat of auctioning off the land is very real.

Respondent A has four attached farm servants (AFSs), three of them newly engaged in the last week of May 1981. Two others who had been under contract earlier left at that time in order to attend to their own farms. He was already acquainted with the three new ones, who had also been engaged in cultivation. He obtained their services without difficulty, paying the going rate of Rs 500 in cash plus clothes annually, 30 kilograms of grain monthly, and some tobacco daily, equivalent to about Rs 900 a year. The whole cash amount is paid in advance, without interest. If an AFS leaves prematurely, the balance is converted into a loan, with interest payable from the end of May at the annual rate of 18 percent. The daily rate for casual laborers is 3–4 kilograms of grain.

Respondent B owns 20 acres, two of which are irrigated and all inherited. His livestock comprises 3 pairs of bullocks, 2 she-buffaloes, 15 "useless" cattle (that is, not currently giving milk—they calve every three years or so), and 3 young animals.

His father died many years ago, leaving him with an outstanding debt to the LMB. He made no payments for some time, and then the officers appeared and threatened various legal steps to recover the dues. He paid off the last amount six years ago. The experience made him chary of dealing with banks, and he has not applied for any loans from public institutions since then. During the past year, several of his friends approached the banks for loans. Their difficulties have confirmed his reluctance to make an attempt of his own.

He has three AFSs, all engaged for the past three years. One is a cousin, the second is the son of a maternal aunt, and the third is a scheduled caste from another hamlet. He does not want more than three AFSs and found these particular people easily. The terms are Rs 500 annually, paid wholly in advance, and three meals a day. He also advanced loans to them as follows: Rs 500, Rs 200, and Rs 2,000, all bearing the interest rate of 24 percent (simple) a year. The only security is a promissory note. When he gives such loans, he satisfies himself that their needs can be met. He does inquire into their debts to others. He said that he borrowed the sum of Rs 2,000 from a brother-in-law living in another taluk. (The survey investigator disputes this.)

He has also made in-kind loans to three other people, each in the amount of two bags of grain, at the own rate of interest of 50 percent a season.

The father of the AFS who borrowed Rs 2,000 now appears and enlarges on the story. It was he who had borrowed the sum in question, for the purposes of marrying his older son, indenturing the younger son for 12 years in order to do so. He claims that repayment will be complete in three years. He obtained additional loans one and two years back, respectively, which he should be able to pay off within a year. (The family has 5 acres of dryland.)

Households: Village 6 (January 28, 1982)

All four respondents belong to households in the sample.

Respondent A is a trader (shopkeeper) and moneylender. He went to Mumbai in his teens to work in the textile industry, joining his brother-in-law, who was already so engaged. After about 10 years, he decided to return to his native village and go into moneylending. He had accumulated about Rs 10,000 in the provident fund, but no other savings. The idea of going into this line of business was not new. Earlier still, when he was about 12, he had worked for such a trader as an assistant. The practice is to lend cash to people who will repay in kind, which the trader processes and then sells retail.

In the past year, he took deliveries of the following quantities in payment of principal and interest: 600 kilograms of jowar, 1,200 kilograms of paddy, and 300 kilograms of castor. In addition, he purchased 6 tonnes of commodities on own account as a trader; 6 tonnes of paddy were processed and sold locally. He always has the option of reselling the paddy obtained as payment, instead of processing it into rice for retail sale. Most of his income is derived from trading.

In the business's first year, he lent money to about 10 people, all of whom were well known to him. He has not suffered any defaults thus far. His present clients, about 10 in all, have been with him for about five years. In an emergency, his borrowers may approach other parties, but if a loan is taken from a third party, all outstanding amounts due to respondent A must be settled within a few days. This applies even if the third party is the bank.

His specific dealings with respondent B include three loans: Rs 600 in May 1976, Rs 200 in October 1979, and 100 kilograms of paddy in September 1981. When B approached him for the first time, B asked for Rs 600. He was given the full amount because A knew that B had some irrigated land, which gave him confidence that the loan would be repaid [presumably in paddy]. What is more, his information was that B had no outstanding loans to anyone else. The second loan was for debt consolidation. It seems that B pays only interest on the first two loans, which A finds perfectly satisfactory, since B is a reliable fellow. Under the agreement, repayment in cash is allowed, but A has insisted on payment in kind.

In the past year, some 15 people approached him for a loan. He told them that he had no money to lend, and this was indeed so. His revolving fund for loans is about Rs 14,000, and his inventories in the shop are worth about Rs 7,000. He would lend more if he had more resources and would take on new clients; he even has some people in mind. Four of his established clients asked for sums he was unable to give and had to settle for about half those amounts.

If he does not have enough cash or goods on hand to meet his regular clients' immediate needs, he will try to borrow from a third party. This he has had to do half a dozen times in the past few years. There are eight traders in the village, and they have formed a loose association to help one another out in times of such need. These loans do not carry interest, but they must be repaid within a week. All eight have shops, but he is the only moneylender among them.

It appears that the bank is the only other source of credit in the village itself. The banks have not affected his lending business, nor does he fear competition from them in the future. Besides, he has his trading business, which is quite profitable.

Respondent B took over cultivation from his father eight years ago. Since then, he has neither bought nor sold land.

His father had known A for many years, so when he learned from someone else that A had started up in business, he decided to approach him for a loan; at that time, he had no other sources of finance. The first loan of Rs 600 sufficed for the repair of his well, and he did not want a larger sum. The second loan of Rs 200 was used to settle the electricity bill for his pump. He signed a statement for the first loan; his word was enough for the second.

The interest on these accounts is supposed to be settled every season. The whole of the principal was outstanding at the start of 1979–80, but there were no arrears of interest. He made no payments at all that year or in 1980–81, due to drought. During this period, he did not approach A for a new loan, for fear that he would demand repayment in full. He does not know exactly what the position is now. He recently delivered 150 kilograms of paddy; the account will be settled at the end of rabi. It is respondent A's choice that repayment be made in kind. He has sold only to A because his prices are competitive, and he would refuse a better offer in order to preserve good relations with him. [Respondent B's options in the commodity market were very likely restricted by his outstanding debt to A, the traders' network being close and active.]

He borrowed from the local bank for the first time in February 1981. The former sarpanch (village headman) filled in the application form, with the "fee" payable only after the loan was received. He wanted Rs 2,000, but, on the latter's advice, he put in for Rs 1,000. He needed a no-dues certificate and the serial numbers on unencumbered land from the patwari, to whom he pays 16 kilograms of grain a year for this and other services rendered. The loan was used wholly to desilt his well. His paddy crop will suffice to pay the installment that is due in a few weeks.

He is sure that A has come to know of his bank loan from other parties, although he himself has kept quiet about it. In fact, he wants to break off his relationship with A and shift all of his borrowing to the bank, whose terms, especially the interest rate, are more attractive. He believes that the patwari's help will suffice for a successful application. He will not be able to switch entirely, however, until he has paid off the existing loan, unless he pledges additional land.

The supplies of fertilizers are quite good, although the dealer does not give credit.

Respondents C and D are landlord and tenant, respectively. C has known D since childhood. They are neighbors and also have neighboring plots.

The contract, which is an oral one, was closed in April 1980. C had been cultivating the land himself, but his bullocks became weak and there is no market for draft power services in this village. Knowing all of this, D suggested the lease.

The practice in this village is sharecropping on wetland and fixed rent in kind on dryland. It is claimed that cultivation is just as risky on wetland as on dryland, due to pests and the possibility that the wells will not fully recharge.

C provided the seed and supervised preparation of the paddy nursery. They plowed and irrigated the plots together (from his well), but he purchased the fertilizer and supervised its application. He also hired and paid the casual laborers. All of these expenses were deducted from the gross output at harvest, with the residual split 75:25 in his favor. He did not ask D to finance any part of these expenses: there is no such arrangement in the village, even when the shares are 50:50. A striking feature of the contract is that the tenant works as a laborer, without pay, in all operations, although his wife is paid if she works. To sum up, the tenant receives 25 percent of the net revenue in exchange for supplying labor services and draft power throughout the cultivation cycle; for his part, the landlord manages and finances the whole undertaking. In this connection, C says that he will not entertain leasing out land under a fixed-rent agreement because cultivation is his profession.

He has recently purchased a new pair of bullocks for Rs 1,000, but the lease still had a season to run.

He borrowed from the Central Bank of India branch for the very first time in March 1981, following an unsuccessful attempt to obtain a loan from Grameen Bank a month or two earlier. It seems that he had no need of finance until then. The whole of the loan was used to desilt his well. He gives the patwari 15 kilograms of grain a season for services rendered (seasonally, not annually, because he owns wetland), but he also paid Rs 15 on this occasion. All of his plots fall under one survey number, so he must pay off this loan before he can take another secured by land. He paid no "fees" to the bank's officials. He will be able to pay the installment that is due in one month's time.

He has been borrowing from a cultivator in another village for several years, having obtained an introduction through one of the lender's existing clients. The first loan was for Rs 2,000, which is the amount he had sought. The lender did not inquire into his financial position (in fact, he had no debts at that time), nor did he have to pledge any security or sign a promissory note: the mediator's word sufficed. The annual rate of interest was 18 percent. He took a similar loan on the same terms each year until 1980, when he borrowed just Rs 1,000. Most of the money went into deepening his well, which was originally 24 feet deep and is now 42 feet deep. This investment has been profitable.

He did not borrow from this party in 1981 because the bank loan sufficed. He has not repaid the loan taken in 1980. He intends to pay it off at the end of 1983, after the kharif harvest. The lender has not pressed him yet. It is quite probable that the lender knows that he has obtained a loan from the bank, since the lender comes to the village daily.

Respondent D has been leasing in land for about 10 years. During this time, he has had three landlords. Two leases involved wetland plots about 1 kilometer away, which he eventually found too troublesome to continue cultivating. He had indeed proposed to C that he lease the plot in question. Dryland plots are even farther away, and it is not worth his while to lease them.

His own account of the operations on C's plot runs as follows. The landlord was not present at any of the principal operations; he would simply turn up every six days or so. He provided D with the seed, in the expectation that D would honor the obligation to use it properly. D did so, in the expectation that the lease would be renewed. The landlord's AFS did the plowing; he also assisted D in irrigating the plot. The landlord provided 15 cartloads of farmyard manure to D's 5 cartloads and also supervised the operation. D helped to transplant the plot and was engaged in harvesting and threshing the crop—all without wages. His wife received the usual daily rate; there was no tying.

The plot of 1 acre yielded 1,800 kilograms of paddy. The expenses amounted to 600 kilograms, including interest of 36 percent a year on the cost of any inputs that he, the tenant, was unable to supply at the time when they were to be applied. D is unclear how large these charges were. His 25 percent share of the net revenue, so defined and calculated, was therefore 300 kilograms. These terms, which are traditional, were imposed by all three landlords. D himself prefers fixed rents in kind, because he would then get the whole of the reward for his efforts, adding that he would also be able to obtain finance from other private parties.

He also borrowed Rs 400 from C four years back. He has paid off Rs 200 of the principal and all of the interest, at 24 percent a year. He has been making these payments in cash from sales of castor.

He and his two brothers share a well, which is 36 feet deep. They would like to borrow from the bank in order to deepen it further, but the deed of ownership has not been registered, even though partition took place three years back. Their father borrowed from the local bank in March 1981. The loan was used to deepen the well from 30 to the present 36 feet.

KALVAKURTHY TALUK

Land Mortgage Bank (January 5, 1982)

The principal programs are (a) minor irrigation, pipelines, and water management; (b) sheep, poultry, and dairy; (c) tractors (only five loans were sanctioned in 1981); and (d) land development for wells financed by the LMB. The first program accounts for about 70 percent of all lending by value. The norms prescribed by the ARDC are followed. The discussion was concerned largely with the financing of wells, although important general points and procedures emerged in its course.

The norm for a well in this area is Rs 7,500. If a technical officer so recommends, more may be provided. In fact, about Rs 15,000 to Rs 20,000 is needed get down to 50 feet or so, this being the desirable depth. The wells are generally rectangular, measuring 30'× 20' × 50', which will command about 5 acres of castor or 3 acres of paddy in kharif and 3 and 2 acres, respectively, in rabi. Bore wells are suitable in a few villages near rivers; these cost Rs 2,500. Loans to deepen existing wells are limited to Rs 2,000.

The stages of application for a loan are as follows:

1. The applicant must provide land revenue records for the past two years. These records are obtainable from the tehsildar. Only those applicants whose holdings fall below the corresponding ceiling in the Land Ceilings Act are eligible for loans. If the land has been sold recently, a deed of sale is required. If the land is held jointly, all relevant members of the family must execute the deed. If any part of the land is under a protected tenancy, the nature of the encumbrance must be noted. If the landlord wishes to take a loan, both parties must execute the deed.

    The applicant must also provide certificates of "no overdues" from the Central Cooperative Bank and local banks. All of these evidential requirements are verified by the LMB officer. The applicant's capacity to repay is also assessed, on the basis of expectations about what his undertakings will be after the well has become operational. This first step normally takes about one month, but it drags on for two to three months in roughly 30 percent of all cases.

Only those applicants owning more than 10 acres must pay the standard fee of Rs 22 for the encumbrance certificate. An administration fee of Rs 5 per Rs 1,000 sanctioned is charged, up to a maximum of Rs 30, plus an admission fee of Rs 5.

2. Field inspections are carried out by subregistrars or assistant development officers with the patwari. The characteristics of the soils and suchlike yield the value of the land in accordance with the established scales for local conditions. (Each taluk has a committee, which meets every three years.) The proposed location must not be closer than 525 feet to any existing well. If an exception is sought, the performance of the latter is taken into account. A comparison also is required when the spatial condition is met, but the loan sought exceeds Rs 7,500. These field reports—technical and verification— take only a day or two.

3. Legal scrutiny follows. This step takes about four days. There is no fee.

4. The president of the LMB sanctions the loan if the file passes legal scrutiny. The managing committee then ratifies the president's decision.

5. The borrower then executes the mortgage deed in favor of the LMB. Small farmers are exempted from stamp duty, which is Rs 3 per 100.

6. Disbursement proceeds in stages. One-quarter of the sanctioned amount, up to a limit of Rs 1,000, is committed for digging a trial pit measuring 10' × 10' × 15' to ascertain the depth of the water table. If water is not found, the depth is increased to 20–25 feet; in the event of further failure, work and disbursement stop. The sum committed at this point is usually about Rs 1,000. The borrower is wholly liable for it, but small farmers are granted a subsidy of 25 percent. Success must be verified, after which the remaining amount is usually disbursed in two steps. The well must be dug within three months of the first installment, and this limit also applies to the disbursement of the final installment. At the latter point in time, there is a visit to verify that the work is complete. If it is not, a notice is issued to the effect that the entire loan will be foreclosed on a specific date, usually in about three months. Failure to settle all outstanding amounts will result in the land being auctioned off.

7. Borrowers enjoy a grace period of one year before repayment begins. The subsequent maturity periods are 8 and 11 years for big and small farmers, respectively.

All villages are electrified, and virtually all borrowers opt for electric motors. The government has recently specified a list of prices and recommended manufacturers. A 5-horsepower motor, for example, has an upper price limit of Rs 5,000. Repayment is made in nine annual installments, with no grace period.

Various measures, of increasing severity, are employed when payments fall overdue. After several attempts to obtain payment have failed, movable assets may be attached, including bullocks in excess of one pair, standing crops, gold, and utensils. If these measures fail to cover the contractually scheduled payments, then after a waiting period of three years, the entire outstanding amount will be foreclosed and the parcels so mortgaged auctioned off.

In the past five years, only two foreclosures have occurred. Auctioned land often fetches a better price than the original valuation [small wonder, when the latter is based on the plots' original condition]. Villagers are sometimes reluctant to bid in these auctions, out of solidarity.

There followed a more general discussion of the LMB's current practice, operations, and experience. Supervisors are given lending targets, so they commonly go around the villages touting the LMB's offers. It is therefore in their interest to help illiterate farmers to fill in the relevant forms. Supervisors usually have no difficulty meeting their quotas. In the period April–June, most of the effort goes into collecting the payments due, with the specific aim of reducing the overdue rate below 25 percent. The bank then attains, or maintains, an "unrestricted" status where lending capacity is concerned. Total lending in the current year is limited to Rs 5.2 million, a consequence of substantial overdue payments in the previous drought years, especially 1980–81.

Lack of working capital contributes to the problem of overdues. Yet, although the LMB's position is affected by the decisions of the cooperatives and branch banks, there is no attempt at coordination.

It is claimed that there is no corruption in the bank itself, but there may well be corruption at the patwari level. The officer conceded that the procedures are very burdensome and must be cut down. The issuance of passbooks and encumbrance certificates would suffice.

United Commercial Bank (January 5, 1982)

This branch opened one year back. It has adopted, among others, village 7. "Adoption" is a formal procedure, which involves notification by the designated "lead bank," which is the State Bank of India in this area. Adoption grants the bank exclusive rights to branch banking in the village in question. About 40 villages are located in the branch's catchment area, but only a few have been adopted to date. The respondent is the manager.

The chief program is crop lending to meet cultivators' working capital requirements. There are two special programs for scheduled castes: social forestry, currently covering 48 acres, and sheep herding when the families have access to common wasteland [without regard for the ensuing common property externalities]. Credit is also available to fertilizer dealers and small traders.

Crop loans are advanced for paddy and groundnut, up to Rs 600 an acre with a maximal loan of Rs 10,000, both limits set by the lead bank. Sixty percent of the loan must be taken in the form of fertilizer from a dealer of the borrower's choice. The balance of Rs 240 an acre may be taken in cash. The annual rate of interest is 12.5 percent, which is charged from the date of the "pay order." The normal term is six months.

The patwari's recommendation of an application is important. In a few cases, he will conduct an investigation of his own. The certification procedures are exactly the same as the LMB's. Once a farmer has obtained a signed mortgage deed, the bond holds good for 12 years, and he is burdened with only one such transaction. It is a requirement that all crop loans be so secured, and there have been no exceptions. The manager himself fills out the application forms. Once a client is known to him, one visit a season usually suffices to complete the transaction.

Some 240 crop loans distributed over five villages have been made to date, with a total value of Rs 5 million. Repayment so far has been good. Once an existing loan has been paid off, a new one can be issued at once, and farmers, being well aware of this, are repaying on time. In the event of nonpayment, help is sought from the Revenue Department.

The branch has already advanced 1,028 loans secured by gold, with a total value of Rs 2.4 million, also bearing the rate of 12.5 percent a year. It is claimed that the notional valuation of the items is superior to that offered by private lenders—75 percent as opposed to 50 percent of the assessed value. The manager estimates that at least three-quarters of this sum has been invested in agricultural development.

Two tractors are to be financed in the coming year, and draft animals may become eligible too. The move into long-term investments will be made only as experience is gained. The sole quota requirements are the provision of loans to scheduled castes, 60 annually. No (explicit) consumption loans have been sanctioned to date.

On the deposit side, there are about 1,000 accounts, with a total value of Rs 5 million. Some of the holders are not members of adopted villages.

The discussion concluded with some comments about village 7 and other lenders. There are some big traders in village 7, but the branch is not dealing with them. There are four or five powerful families [presumably overlapping with the big traders], and their moneylending operations have been severely affected by the bank's entry. It is possible, however, that commission agents have benefited from the infusion of new funds. It is also possible that the revival of cooperatives has been likewise assisted.

Households: Village 7 (January 5, 1982)

The cooperative society, which has 65 members, was a prime topic of discussion. It was dormant between 1971 and 1978, there was no executive in later years, and so no new loans were made. In 1977, overdue payments had reached 70 percent of the value of outstanding loans, bringing operations to a complete halt. The government then began to pay the executive secretary's salary, and the rules were relaxed to permit those paying off their overdues to take out new loans. About 45 members repaid. It was asserted that repayment followed threats of attachment of movable property, not collective action among the membership. Subsequently, new members obtained loans under "cyclone relief," which was followed by drought relief, enabling those in arrears to convert their short-term loans into long-term ones. The total value of outstanding loans is currently Rs 90,000; Rs 22,000 are still overdue (most for the past decade or so). Since this revival, only crop loans have been sanctioned.

The second topic was the recent adoption of the village by United Commercial Bank, which has resulted in about 40 loans. For some respondents, this is the very first loan from a commercial bank. The procedure is fairly efficient; the main drawback is the time involved in the round-trip journeys. The government and the banks, it is claimed, are now virtually the only sources of finance for small farmers. Even with the associated demands on these farmers' time and purses to pay bribes, it seems that official sources now offer better net terms than private ones. [Is this an implicit confirmation of the manager's claim that the bank's operations have spoiled the big families' moneylending business?]

It appears that farmers have found a way to skirt the provision that 60 percent of a crop loan be taken in the form of fertilizers. They reach an arrangement with dealers to exchange fertilizer for cash at a discount on the list price, obtaining the requisite certificate of purchase as part of the deal. Such ingenuity is only to be expected. There is presently no black market in fertilizers.

There followed six individual accounts, in varying detail, of dealings in formal loans. Respondent A spent Rs 320—Rs 300 in the form of a deposit in a fixed-term account for three years—getting a loan of Rs 3,000, the deal apparently handled through the patwari. He repaid this loan and took another, this time without the "investment" of Rs 320. A partial crop failure followed, so he had to pledge gold against an additional Rs 1,000 to retire the first loan. (There are some doubts about this man's story.)

Respondent B possessed certified parcels comprising 20 acres in all, valued at the meager rate of Rs 250 an acre. He paid Rs 100 into a fixed-term account. He claimed that the in-kind provision of 60 percent had not been enforced in the first round, so he took a loan of Rs 2,000, spent Rs 1,200 on a boring, and managed to repay the whole (plus Rs 65 in interest), before taking out a new loan. His "investment" in concluding these transactions was Rs 300.

Respondent C took a loan of Rs 1,000, deposited Rs 50, which he later withdrew, and repaid on time. On the second occasion, the bank's officials forced him to deposit Rs 100 into a fixed-term account for three years.

Respondent D borrowed Rs 1,000 on his personal surety in kharif, his holding being inam (land grant) land; a loan of Rs 1,500 followed in rabi.

Respondent E took loans of Rs 5,000 in the first round and Rs 10,000 in the second. He was required to put Rs 200 into a fixed-term account for three years. His total expenditure to conclude these transactions was Rs 700, of which Rs 600 was lawful.

Respondent F obtained a loan of Rs 10,000 under DPAP, Rs 4,500 of which was in cash. Rs 600 was spent to purchase shares. His expenses amounted to Rs 500.

Households: Village 8 (January 4, 1982)

The cooperative provided the main topic of discussion. It has not functioned for the past two years, but elections were held recently and overdues have been paid off. The president of the society is the patel (village leader) of a nearby village; as president, he is ultimately responsible for such debts. Meetings were held in which defaulters were persuaded to make good their earlier failures to repay on time. The years 1979–80 and 1980–81 were poor ones, so many had to borrow from private sources to clear their debts, and several lost land in consequence. One took a loan from a private lender in the expectation of obtaining a new loan from a revived society, but no such loan was forthcoming. In order to settle the private debt, he had to sell his land.

A bank adopted the village recently, but it is unclear whether there has been any effect beyond the (cheap) refinancing of existing private debts.

Digging a successful well involves an outlay of between Rs 20,000 and Rs 30,000, but the LMB sanctions only Rs 10,000 or so. Water is often not struck, and a demand for repayment of disbursed funds then follows. One small farmer sold some land to augment the initial disbursement, but still met with ill-luck. His pit is now 30 feet deep, but a further deepening of 20 feet is needed to ensure success.

Respondent A is a member of a sample household. The family owns 4 acres of dryland and two cows, which are used as draft animals, since they are not presently giving any milk. He and his brother alternate as an AFS. He is presently so engaged, while his brother manages cultivation, having served the previous two years. His wife and mother work as casual laborers as well as on the family's holding. Entering into an AFS contract was a response to the crop failures that have plagued the family in recent years. His father, who died six months ago, had taken out a loan of Rs 300, at an annual rate of 30 percent, about a year back.

VAYALPAD TALUK

Land Mortgage Bank (January 12, 1982)

This branch was recently established following the bifurcation of an existing one. Its exact assets and liabilities will become known only after March 15, 1982, when about 4,000 accounts, held by some 3,500 borrowers, will be transferred to its books. Due to the drought, 70 percent of the parent branch's loans are overdue, so it is not lending this year (1981–82). This new branch is able to lend only because it has been granted special status.

The ARDC has allocated Rs 0.75 million, purely for minor irrigation—new wells, well repairs, land development, and engines. Lending began in March 1981, covering 65 villages; the target has been met. The following advances have been made: 63 new wells, a credit limit of Rs 7,500, but with provisions for relaxation; 217 repairs, with a limit of Rs 3,000 for repairs and Rs 2,000 for desilting; 16 engines (15 electric), totaling Rs 57,000. Small farmers (defined as those owning less than 7.5 acres of dryland or 3 acres of wetland) are eligible for subsidies under DPAP and the Intensive Rural Development Programme (IRDP). These loans amount to about Rs 0.6 million.

The stages of application for a loan are as follows:

1. The completed application form, which costs Rs 3, must be accompanied by a certificate from the kurnam (village accountant and land records keeper in Chittoor Taluk), based on the village accounts. The LMB then files for an encumbrance certificate. The applicant must also pay Rs 10.5 as an entrance fee and for the first share. Applicants normally require up to four trips to complete the process. It appears that kurnams are demanding between Rs 5 and Rs 10 for their services.

2. The LMB supervisor and the engineering supervisor go to the village to collect the documents. If all is in order, the LMB subregistrar returns with the supervisor to inspect the plot. Each of these two steps takes about one month. The subregistrar has responsibility for five taluks, so the process is abnormally lengthy.

3. Legal scrutiny takes 10 days, following which the bond must be executed, which usually takes another 10–15 days. The applicant must purchase share capital at the rate of 6 percent on the first Rs 7,500 of the loan amount, and 7.5 percent on any excess. He may not use the loan to meet this expense. Small farmers may contribute their share capital in installments; this is the only exemption they enjoy.

4. The application goes to the board. If it is approved, the bond is registered.

5. Since the branch has no funds of its own, the loan must be cleared with the regional office in Tirupati. The first disbursement then follows. Steps 3, 4, and 5 take another month. Each subsequent installment takes another 15 days.

The samithi must identify those eligible for subsidies and submit the list to the LMB. Since the samithi makes the recommendations, local politicians can influence the allocation of subsidies. Elsewhere, the LMB's scrutiny has revealed anomalies in these lists, but this branch has found none thus far.

The subsidy should be paid at the time of the final disbursement, but interest is paid on the full amount of the loan, even if the disbursement of the subsidy is delayed. About 40 eligible farmers have completed wells, as verified by the LMB's inspectors. Yet no subsidies have been paid out, since the samithi has yet to carry out its own inspection.

Most wells measure 24' × 24' × 24', which costs about Rs 10,000 to Rs 12,000. The trial pit measures 6' × 6' × 18'. The amount of Rs 1,000 is advanced to small farmers for this purpose; big farmers must finance their own trial pits. If water is not struck, no further disbursements are made, and the borrower is stuck with a liability of Rs 1,000. In the event of success, the loan is made in two further disbursements. All 63 trials to date have been successful.

The engineer prepares the cost estimate—almost always for Rs 7,500, presumably to satisfy the administrative ceiling. Farmers therefore usually require additional funds. [The silence that greeted our questions on this point was an implicit admission that the rest comes from private sources, perhaps including self-financing.] Few loans have been advanced for land development (grading) and engines, so it is quite probable that these wells are not able to command their full rated areas—if at all.

Two equal disbursements are made for desilting and deepening. No subsidy is allowable, and a loan cannot be given for both.

The branch has applied for Rs 2 million to lend in the coming financial year 1982–83. The outcome will depend on the apportioning of assets and liabilities following formal bifurcation on March 15. Presently, 240 applications are pending for want of funds. Even if the full amount of Rs 2 million becomes available, it appears unlikely that this backlog will be cleared. In such circumstances, loans are not disbursed on a first-come, first-served basis, as given by the date of application. If the date of inspection is the same for two or more applications, the date of application is disregarded. The LMB's officers therefore have some discretion in allocating funds under these conditions of excess demand.

Households: Village 11 (January 13, 1982)

Both respondents belong to households in the sample.

Respondent A was, until recently, president of the Cooperative Society, which covers three villages. He took a crop loan for Rs 4,000 in 1978, secured by 2.5 acres of dryland valued at Rs 1,000 and bearing an interest rate of 11.25 percent. Even though he was the president at that time, the whole process lasted six weeks. Following the drought in 1979–80, all short-term loans were converted to a three-year term at the same rate of interest. He paid one installment, but missed two more as the drought continued. The associated penalties were waived when a further government ordinance extended the term to five years. He will pay another installment soon.

Many years ago, he obtained a loan from the LMB. At that time, the branch was 50 kilometers away, and he had to make four or five trips to conclude the deal. The documents were filed quickly, but there was a long delay in the field inspection. The first disbursement followed 15 days later, but the whole process took about four to five months. He purchased the prescribed share capital, but paid no ex gratis "fees" to anyone. He has deferred payments at least twice (in 1973 and 1979); penalties were imposed.

During a recent trip to the LMB, he inquired about purchasing a tractor. It is possible to hire tractor services, but he reckons the current rate of Rs 30 to Rs 40 an hour for about 2 acres to be rather costly compared with using bullocks, either his own or hired.

In any event, he has had second thoughts: he would have to purchase Rs 10,000 in share capital, and there is the risk of crop failure. [The two consecutive droughts must have been on his mind.]

In 1970, he borrowed Rs 10,000 at 12 percent from the Finance Corporation, a private bank, in order to purchase some land. No collateral was required, since he had known these bankers for some 20 years in connection with the marketing of groundnut. They were also commission agents at that time, but gave up that business four years ago following what seems to have been a financial failure. Collection of loan dues was irregular at first and then stopped altogether. They renewed the loan in 1979 and again yesterday. He has made no repayments, and he will not pay up unless all four of them turn up at the same time to execute the bond. (According to my calculations, he now owes about Rs 40,000.) It seems that they would be happy to recover just the principal, but he does not wish to blemish his good name. In fairness, he would pay interest of 12 percent (simple): the courts will entertain nothing else.

He proceeded to buy 3.5 acres of dryland for Rs 12,000 plus an additional Rs 3,000 in fees of some sort, although he reckons that only Rs 200 to Rs 300 of the latter was for bribes. He financed the additional Rs 5,000 with sundry private borrowings and the sale of some sheep. The land in question belonged to merchants living in a nearby village. He had been leasing the land on a fixed-rent basis for 10 years, and the rent in kind of two bags of groundnut was so low that they were happy to sell. [I presume the tenancy was registered.] Three years ago, he established an orchard of 200 lemon trees on 2 acres, which he irrigates from his own well nearby. He invested Rs 1,600 of his own money in the first year, supplemented by part of the crop loan from the cooperative. The trees have now matured, but prices have collapsed, and it is not worth his while to market the crop. The quality is poor, due to pest attack, but with prices so low, it was not profitable to spray. He must now apply fertilizers, which will cost Rs 500.

His main commercial crop is groundnut. In earlier years, there was no marketing yard, and traders were active in purchasing in the village and providing small loans.

He is not in the habit of selling to a particular trader, nor has he ever borrowed from them. He expects to sell 60–70 bags this year, at about Rs 140 per 40-kilogram bag. Some farmers intend to sell through a new husking mill, but he is not persuaded. A marketing yard is about to be established in Vayalpad. He has been elected to the marketing committee, but he will sell in the village this year.

He fears incurring large debts and will try to get by with his present sources of finance. Besides, moneylenders are much tighter with loans nowadays. The banks are proposing sheep loans, and if he can get one, he will put it to other uses, having plenty of sheep to show the officers on inspection.

He has two AFSs under contract:

- The first, KN, is now in his second year. His salary is Rs 400 a year in cash, and three meals a day, the same as last year, when he took a loan of Rs 100 and then subsequently, as needed. No interest is charged, and he will not abscond. Respondent A has known KN since childhood. He is not the head of the household, but his father has become an ascetic, so KN is effectively alone. He works 365 days a year, with all sorts of tasks and variable hours. In the event of sickness, he is paid as usual for up to 10 days. KN is now threatening to leave unless he gets a raise—"But let's see," remarks A.

- The second, SV, is a neighbor, also in his second year. He, too, does all sorts of work. He may get a small raise this year, to Rs 320 plus clothes annually and three meals a day, but it is not clear that he will continue.

People have their own land, and although A is prepared to pay up to Rs 500 in cash annually for an AFS, even at that rate, he may not be able to engage one. If KN and SV leave, he will try to replace them. Failing that, he will get by with casual laborers. There are no labor unions here.

A shortage of labor has induced him to reduce his area under paddy from 6 acres to 2.5. Yields were very poor in the past year, mainly due to late planting. Indeed, he will purchase rice for the first time in 40 years. (At this point, he was called away.)

Respondent B is SV's father. He has five sons, of whom SV is the eldest. He obtained his land some 15 years ago, paying Rs 6 an acre for the patta (proof of ownership). About three-quarters of the households in the village got land in this way.

In 1973, he was successful in getting a loan from the cooperative, for Rs 700. He has made no repayments thus far, and although he had pledged land as security, he has received no threats of foreclosure. As in other cases, there has been some rescheduling of the debt, but the villagers have been pressing him and other defaulters to repay so that the level of overdues will not threaten the society's operations.

Two of his four private debts are to fellow villagers. He executed promissory notes for Rs 400 each with two outsiders, in 1976 and 1978. He has been able to reschedule these notes because it is not worth the lenders' time to recover such small amounts through the courts. He has therefore exhausted all lines of credit in this village.

He had work animals until about three years ago, when he sold them due to the financial difficulties caused by the first of the two droughts. (He engaged SV to respondent A at that time.) He plans to buy some replacements soon by borrowing from other cultivators. (Banks will demand land as security and pose other difficulties.) He has also been grazing another farmer's cow for a year. Half of the increase in the animal's value will accrue to him, in the form of its mature calf. He will then repeat this process to get a work-pair. [This tortuous plan is not only very long term, but also carries the risk that the calves will be female. It puts me in mind of similar arrangements in northeast Bihar a decade earlier.] In the meantime, he will try to obtain the services of work animals in exchange for casual labor. The implicit wage rate apparently is not lower than the standard spot rate, a customary obligation respected by cultivators in these parts.

In any event, following the droughts, he has left his land fallow this year, so the family has had to depend on earnings from labor. He had engaged SV as an

AFS because he needed a lump sum to cope with the difficulties ensuing in 1979. The decision was his alone, and he did all the bargaining. He will now withdraw his son, who will then work as a casual laborer and be able to enjoy a little leisure. He also dislikes the ties involved. Even with the risks attached to casual labor, he thinks that this course is preferable to continuing the AFS contract. He and his sons may seek work in other villages during the peak season.

Households: Village 12 (January 14, 1982)

All four respondents belong to households in the sample.

Respondent A borrowed Rs 5,000 from the LMB in 1976 in order to sink a well. It took about a year in all to get the money, and he made at least 10 trips to the office in the course of doing so. He pledged 7 acres as collateral.

On hearing that loans were being made, he obtained an application form from the office, which the kurnam filled out for Rs 15. On filing the papers, he paid Rs 30 in legal fees and Rs 20 in bribes. It took some time for the inspector to visit the field, but no "fee" was demanded. The LMB did not provide him with an estimate of the cost, but did inform him that Rs 5,000 would be sanctioned. He had a trial pit dug at his own expense. It turned out to be a cheap undertaking—just Rs 50 to Rs 100—because the soil is soft and he struck water at 18 feet. Three months then elapsed before he received the first installment of Rs 2,500, having purchased the required share capital and paid a bribe of Rs 150. Upon completion of the work, it took another two months, as well as another Rs 100 in bribes, to get the second installment of Rs 2,500.

The loan is repayable in 10 installments of Rs 800, four of which he has made, incurring a penalty for late payment on one occasion.

His brother gave him a loan in order to purchase an electric motor. The bribe for making the connection was Rs 100.

He spent a total of about Rs 6,000 on the well at that time. Subsequently, there were severe droughts, so he had to deepen the well progressively to the present 42 feet, bringing the total cost to about Rs 20,000. He financed part of the additional investment out of his own funds and the rest by borrowing from other cultivators in the village. The cooperative society refused to sanction a loan.

He was able to irrigate about 0.75 acre in the first year; the well now commands 2 acres quite effectively.

He sells groundnut directly to traders, many of whom come to the village and pay cash on the spot. Individuals seem to move into and out of the pool of active traders. Four or five approached him last year. It is not worth his while to transport his crop for husking. He has 11 acres under groundnut this year; the crop is not yet in.

He had two AFSs, but both left his employ recently. He will engage two more—without difficulty, he claims. Such relationships seem to turn over quite frequently: the parties grow tired of each other, so they say. The cash rate is Rs 100 a month, but those who attend to the motor get Rs 125 and 25 paise a day for tobacco. The in-kind rate is seven bags of paddy and clothes annually, plus three meals a day. He prefers the first system. Having an AFS possesses the advantage that the servant is always available, 365 days a year. The other members of the AFS's family are not, however, under a first-call obligation as casual laborers.

Respondent B was, until recently, respondent A's AFS. He is the head of the household. His wife and brother-in-law work as casual laborers. He took up employment as an AFS because of the drought and then with the intention of doing so for just one year. Earlier, he had worked for respondent A as a casual laborer now and then; this was his "introduction." (His brother-in-law has resided in the village for only a short time and thus could not get such a contract.) Respondent B wanted payment in kind, but A insisted on cash, another consequence of the drought.

In any event, he had a dispute with A about six months ago, after which he went back to casual labor. The dispute arose as follows: B wanted some seed to grow groundnut on his own small plot. He was owed a month's wages and offered to give up another month's wages as payment for seed. He then spent Rs 30 to get the land plowed, but when all was ready, A reneged on the promise to supply the seed, and that was that. (B added that the prospects for casual labor also seem better this year.)

He purchased the plot from some people in a village nearby about 10 years ago. At that time, he and his two brothers formed a joint family; when they separated eight years ago, he got his one-third share. The plot is served by a well, which even then was not in good condition and now is dry. In 1978, he pledged the plot as collateral to secure a private loan of Rs 1,000. He had also taken a crop loan from the cooperative society. [It is not clear whether he had managed to pledge the plot to both lenders.] At all events, the private loan contract ruled out an approach to the LMB or cooperative society for a loan to desilt the well. Another, final installment of the cooperative loan, which had been converted into a medium-term loan, is due in March, but he will be unable to pay it. What is more, he will have to clear both debts before his brothers will join him in seeking a loan for desilting.

To compound matters, the private party is also demanding full repayment, within two or three months, failing which the land must be sold. In fact, the creditor himself wants to acquire the land, since he owns plots close by, which motivated him to offer the loan to B in the first place.

Respondent C leased in an irrigated plot of 0.7 acre about three years back, under the terms of a usufructuary mortgage, whereby he lent Rs 10,000 to the owner, who lives in the same hamlet. C cultivated the land for one year, but found the additional burden too much. He therefore decided to sublease the plot, on a sharecropping basis, to a party recommended by the owner, but not of his own acquaintance. As it turned out, the subtenant and the owner colluded to deprive him of his rightful share.

He chose a sharecropping lease because he thought it would be profitable. Among other things, he gave the subtenant the use of his draft animals; they were abused to the point of becoming useless. He also provided some fertilizer, to be repaid after the harvest. The agreement was to share all outputs 50:50. In the first year, paddy, tomatoes, and sugarcane were grown, but all he got was one-third of the jaggery and then only because his son-in-law supervised the conversion from cane. The subtenant's family are tough, difficult people, so he could do nothing. It seems that the owner himself then leased back the plot for one year. [Respondent C's son had been murdered before this whole affair. His troubles have apparently disturbed him so much that his account is confused and inconsistent. See respondent D's account below.]

Respondent D obtained a loan from the LMB in 1970, having heard from the kurnam about its program to finance wells. It took about 15 days to file the documents. The whole process lasted about three months and involved transportation costs totaling Rs 125 for 25 trips to the branch office 50 kilometers away.

He paid the supervisor Rs 25 to issue the encumbrance certificate and another Rs 100 at the time of the first disbursement. Despite being a small farmer, he had to finance his own trial pit, which struck water at 18 feet and cost about Rs 400. The total cost of the well was Rs 2,900, but the LMB sanctioned only Rs 2,000. He financed the rest by selling his large bullocks and replacing them with smaller ones. The well commands about 0.8 acre, but it needs desilting.

The final installment was due last year, but the drought was so severe that he decided not to pay it. There was also another, earlier overdue payment. All told, he now owes the LMB about Rs 700, which, he claims, he will pay off soon. He will not approach the LMB in future, however, since the bank is always pestering him for repayment.

In September 1980, he obtained a loan of Rs 800 from the cooperative society. He had to purchase Rs 80 in share capital and pay the secretary a "fee" of Rs 20. A certificate of landholding sufficed, since the amount was less than Rs 1,000. He had a pressing need for credit at that time, and the cooperative was the only source available. He has received a due notice dated November 30, 1981, demanding repayment on pain of 3 percent penal interest on the principal.

He has more than one outstanding private debt. His creditors are cultivators in neighboring villages, whom he had known from the past or to whom he had obtained an introduction. He always goes outside his own village for this purpose. [Perhaps he is concerned to save face.] The creditors make inquiries about borrowers' liabilities, both directly and through third parties. They insist on a promissory note. The annual rate used to be 18 percent five years back, but is now 24 percent. Some work is involved in getting private loans nowadays, due to the drought and government moratoria on repayments.

He is currently renting 0.18 acre of irrigated land from a widow. He hinted that she seems to prefer a nonrelative as a tenant—to be sure of getting the rent. The contract is oral and has run for two years. The rent is 80 kilograms of paddy; she pays the land revenue. He would prefer to pay in cash, but she insists on payment in kind. Sharecropping is ruled out because she cannot supervise cultivation (especially harvesting). Despite the risks, he would prefer to get the whole return from his investment as residual claimant under a fixed-rent arrangement. Generally, sharecropping is chosen on wetland and fixed rents on dryland. [The explanation for this apparently paradoxical practice is that percolation wells depend on recharge from the rains. If the monsoon is poor, there will be little or no water for irrigation and hence no cultivation of paddy, or—worse still—a failed crop. Other crops grown on dryland are more robust to this hazard.] He would like to lease in more land, but owners seem set on cultivating themselves.

Three years ago, he was indeed leasing land from respondent C. He claims that he planted sugarcane, with his share of output to be two-thirds, since he was to meet all of the expenses of cultivation. After the harvest, C demanded that the land be returned, no doubt in order to get the benefit of the first ratoon crop. He realized Rs 2,000 from the sale of his share of the jaggery.

In January 1981, he managed to purchase 0.5 acre and a half share in a well from a fellow villager for Rs 6,000, financed in part by the proceeds of the jaggery sale. At present, Rs 3,000 are still due, and the deeds have yet to be transferred. The land is under sugarcane.

He sold the jaggery to retail outlets in two places, getting about Rs 3 per kilogram. No trader came to purchase it, so he had to market it in this way.

Traders do not seem to be active in the market for jaggery, and if no traders approach him this year, he will sell to retailers again. As for groundnut, there seem to be as many traders as cultivators, but his crop this year will suffice only for seed purposes.

The members of his family do not work for any particular landlord on a first-call basis. AFS contracts are ruled out as a matter of principle. He himself hires labor only for transplanting paddy.

CHITTOOR TALUK

Land Mortgage Bank (January 7, 1982)

Since 1970, the ARDC has declared the taluk to be a "dark area" due to "excessive exploitation" of groundwater, so ruling out any lending for irrigation other than the laying of pipes to serve existing wells. This limitation aside, this branch is the only "unrestricted" LMB in the whole of Rayalaseema.

The current programs cover dairy, sericulture, sheep, orchards, tractors, carts, and bullocks (for villages within 16 kilometers of the sugar factory) and a few cases of electric motors to replace diesel ones. Total lending in 1980–81 was Rs 2.7 million, comprising Rs 1.3 million for coconut and mango orchards, Rs 0.4 million for carts and bullocks, Rs 0.3 million each for dairy and sheep, and Rs 0.4 for sundry other purposes.

The stages of application for a loan are naturally much the same as those in other taluks, but there is enlightening variation in some details.

1. The farmer must first approach the bank. The application form, which costs Rs 3, is to be filled out by the village kurnam. The latter will provide certificates of "no dues" owing to the cooperative and other credit institutions, as well as the survey numbers and status of the plots to be pledged as collateral. Also required are the title deeds, in the case of sale, patta, or (family) partition. On submission of all these documents, the applicant must pay an admission fee of Rs 10.5 and Rs 5.0 per Rs 1,000 of the sum to be borrowed, up to a maximum of Rs 25. Lastly, an encumbrance certificate is applied for; the fee for big farmers (those possessing at least 10 acres of wetland or 20 acres of dryland) is Rs 16. This stage normally takes about 15 days.

2. A supervisor carries out the field inspection to ascertain the plots' condition, whether they are under cultivation, and suchlike. More senior officials are involved if the loan sought exceeds Rs 5,000: the assistant development officer must concur for loans between Rs 5,000 and Rs 15,000; for those above Rs 15,000, the registrar himself must accompany the supervisor when making the field inspection. Since this bank serves two taluks and staff are short, this stage may take up to one month.

3. Legal scrutiny is conducted.

4. If the application passes legal scrutiny, a bond is executed and the loan is sanctioned. Share capital must be purchased at the rate of 6 percent of the loan up to Rs 7,500 and 7.5 percent on all excess thereafter. These purchases must be made from the borrower's own funds, not from the loan itself. Steps 3 and 4 take a few days.

5. Disbursement is made in stages, depending on the nature of the investment. For mango orchards, the rate is Rs 750 per acre in the first year (for saplings, planting, fencing, and so forth) and Rs 300 per acre for each of four years thereafter. For coconuts, the rate is Rs 1,000 per acre in the first year and the same as for mangos thereafter. There is an inspection before each disbursement to ensure that the orchard is being developed and maintained properly. In the event that the work is assessed to be not up to scratch, foreclosure of the whole loan follows. In 15–20 percent of all cases, the first installment is not used to establish the plantation, so some persuasion is called for, with the exercise of due discretion, to avoid the process of foreclosure. When livestock is to be purchased, the manager and a veterinarian accompany a group of applicants to a local market. These markets take place weekly.

The terms of loans are as follows: the interest rates for small and big farmers are 10.50 and 12.25 percent a year, respectively; these rates went into force in June 1981. For mango orchards, only interest payments are due in the first five years; both principal and interest are due in the next seven. The corresponding schedule for coconuts is six years each. For all other loans, both principal and interest are due throughout. The repayment schedule is four years for cows and buffaloes, five for sheep and bullocks, and seven for tractors, pipelines, and crushers.

The taluk committee sets the value to be placed on land pledged as collateral: the current rates are Rs 1,200 an acre for dryland and Rs 3,000 for wetland. They may be modified in light of the subregistrar's statistics if a higher value is sought. These rather low valuations contribute to the above-noted failures to use first disbursements to establish mango and coconut plantations. The valuation norms are fixed too low to yield satisfactory levels of financing at this stage of such investments.

Although there is no restriction on aggregate lending, the target for the current year (1981–82) is Rs 30 million. The associated allocations for designated groups are 15 percent for scheduled castes, 3 percent for scheduled tribes, and 60 percent for small farmers, whereby the ARDC defines the latter as owning at most 5 acres of wetland or 11 acres of dryland. Only small farmers are eligible for cart and bullock loans. Livestock loans are now restricted to the relevant castes, since others have failed to do well.

In the April–June quarter, there is a collection drive to ensure the repayment of dues, and there are no advances of new loans. In earlier years, 98 percent of dues were actually paid. Indeed, there have been only 43 foreclosures in all since 1936 and none last year, despite the drought. The overdue rate, however, rose to 15 percent, and the manager made a personal decision not to proceed with the attachment of movable assets. The incidence of overdue payments was much the same across all categories of borrowers.

This recent shortfall in repayment—about Rs 0.4 million all told—has affected the branch's current operations. It used virtually all of its own reserves to retire the debts in question with the central LMB; so that documents must now be sent to headquarters for disbursement. The branch is also short-staffed: four posts are vacant due to lack of funds.

The manager claimed that, generally speaking, farmers are approaching the bank for loans without any particular encouragement or pressure from the field officers. Like his counterpart in Kalvakurthy Taluk, he suggested that some village kurnams are extracting ex gratis fees from applicants.

Andhra Bank (January 8, 1982)

This branch was established in 1964, but made no loans to agriculture until 1978. Andhra Bank was nationalized in 1980. Its lead bank is Indian Bank.

"Adoption" of villages is an important feature of the new regime. All short- and medium-term loans are covered, but not long-term ones, which are the LMB's province. The term of adoption runs up to seven years. Villages are selected in consultation with the block development officer, involving an assessment of the villagers' repayment capacity and reliability. Villages with well-functioning cooperatives are not eligible. Eight villages have been adopted to date; one of them is village 13. There are about 430 customers in these villages.

In the current year (1981–82), crop loans have amounted to Rs 0.35 million (against a target of Rs 0.4 million); term loans have amounted to Rs 0.5, covering dairy, sheep, deepening of wells (about 20), and replacement of diesel with electric motors (about 20). According to a government circular, at least half of all loans must go to small and marginal farmers, defined as farmers owning less than 5 acres of dryland.

All borrowers must first open an account—a nominal deposit of, say, Rs 5 will do. A new client must also name a few existing customers from his village and, having opened an account, can then apply for a loan. The process culminating in sanctioning of the loan usually takes 10 to 15 days. Existing clients need one visit to pay off any outstanding dues. An officer of the bank then inspects the plot, usually within 10 days, and a new loan is issued upon a second visit.

All applications for crop loans must be accompanied by a certificate from the cooperative that there are neither overdues nor current crop loans. A corresponding certificate from the LMB is not required, even though loans must be secured by land as collateral. The current rate of interest is 12.5 percent per year.

In an innovation, a group guarantee scheme (GGS) was introduced at the behest of the RBI in 1981, in order to simplify procedures, although certificates of landownership are still required. Each group comprises three members, with a credit limit of Rs 5,000 per member. These loans are mostly for the cultivation of sugarcane and have a term of one year; the current ones are due in May 1982.

Loans for the purchase of milch animals are restricted to small and marginal farmers who possess some land of their own. The program envisages the purchase of one animal, with another to follow if things turn out satisfactorily. Each animal costs about Rs 2,700, one-third of which the bank pays as a subsidy. A purchase committee accompanies borrowers to Bangalore, where the animals are bought. The animal itself stands as collateral for the loan. If it dies, insurance is paid on the entire purchase price. The annual insurance premium is 2.25 percent, which is debited to the borrower's account. Thus far, some 40 eligible beneficiaries, 12 of them scheduled castes, have been identified. Interest is charged at the rate of 10.5 percent per year from the date of purchase, for a term of three years.

Milk marketing is handled by an agency. Until recently, farmers were organized in groups of three, with one taking responsibility for all three repayments. The milk collection center enforces exclusive delivery of the milk, but there is only one "leader" in each village for this purpose, and he is not easily controlled by the bank. This is the weak point in the loan program. As a recent countermeasure, a list of the beneficiaries is submitted to the Dairy Corporation, which makes deductions from the individual accounts in the bank's favor—but only after the Dairy Corporation has deducted the cost of the feed concentrates it supplies to the dairymen. This is a reversion to the scheme in force three years ago.

Loans for the desilting or deepening of wells are limited to Rs 1,500 per borrower, but this suffices to finance the whole work under the GGS when only one member of the group makes such an application. The purchase of an electric motor (about Rs 4,000) requires land as collateral, with the usual procedures. Although the new government circular permits such loans under the GGS, land as security is still demanded. In fact, many of these borrowers have also taken a crop loan. Land is valued at eight times the net incremental income from an associated investment or at its market value, whichever is lower. Most land would fetch Rs 12,000 to Rs 15,000 an acre, but the bank's upper limit is Rs 10,000.

The bank also advances loans against gold as security. About 140 people have such loans currently, with a total value of Rs 0.5 million. Some 50 to 60 of these borrowers belong to the eight adopted villages; it is claimed that the money has been used to finance agriculture. The bank's valuation is set at 75 percent of the appraiser's, up to a limit of Rs 100 per gram for a total value less than Rs 2,500 and Rs 80 per gram in excess thereof. The appraisal fee is 25 paise per Rs 100 of the loan amount. The recent drought has greatly encouraged clients to take out these loans.

This brought the discussion to the general topic of the drought's effects on the bank's operations and its clients' repayment morale. Collection of dues was suspended in 1980, and second milch animals were not sanctioned in that year. Three of the animals purchased since 1979 have died, milk yields have been poor, and the animals have not calved well. The group leader in each village is supposed to make payments for the rest, but overdues now amount to Rs 30,000 on loans totaling Rs 78,000. For all that, it is claimed that the loans represent no great risk to the bank because the animals are insured and the milk marketing agency enforces collection through individual accounts. This claim is somewhat at odds with the decision that only 20 of the 40 beneficiaries are eligible to purchase a second animal. [Even with this retrenchment, such is the level of overdues that the manager's view of the position seems rather optimistic.]

Eight clients belonging to the eight adopted villages have defaulted on loans taken in 1980–81. Three of the 28 clients borrowing for sugarcane cultivation in village 13 in that year have overdues, totaling Rs 6,000.

The officer expressed opinions on various related matters. There is some diversion of funds to purposes other than that stated in the application—perhaps as much as 25 percent in the case of crop loans. Yet there is no insistence on the provision of fertilizer purchase receipts. Farmers are keen to invest in fixed assets and spend generously on marriages; they see to these expenditures rather than meeting their installment payments.

The restrictions recently imposed by the RBI are biting; without them, total lending in rabi would have been Rs 0.5 million to Rs 0.6 million. The GGS will strongly expand the [notional] demand for loans [thus intensifying rationing until the RBI's restrictions are eased]. The commercial banks are certainly displacing moneylenders and commission agents. They are also putting the cooperatives under pressure—those that are not already dormant or defunct. In this connection, the rule that a society can continue to lend until the level of overdues exceeds 50 percent is a powerful incentive for free riding among its members.

Corruption is rife, not only in the LMB branches but also in the cooperatives, so people are now coming to the banks instead. The officer added that issuing farmers passbooks that specify their landholdings would reduce the kurnam's ability to extract bribes.

Cooperative sugar mill (January 7, 1982)

The share capital of Rs 1 million was raised over a period of some years. The government contributed Rs 2 million, and the balance of Rs 7.5 million was provided by the IFCI (previously the Industrial Finance Corporation of India) as a loan.

Production began in 1962–63. The initial installed capacity was 1,000 tonnes a day; this was raised to 1,600 tonnes in 1974–75, for which additional loans were taken. The recovery rate was about 11 percent in 1962, but now is only 8.6 percent. The radius of operation is about 50 kilometers; this should be reduced in order to improve the recovery rate. The normal working period is 150 days, corresponding to an annual capacity of about 210,000 tonnes. In 1980–81, however, operations lasted just 63 days and only 60,000 tonnes were crushed, as high jaggery prices induced members to divert their cane into home production and subsequent sale in Chittoor's market, which is the leading one in Rayalaseema and the neighboring areas of Tamil Nadu.

There are presently about 9,300 members, but only about 2,000 are providing cane. Any dividends resulting from a year's operations are distributed one year later. Contracts were closed on October 31, 1981, even though the full quota of 208,000 tonnes had not been met. The targeted throughput for this year is 186,000 tonnes; any excess will be allocated to loyal members.

Members are contractually obliged to deliver 8 tonnes of cane for each share they own, but those who do not grow cane are exempt in that season. The penalties for failing to comply are as follows: upon the first default, Rs 5 per tonne on the next delivery; upon a second and third default, Rs 10 and Rs 25 per tonne, respectively. This tariff has ruled for the past 15 years, and there is no prospect of making it stiffer. A fourth default results in the member losing his supplier status, and his shares will be converted into nonsupply status. A nonrefundable deposit of Rs 5 per tonne is levied on all deliveries to pay off the mill's past loans and support applications for new ones.

The mill gives certificates to those members who wish to obtain crop loans from banks. The financing rate is Rs 2,000 per acre, Rs 500 of which is for fertilizers. About 2,500 members have availed themselves of this facility; 1,500 of those 2,000 actively supplying cane have done so. The mill itself has provided fertilizers directly in the value of about Rs 0.4 million. [This is small beer.] The previous year was poor and left the cooperative with such low financial reserves as to rule out heavier provision. It is claimed that the link between private credit and the supply of jaggery does not influence farmers' decisions concerning whether to deliver cane to the mill—only the relative price of jaggery to cane matters.

The latest plan to improve matters is two-pronged. The first, on the supply side, is to introduce a short, early crushing season in August and September, when temperatures have fallen a bit, to supplement the main season from November to March. Jaggery production is not feasible in the former season; however, short-period varieties are needed, although their yields are rather low. There is already an active extension effort, especially in pest control. On the whole, the members are conscientious cultivators, who do not go beyond a third ratoon crop.

The second is aimed at improving deliveries directly. Every year, proceedings are launched against 500 or so members for noncompliance or default on fertilizer loans. Attachment of movable assets has been quite common, but a special ordinance prompted by the drought put a stop to this in 1981. Big farmers comply better with their delivery obligations than do small ones, because they find it harder to prevent pilferage of cane during the production of jaggery. The central problem, however, is that the levy price is not based on local costs of production. [It would be better to keep an eye on world prices, which influence those of jaggery.]

It is claimed that the chance, joint occurrence of the drought and boom in jaggery prices has led to most of the improvement in farmers' earnings going into the deepening of their wells: the protracted drought has virtually forced these investments.

Jaggery merchant (January 9, 1982)

The discussion took place in the merchant's shop, which is one of many such establishments in a long street. Although it lasted for quite some time, the merchant was eventually called away on pressing business, so the following account is incomplete. Some interesting points and questions that arose in the course of the discussion could not be pursued.

About 45,000 acres in Chittoor District are currently under sugarcane. There are two factories, whose joint requirement is about 15,000 acres. There are about 250 registered dealers, most of whom deal in groundnut as well as jaggery. Some of them have as many as 700 clients, and 90 percent of them are also landlords—in contrast to their counterparts in the other main centers of India's jaggery trading. There are also some petty dealers, who buy directly in the villages or act as middlemen (agents) for registered dealers. The latter are financing cultivation in Chittoor and Vyalpad Taluks to the tune of Rs 30 million to Rs 40 million a year, which dwarfs public sector lending.

Trading in groundnut is seasonal; that in jaggery is year-round. The commission rates are 2 percent (ad valorem) for groundnut and jaggery and 5 percent for mangos. The merchant claims that the commission agent protects the seller's interests in the sales transaction at auction. The banks are not effective competitors because the dealers offer more flexible terms.

He took over his father's business, with about 400 clients, in 1958; he now has about 500. An existing client who seeks a loan will simply sign a statement to the effect that he will deliver a certain number of quintals of jaggery at the end of the crop cycle. The merchant assesses the size of the associated loan in light of the current price. [The contractual delivery and the loan are jointly determined, so one presumes that the client is aware of the basis of the assessment.] New clients are usually required to sign a formal agreement covering all aspects of the transaction. The annual interest rate ranges from 12 to 18 percent, depending on the size of the delivery; it is charged only on advances outstanding for four months and more. For new clients, the rate is contractually fixed in their agreement. For existing clients, its level is "understood" between the parties, but the actual level in the event ultimately depends on the merchant's goodwill. If he agrees to roll over the loan, the interest rate is unchanged, without compounding. If a client delivers cash instead of quintals of jaggery, the commission on the contracted amount is deducted, along with principal and interest.

Storage is important in this market. Jaggery can be stored for long periods with the right facilities, which are rare in villages. Yet farmers persist in storing jaggery at home. He provides storage, at no charge, when he has space, but for no more than 10 or so clients at a time.

The market yard itself is not regulated. Such a development would improve the exchange of information among clients. It would also ease his life with the income tax officials, since his dealings would be recorded.

There are legal means to enforce delivery: the merchant can go to court to recover the contractual commission if a client fails to deliver the agreed quantity. Such a recourse is not always the last resort; for much information about clients' doings circulates among the dealers themselves, who meet informally on social occasions and collaborate quite extensively. The merchant claimed that if he sees a "bad" client approaching a neighboring dealer, he will immediately warn the latter. More generally, commission charges on a delivery to dealer B, but contracted to A, will be restored by B to A if they are well known to each other. [Even so, enforcing exclusive contracts on clients is not that easy.] If a client is also engaged with another dealer and our respondent gets wind of it, he will send his man at once to secure the contracted amount. If that fails, he will recover the loan (at length) and terminate his relationship with the client. In recent years, partial defaults on deliveries have risen to about 10 percent of all deliveries.

In this connection, the cooperative mill is, in effect, a second dealer, which imposes its own contractual obligations on its shareholders. About one-fifth of his clients are shareholders, and there is some tension here. Following the drought, the cooperative withdrew its court case against defaulters last year, which relieved the situation. He accepts new clients who are shareholders, provided their current areas under cane are sufficient to meet both obligations. He himself owns 12 shares. What is not delivered to the mill, his tenants convert into jaggery.

Although the collection of debts and commission fees occurs, in principle, in one action, debts are subject to a special hazard: "forgiveness" by government decree. Four years ago, in the aftermath of another drought, the government enacted an ordinance under which cultivators owning less than 5 acres were allowed to default without legal penalty. About 40 of his clients seized this opportunity, and he incurred expenses in unsuccessful litigation against them. Thereafter, he has concentrated his business on clients with medium to large holdings, although those small farmers who did meet their obligations are still with him.

Where current operations are concerned, he does not employ people to keep an eye on his clients' crops. When he goes to a village on other errands, he takes the opportunity to inspect the fields himself. When clients come to see him in Chittoor, which they do frequently, they report on crop conditions in their villages.

The costs of doing business comprise those of his establishment (shop) and financing, including risks. They are roughly equal and have risen over the years. In 1958, the interest rate was a flat 12 percent a year [and the inflation rate was much lower]. When the need arises, he resorts to loans from private banks, which now charge 24 percent a year. (It appears that he uses these funds mainly to finance his speculative activities, in which case, they should not bear on his clients.) If, as he wishes, he does take on more clients, his funds may not suffice to meet all of their needs in the event of a drought. He would then restrict the amount that he lends to each and every one of them and attempt to secure for them additional loans from other private sources.

He owns 10 acres of land, on which he has installed five or six tenants, whom he rotates every two or three years in order to avoid their acquiring permanent tenure rights. All of them also have land of their own. The terms of these share-cropping contracts are as follows: output is 60:40 in his favor, he pays for electricity (for pumping) and fertilizers, and the tenants supply bullocks and labor. The choice of sharecropping stems from the balance of reward and risks: no farmer would offer more than Rs 1,500 per acre on fixed-rent terms, but the present arrangement yields him Rs 2,000 per acre [presumably a long-run average]. The allocation of these tenancies is not disturbed during the cycle of the main and ratoon crops, whereby at most two cycles of ratoon are taken. (Sugarcane is an annual crop.)

Where trading conditions are concerned, he claimed, at one point, that jaggery prices are no more volatile today than 25 years ago. Yet a question posed a little later elicited the information that, having reached an all-time high of Rs 400 per quintal in 1981, the price ruling on this very day stands at Rs 160. [Volatility on this scale prompts the question, Was the size of the loan really assessed on the basis of the spot price then ruling, as claimed above?] He estimates that about 90 percent of the cultivators' earnings from this boom went into deepening their wells. He himself does not get involved in financing pumps and well digging. For these purposes, he directs his clients to the banks.

This account of the terms of loans is at odds with that of the cultivators on several points. First, cultivators claim that they have paid commission rates of 4.0 to 4.5 percent; only those who do not borrow pay 2 percent. Second, the interest rate charged is more commonly 18 to 24 percent than 12 to 18 percent. Third, interest is charged from the date the loan is taken, not four months later. (The four-month rule may simply trigger interest payments from the date on which the loan was taken; since farmers cultivating cane normally borrow for the whole crop cycle of one year, the trigger will then be in effect.)

Cooperative society (January 9, 1982)

The respondent is the president of the cooperative society of a village 2 kilometers from village 13.

This cooperative had earlier served just three villages. In 1978, several societies were merged to form a single society covering some 20 villages, including village 13. There are 570 members, 80 percent of whom have current loans; 75 percent are small farmers. He has spent his own money to purchase memberships for scheduled castes in order to meet the society's quota. The value of all outstanding loans is Rs 0.5 million, of which almost Rs 0.2 million is due. The latter is to be collected over the next four months. The outstanding amount exceeds that due because short-term loans were converted into medium-term ones following the drought, as required by a government ordinance.

Land must be pledged as security in order to obtain a loan, even from the society. This requirement has been in force for at least 10–15 years. There have been about 100 cases of foreclosure in the past four years, which resulted in the attachment of movable assets; but after the ordinance went into force, they were returned to the households. There have been no cases in which land was attached and sold.

Following the merger, only crop loans have been sanctioned, although a recent circular sets the provisions for medium-term loans. Markfed supplies the fertilizers as soon as the Central Cooperative Bank clears the check. Farmers receive these supplies in good time. Backward castes and scheduled castes can apply through the society's registrar for loans to finance draft animals and carts. No such loans have been advanced by this society, mainly because no corresponding government order has gone into effect.

All villages in the area have been adopted by banks, which has put the cooperatives under increasing pressure. The free-riding problem arising from the provision allowing cooperatives to continue lending until overdue loans reach 50 percent of the total amount outstanding had already weakened their operations for some time. This had encouraged farmers to approach the banks for loans, even before the adoption program got under way. The cooperatives' processing procedures are also very cumbersome.

More than a few farmers take loans simultaneously from the cooperative sugar mill, the society, and commission agents, all for the same plots of sugarcane. [The commission agents are naturally well placed to enforce debt seniority in their favor.] As elsewhere, there is much refinancing of institutional loans using credit from private sources.

Households: Village 13 (January 9, 1982)

Both respondents belong to households in the sample.

Respondent A has various dealings on both sides of the credit market, as cultivator and employer. He recently made a successful application to the LMB for a loan of Rs 9,000 to finance a mango orchard on 4 acres. He had paid off an old loan to the LMB and did not have to purchase any additional share capital. The land that had been pledged as collateral sufficed to cover the new loan. The kurnam, who is an old acquaintance, filled out the application form on the same day, provided the necessary documents, and demanded no "fee." (Respondent A added that others are less fortunate.) A fellow villager has a son who works in the LMB office, and he helped to expedite the whole process. Respondent A does not remember exactly how long it took to go from filing the application to getting the first disbursement. It may have been about six weeks, but he was not unhappy about it.

The schedule of disbursements is an initial Rs 4,000, followed by five annual ones of Rs 1,000 each. These amounts are sufficient for development of the orchard. He had no difficulties with the LMB's inspecting officer in the first stage. Installment payments will begin only once the trees are mature, but he is otherwise unclear about the maturity of the loan. The planting density is 100 trees per acre, and each tree should yield an income of Rs 100 to Rs 150, implying a gross income of Rs 10,000 to Rs 15,000 per acre.

The adoption of the village by Andhra Bank induced him to switch commercial banks. About one month after Andhra Bank officials had come to the village to assess it, he went to the branch office in Chittoor to obtain a loan. The officials and his friend the kurnam helped him to file the application. He had to visit the office several times, but there is always other business to settle in Chittoor and the whole process took just 15 days. Since his own land is pledged to the LMB, his son-in-law had to stand guarantee for him. The first loan was for Rs 5,000, which he repaid on time one year later. He made one trip to repay and another a week later to pick up a new loan of Rs 5,000. A repayment is due in a few months, but he is not sure that he will be able to manage it. A shortage of groundwater has limited irrigation, and if the crop itself does not suffice, he will borrow from friends in order to remain in good standing with the bank and so obtain a third loan.

He wound up his account with Syndicate Bank by paying off a loan secured by gold. He is very happy with Andhra Bank and claims that its dealings are free of corruption—not that those of Syndicate Bank were so tainted.

He has five shares in the cooperative sugar mill. The factory gate price is Rs 191 per tonne, but he must pay transport costs (he will finish his deliveries today). The balance of the crop will be converted into jaggery. Last year, he delivered 16 tonnes to the mill and converted 60 tonnes into jaggery. [The contractual delivery is 8 tonnes per share, which implies that, holding five shares, he defaulted on 24 tonnes.]

He has current dealings with three commission agents, all of whom are related to him. He has not revealed to the third that he has loans outstanding with the other two; he does not know whether they have put the third in the picture, although that is likely. Morally, he is obliged to sell only through his present lender(s) or agent(s). Since Andhra Bank has set a credit limit of Rs 5,000, which is insufficient for his needs, he must continue to deal with commission agents.

He is charged a commission rate of 4 percent. Malpractice in weighing jaggery also abounds. The timing of the sale is his decision, and he leaves instructions with the agent about the minimum acceptable price at auction. The interest rate is 18 percent, specified orally when the loan is taken, and interest charges accrue at once.

He expects to produce about six cartloads of jaggery this year. At today's spot price of Rs 160 per quintal and 750 kilograms per cartload, this quantity would fetch Rs 7,200.

The Christian Society is yet another source of credit. His friend the kurnam helped out once again, this time by providing a fraudulent certificate stating that he owns less than 4 acres. The Christian Society has now come to know that he owns much more and has demanded that he execute a bond for 4 acres in their favor. Since all of his land is pledged to the LMB, he will have to settle the account.

Respondent A's own dealings as a lender to laborers have been dogged by enforcement problems. Petty loans to casual laborers are essential, or they will not come and work when asked. He is currently advancing loans to 10 laborers, each of whom seems to have a similar arrangement with other employers. The amounts in question are usually about Rs 60 to Rs 70. This attempt to tie labor is not especially successful. Other family members are exempt from this obligation, and the borrowers themselves appear on demand only half the time.

A heavier loss occurred two years ago. He advanced the sum of Rs 470 to a laborer he had engaged as an AFS. The laborer absconded 10 days later, taking with him a similar sum obtained from a cultivator in another village. Enforcement has become such a problem in AFS contracts that even paying monthly is not fully effective.

Respondent B has taken two loans, at separate times, from Andhra Bank, the first to purchase a milch animal and the second to purchase an electric motor.

He paid the kurnam Rs 20 to fill out the application; three months elapsed before the loan was sanctioned. The animal cost Rs 2,600, less a subsidy of one-third. The purchasing procedure ran as follows. A group of about 10 people went to Bangalore for the transaction and paid the veterinarian Rs 70 for his services. The whole trip was very enjoyable, took three days, and cost Rs 60 to Rs 70. The trucking fee was Rs 100 for each animal. He made a small profit from selling milk, after expenses for feed and such; he also confirmed the bank officer's account of the marketing arrangements. Maintaining the animal proved to be very time-consuming.

The bank was unwilling to advance a loan for the electric motor while the first loan was still outstanding. He therefore sold the animal, for Rs 1,800, and paid off the first loan one year early. All in all, the subsidy just about bailed him out. In order to obtain the second loan, he had to deposit the land title deeds with the bank. The loan was sanctioned one month after he had filed the application. The motor itself was delivered 15 days later, and the connection followed 10 days afterward, with a payment of Rs 25 to the lineman who made it. Despite power failures, the switch from a diesel pump to an electric pump has been profitable. A subsidy of one-third also applied, this time under the DPAP.

His current cane crop is in poor condition, a fact noted by the inspector from the cooperative mill. He had neglected to desilt his well, choosing instead to improve his house. As things stand, he will be lucky to get enough output for seed purposes. To compound matters, the jaggery he produced last year suffered severe damage in storage: he realized only Rs 4,000 instead of the Rs 12,000 or so expected.

Earlier, he had no need to borrow, but facing difficulties, he asked his brother to introduce him to an agent with whom the latter has had a long-standing arrangement.

He contracted to deliver five cartloads of jaggery in the first year, did so, and renewed the contract. The commission rate is 4.5 percent (2 percent applies only for nonborrowers), and the interest rate is 18 percent. He will not be able to meet his delivery obligations this year, and the agent has rolled over the loan. The commission on the contractual delivery still applies, however, and has been added to the due amount rolled over. The tie between credit and delivery is firm, with enforcement as described by the jaggery merchant in Chittoor.

Households: Village 14 (January 11, 1982)

All three respondents belong to households in the sample.

Respondent A's affairs have been complicated by the recent partition of the joint family. Before that event, the family was unable to obtain sufficient finance from one agent alone. The prime agent directed them to a second to get additional finance. On some occasions, the family was unable to deliver the contractual amounts to both agents. They then met their obligations to the first, who is the more aggressive of the two, and rolled over the shortfall with the second, who naturally charged full commission on the contracted amount. Since respondent A was on better terms with the second agent, he maintained this relationship after the family's separation.

As a result, he inherited some sundry debts, which he repaid out of the proceeds of jaggery sales in March 1981. At that time, he met his obligation to deliver eight cartloads, but the proceeds were insufficient to pay off all his debts. The agent deducted interest and commission charges and rolled over the principal. He does not remember the exact commission rate on that transaction. The interest rate was 24 percent per year, which will also apply to the amount rolled over.

What remained after these deductions was used to pay off the debts to third parties. He is not always paid on the nail. If the auction takes place on the day of delivery, he may be. Otherwise, he picks up his money in dribs and drabs, not wishing to press his case when he has an outstanding debt.

Since his seedlings had already shriveled in the field and the crop was doomed to failure, he did not bother to take an additional loan in 1981. He will be unable to meet his obligation to deliver eight cartloads this year. In a few months, therefore, further interest and commission charges will be added to the amount already outstanding. He expects to have to pay about Rs 3,000 $(2,000 \cdot 1.24 + 12,000 \cdot 0.045)$. In order to finance this year's crop, prospectively of 3 acres, he will sell milk and borrow from friends. His application for a loan of Rs 4,000 from the cooperative society is likely to be approved soon (he has no outstanding dues).

The joint family had shares in the cooperative sugar mill, but not in his name. He helps out with those contractual deliveries when he can.

On jaggery transactions more generally, he knows of no one in this village who can deliver in such bulk as to enjoy an interest rate as low as 18 percent. More important, in the absence of a marketing yard, the traders will always deal with the commission agents, because there is no place where the cultivators can display their product except in their agent's shop. If there were a regulated market, A would certainly use it. He knows of no one who sells directly to traders.

He does not sell his groundnut in Chittoor, even though his commission agent there deals in both commodities. He has a long-standing relationship with another businessman, who organizes a truck pickup in Chittoor District, for subsequent dehusking at his site in neighboring Tamil Nadu. The trucking charge is Rs 200 for about 60 bags of 40 kilograms each. The conversion rate is 120 kilograms of pods into 75 kilograms of kernels, for which Rs 5 is charged. The kernels must be transported to the shop, which costs a further Rs 2 a bag. He appears to get the spot price ruling that day, as reported in the newspaper, less some Rs 30 a bag. A commission of 4 percent is charged on the net amount, and he is paid on the nail. Since he does not grow groundnut every year, he does not borrow from this businessman.

The commission rate last year was 2 percent. The agents then pleaded that increases in their costs have made a higher rate essential. Respondent A thinks there is a cartel.

Groundnut mills buy only in bulk from the agents. Petty traders serve as middlemen between farmers with small lots for sale and the big commission agents.

As noted elsewhere, he is advancing loans to a laborer in the sample, as are several other cultivators. His first call is generally successful. If not, a second call on an agreed date is invariably so. Such a practice is very common in this village. He charges no interest on these loans, which are recovered through partial withholdings from wages.

He buys fertilizer from shops for cash; they do not sell on credit. He thinks the bags are short-weight.

Respondent B also has diverse dealings. He started off with two shares in the cooperative sugar mill in 1962 and purchased eight more about five years ago. He claims that fluctuating jaggery prices induced him to do so, although he admits that they are no more volatile today than before. It seems that he did not have the money to purchase enough shares at first (an implausible story!). He has been borrowing under the mill's financing facility from the very beginning. The current limit is Rs 500 a share, bearing an interest rate of 11 percent on personal surety. He must make about three trips to obtain a loan, but no special "fees" are demanded, and he is satisfied with the service. This year's crop should just about cover his delivery obligations.

In past years, the balance of output was converted into jaggery. About four years ago, he had a dispute with the two commission agents with whom he was then dealing. This was followed by a dispute with their successor for the same reason—irregular payment. He had been borrowing about Rs 2,000 a year from these agents. Last year, he sold directly to a trader from Tamil Nadu, who paid cash on the nail for 600 kilograms (120 bags of 50 kilograms each), at Rs 3.51 per kilogram.

He has just concluded a contract to lease the whole of his mango orchard for 10 years, for which he has received the sum of Rs 20,000 up-front. In the past 10 years, the orchard yielded between Rs 1,000 and Rs 3,000 annually (last year, about Rs 1,000). He needs the money to purchase a tractor. The price will be about Rs 50,000, for a second-hand machine, so he cannot get a bank loan. He will get Rs 3,000 from the cooperative society (he has Rs 300 in shares) and the rest from other sources.

He uses various channels to market his groundnut crop. Only if a cart happens to be going to Chittoor will he sell to a dehusking mill there.

In 1977, he borrowed from the cooperative society in order to purchase an electric motor. The president filled out the application, with land pledged as security, and he received the loan one month later. Supply is a bit irregular, but electricity is still a better proposition than diesel.

He started a poultry farm about two years back, having seen some near Chittoor Town. The initial investment was Rs 20,000, financed by sales of jaggery. He began with 500 chicks, paying Rs 4.5 a chick, and has since kept his stock at about 400 birds, which yield about 200 eggs a day (he sold 1,000 today for Rs 400). His monthly running costs are about 1 tonne of feed and Rs 40 for electricity. The veterinarian charges Rs 20 to Rs 30 a visit, plus drugs. Feed prices had risen so high as to make the business unprofitable, but following good rains in 1981, they have fallen sharply, while egg prices have remained firm. He will replace the present stock with 1,000 new birds.

With the ending of the drought, he decided to engage an AFS once more. The man, whom he has known as a casual laborer for some years, is 20 years of age, unmarried, and with two dependent parents, who will work on a first-call basis when needed. Fairly assured that the fellow will not abscond, he advanced him Rs 250 in wages. The terms are Rs 600 annually in cash plus clothes and three meals and 10 paise (for tobacco) daily. There was no bargaining over terms, which appear to be competitive with the casual rate of Rs 4 a day.

Respondent C's means are much more modest. Having sold his draft animals two years ago—a serious step forced by the drought—he has since had to rely on the hire market. He needs about 20–30 pair-days a season, depending on the rains. The daily rate is Rs 10 for six hours, but they work only for five. He hires mainly from scheduled castes, who seem to have draft power to spare, having only small plots of land. They get the right to cut grass and straw from the farmers who hire from them. He has not leased out any land, nor has he wished to do so.

He badly needs to get a pair of his own once more, since the hire market is unreliable; the cost will be about Rs 1,500. He has outstanding dues to the cooperative society and the Bank of India, so he will have to resort to private sources.

He borrowed Rs 2,000 from a commission agent in July 1980, paid it off in full, and borrowed only Rs 900 in July 1981. He expected to get low yields in 1981–82, due to drought, so he borrowed less on that occasion. [In fact, the rains in 1981–82 turned out to be normal, but the groundwater supplies may have remained limited.]

4 Contracting: Setting the Stage

Peasant agriculture displays a rich palette of contractual forms and variations, thus providing fertile territory for economic inquiry. Two notable collections of papers are Bardhan (1989), which is devoted to theory, and Hoff, Braverman, and Stiglitz (1993), which is much more empirical in character, yet has streaks of theory running through it. The following chapters revisit this topic, drawing on the interviews with villagers, merchants, and the officers of banks and cooperatives conducted during the two tours. The prime purpose of those interviews was to allow the individuals to speak for themselves, so as to understand their motives for contracting in a particular way—or not at all—in the markets open to them. Although their responses illustrated and confirmed a good deal of received wisdom, they also revealed some gaps, or at least misplaced emphases, in that body of knowledge, and a few intriguing twists emerged. Motivated by those accounts, as well as the data yielded by the formal survey work, each of the following chapters proceeds with formal analyses of certain aspects of rural contracting where the extant literature still seems wanting. Although the empirical material is rather dated (summaries are provided as needed), many of the questions are current, and there may be a lesson or two for policy.

Transactions across periods had a prominent place,[1] all the more so in view of the drought that plagued the whole state of Andhra Pradesh in 1979–80 and many of its districts in the next. These droughts were such as to overwhelm the (efficient) mechanisms for coping with idiosyncratic shocks, as established by Townsend's (1994) pioneering investigation of the International Crops Research Institute for the Semi-Arid Tropics (ICRISAT) villages, one of which is just 10 kilometers from a village visited during both tours. With the summary of the associated household surveys and general background as a backdrop, the chapter turns to a description of the incidence and scale of households' borrowing and indebtedness, distinguishing between private and public sources of credit. These transactions involved not only a substantial volume of rollovers, but also a significant quota of outright defaults, as related by all parties. These possible outcomes play a central role in the formal analyses presented in chapters 5, 6, and 7.

For those households owning little or no land and lacking any real prospects of getting a tenancy, the key decision was allocating its members between employment as casual workers and as attached farm servants (AFSs) for a whole year. Respondents pointed to the obvious attractiveness of an AFS contract as a means of smoothing income within the agricultural cycle.[2] What also emerged from the discussions, however, was the pressing need to smooth income across annual cycles, a need that the substantial credit usually offered by employers of AFSs could meet. This finding motivates the model developed and analyzed in chapter 5, in which smoothing within and across cycles inevitably involves the possibility of rollovers and hence continuation of the contractual relationship.

Tenancy, the subject of chapter 6, was quite extensive, with both sharecropping and fixed-rent leases payable in kind often coexisting in the same village. Inputs of fertilizers and pesticides were subject to cost sharing in the former; the latter could be commuted to sharecropping if the harvest turned out to be poor, albeit at the landlord's discretion. The literature, already vast when surveyed admirably by Singh (1989) and Otsuka, Chuma, and Hayami (1992), teaches us that the choice between them depends on the balance of risk, reward, and incentives, so that one would expect sharecropping to rule on unirrigated land, especially in Andhra's extensive semiarid tracts. In fact—and this is the twist—the reverse held: fixed-rent leases ruled on dryland plots, sharecropping on irrigated ones served by percolation wells. This apparent paradox is taken up formally in chapter 6.

There is the old saying that Indian agriculture is a gamble on the monsoon. Doubtless aware of this adage, owner-cultivators in the dryland tracts had already made quite substantial investments in wells, and the recent droughts spurred them into making new ones. Meeting the entire cost of a well and a pump was well beyond the self-financing capacity of all but a tiny fraction of these households. There was also the attendant risk that the trial pit would not strike water, leaving the household to write off this preliminary, unavoidable investment. By all accounts, private lenders were rarely prepared to act as the principal source of finance, although they often played an auxiliary role. Those bent on digging a new well or repairing an old one had no option but to deal with officialdom, in the form of the publicly owned Land Mortgage Bank (LMB). Its lending procedures involved not only the pledging of land as collateral, which is unexceptionable, but also other actors in various levels of the state bureaucracy, the whole yielding a structure possessing Kafkaesque possibilities, as described in detail in chapters 2 and 3. Compounding matters was the provision of lump-sum subsidies to qualified categories of households, which opened the door still wider to corruption, whose forms and pervasiveness are vividly illustrated in those accounts. The discussion closes with a summary of the findings of an empirical investigation of the various elements comprising the cost of public and private funds, respectively. A theoretical analysis of the profitability of investment in wells is provided in chapter 6, with a numerical example to illustrate the chief factors at work.

The final topic is the nexus between financing the cultivation of commercial crops and the arrangements for marketing them. Commission agents were very active as lenders (Bell and Srinivasan 1989), while attaching to their loans the condition that their clients market a minimum quantity to, or through, them. Interviews with three merchants, as well as some households, revealed much about their system of operations. Two questions arose: first, why would the contract involve both interest charges on the loan and an ad valorem fee on the quantity to be delivered? The cultivation of sugarcane introduces a further option when households are able to transform cane into the marketable sugar known as jaggery in their backyards, as opposed to delivering it to the public sector mill for crushing. The mill competes, in effect, with the agent for the cane, and the game now involves three players, with an additional stage. How does the presence of the mill affect the contract between the cultivator and the commission agent? These questions are addressed in chapter 7.

THE SURVEYS AND BACKGROUND

The empirical material is furnished by the survey work in the 14 villages and interviews with some traders and officials with whom the villagers had dealings. The interviews took place in the course of two tours, the first in September and October 1980. As preparation for canvassing the questionnaires, quite extensive discussions were held with the villagers to inform them about the research and seek their cooperation. These discussions were of the focus group kind, but they were uniform neither in the emphasis on particular topics nor in the makeup of the local participants. Toward the end of the survey work, in January 1982, a second tour involved eight of the villages as well as interviews with bank and other officials in five of the seven taluks (subdistricts). The two travelogues presented in chapters 2 and 3 provide detailed, structured accounts of those proceedings.

The surveys yielded a substantial body of quantitative data. Given the underlying aim, the approach differed quite sharply from what is considered more or less de rigueur nowadays. The villages—two in each of seven taluks—were selected deliberately, so as to capture variations in climate, soil, irrigation, and other public infrastructure. The sampling of households from each village was based on contractual choices. Using the findings of an initial village census conducted for the general purposes of the research, households were allocated among the (primary) occupational categories of landlords, owner-cultivators, owner-tenants, tenants, attached and casual laborers, moneylenders and traders, and others. According to the census round, the 14 villages had a total of 4,657 households, distributed among the occupational categories as set out in the final column of table 4.1.

In the first stage of sampling, 24 households were drawn from these choice-based strata in each village—so far as possible in fixed proportions heavily weighted in favor of cultivators. Sampling from some strata was simple, from others with probability proportional to the size of landholding. When canvassing the questionnaire, the investigators sought the identity of the other party to each and every transaction reported by these 24 respondents. All of the households thus identified and belonging to the same village, but not those already in the primary sample, constituted a pool from which a further 16 households were to be drawn, as a secondary sample. As it turned out, the stratified design at this second stage was not always possible—in a few cases, not even 16 candidates could be found—so the resulting sampling at the second stage is essentially simple in nature, conditional on the household appearing in the eligible pool. Full details of the design and calculation of the sampling probabilities are set out in Srinivasan and Sussangkarn (1984).

Circumstances surely influence contractual decisions. At that time, West Godavari District in the eponymous river delta was relatively developed, being served by an old canal system and other public infrastructure. One area of Nalgonda District, which lies in the upland, semiarid tract in the interior, was served by the new Nagarjuna Sagar canal, the remainder very patchily by tanks and wells. The neighboring Mahbubnagar District was very much like the latter. Somewhat farther south, in the same general tract, commercial crops like cotton and groundnut grown on black and red soils made Kurnool District a bit more prosperous. Chittoor District's upland taluks broadly resembled Mahbubnagar's. Chittoor Taluk itself is low-lying. In a normal year, tanks and wells commanded an extensive area sown to paddy and sugarcane. Chittoor Town exerted a palpable commercializing influence.[3]

As for the rural economy of India's semiarid zone in that earlier period, Walker and Ryan's (1990) account of the ICRISAT villages, two of which belong to Mahbubnagar District, is broad in scope and rich in analysis and insight.

BORROWING AND INDEBTEDNESS

Credit transactions are at center stage in the chapters that follow, which calls for a summary picture of borrowing and indebtedness. The number of households that borrowed in the kharif season (July 1–December 31) of 1980–81, classified by the type and source of funds, together with the average amounts they borrowed, are set out in table 4.1.[4] Three in eight households borrowed in that season; of these, four in five did so only from private sources. Landlords and traders were scarcely active at all as borrowers, presumably having little need and being engaged in this market rather as lenders. Landless laborer households were not very active either, their needs presumably being blocked by their limited credit-worthiness. About 35 to 40 percent of cultivating households, landed laborers, and the residual "other" category obtained credit. As expected, cultivating households were a good deal more successful than other villagers in getting loans from institutional lenders. The other notable feature of the pattern of participation is that the rates for attached and other laborer households exceeded half, both exclusively from private sources. AFSs borrowed heavily from their employers as part of the contract.

TABLE 4.1 **Type and amount of borrowing during the kharif season, by number of survey households, 1980**

HOUSEHOLD TYPE	SOURCE OF CREDIT			AVERAGE AMOUNT BORROWED (Rs)[a]	NONBORROWERS	TOTAL
	INSTITUTIONAL ONLY	PRIVATE ONLY	BOTH			
Landlords		2 (2.4)		3,192	82 (97.6)	84
Owner-cultivators	220 (10.2)	689 (31.8)	64 (3.0)	3,218	1,193 (55.1)	2,165
Owner-tenants	11 (7.3)	46 (30.5)	6 (4.0)	2,750	88 (58.3)	151
Pure tenants		20 (25.3)	9 (11.4)	3,402	50 (63.3)	79
Attached laborers		71 (51.8)		1,902	66 (48.2)	137
Landless laborers		50 (10.2)	3 (0.6)	358	436 (89.2)	489
Landed laborers	3 (0.5)	216 (33.4)	23 (3.6)	577	403 (62.4)	646
Other laborers		80 (54.4)		346	67 (45.6)	147
Traders		2 (1.8)		2,047	108 (98.2)	110
Others	12 (1.8)	200 (30.8)		574	437 (67.3)	649
Total	246 (5.3)	1,375 (29.5)	106 (2.3)		2,930 (62.9)	4,657

Source: Bell and Srinivasan 1985.
Note: The figures in parentheses are percentages of the row totals.
a. Average amount borrowed in kharif from all sources by households that borrowed.

Turning to the level of borrowing in that season, those landlords and cultivating households that did borrow obtained, from all sources combined, about the same average amount—namely, close to Rs 3,000. Village traders, who were typically shopkeepers, obtained about Rs 1,000 less. What is particularly striking is that AFS households obtained, on average, almost as much as traders, whereas the amounts for the other categories of labor households ranged between just Rs 350 to Rs 580. This difference has a prominent place in chapter 5.

Table 4.2 sets out the households' indebtedness positions at the close of that kharif season. Three in five households had outstanding debts at that point in time, only one-quarter of them to institutions, all of which were public ones. Very few landlords and traders had debts, but at least half of all the others were thus encumbered, with the incidence higher among those possessing land. As expected, indebtedness to institutions was higher among cultivating households owning land than among pure tenants, and it was higher among pure tenants than among labor households. Since indebtedness is a stock, this pattern implies that cultivating households had greater success in getting institutional loans (recall table 4.1), but perhaps less success in repaying them.

A comparison of the opening and the closing positions yields a broad indication of whether the scale of borrowing and repayment flows within the season in question were out of the ordinary, whereby much of the borrowing was seasonal. The transition matrix for the sample of all households is set out in table 4.3. It is strongly diagonal: 80 percent of the households experienced no change in their indebtedness status. There was, however, a marked increase in the overall incidence of indebtedness, from 50 to 60 percent, with nearly all it involving private sources. This development was surely the result of the drought. Households sought to smooth consumption and had a much better chance of obtaining loans for this purpose from moneylenders than from banks.

The general pattern of borrowing over the subsequent 15 months from April 1, 1981, to June 30, 1982, was broadly similar to that in kharif in 1980,

TABLE 4.2 **Indebtedness, closing position as of December 31, 1980, by number of survey households**

| HOUSEHOLD TYPE | SOURCE OF CREDIT | | | | |
	INSTITUTIONAL ONLY	PRIVATE ONLY	BOTH	NO DEBTS	TOTAL
Landlords	1 (1.2)	3 (3.6)		80 (95.2)	84
Owner-cultivators	268 (12.4)	792 (36.6)	279 (12.9)	826 (38.1)	2,165
Owner-tenants	34 (22.5)	50 (33.1)	33 (21.9)	34 (22.5)	151
Pure tenants		31 (39.2)	9 (11.4)	39 (49.4)	79
Attached laborers		74 (54.0)		63 (46.0)	137
Landless laborers		217 (44.4)	26 (5.3)	246 (50.3)	489
Landed laborers		387 (59.9)	50 (7.7)	209 (32.4)	646
Other laborers		94 (63.9)		53 (36.1)	147
Traders		7 (6.3)	1 (0.9)	102 (92.7)	110
Others	11 (1.7)	341 (52.5)	59 (9.1)	238 (36.7)	649
Total	314 (6.7)	1,996 (42.9)	457 (9.8)	1,890 (40.6)	4,657

Source: Bell and Srinivasan 1985.
Note: The figures in parentheses are percentages of the row totals.

TABLE 4.3 **Indebtedness: Opening and closing positions during the kharif season, for all survey households, 1980**

OPENING POSITION	CLOSING POSITION				
	INSTITUTIONAL ONLY	PRIVATE ONLY	BOTH	NO DEBTS	TOTAL
Institutional only	160		19		179
	(89.4)		(10.6)		(100.0)
	[51.0]		[4.2]		[3.8]
Private only		1,472	74	136	1,682
		(87.5)	(4.4)	(8.1)	(100.0)
		[73.7]	[16.2]	[7.2]	[36.1]
Both	76	17	332		425
	(17.9)	(4.0)	(78.1)		(100.0)
	[24.2]	[0.9]	[72.6]		[9.1]
No debts	78	507	32	1,754	2,371
	(3.3)	(21.4)	(1.3)	(74.0)	(100.0)
	[24.8]	[25.4]	[7.0]	[92.8]	[50.9]
Total	314	1,996	4,57	1,890	4,657
	(6.7)	(42.9)	(9.8)	(40.6)	(100.0)
	[100.0]	[100.0]	[100.0]	[100.0]	[100.0]

Source: Bell and Srinivasan 1985.
Note: The opening position is as of July 1, 1980. The closing position is as of December 31, 1980. The figures in parentheses and brackets are percentages of the row and column totals, respectively.

allowing for the longer span of time in which transactions could occur. Just over half of the 535 households comprising the sample borrowed in that period: 35 did so only from institutional sources, 186 only from private sources, and 54 from both. These 275 households had 650 transactions in all, 130 of which were with institutional sources and 75 percent of which occurred in the first six months (the main period of operations for the kharif crop). The average loan amounts from institutional and private sources were Rs 2,720 and Rs 750, respectively (Chung 1993, 64–66). The fact that the sample is quite heavily weighted toward cultivating households—and, among them, those with larger holdings—contributed to the higher participation rate in the formal segment of the market in the second period. Yet the general picture of borrowing over the second period that emerges from these unweighted figures is unlikely to be very distorted.[5]

These outcomes should be viewed in light of the attractiveness of the terms offered by the various sources of funds. Institutions charge, as a rule, lower rates of interest than private sources; but other, significant costs of borrowing also enter into the reckoning: registration and documentation fees, travel back and forth twice or more, waiting for final approval, and—not infrequently—the payment of bribes. Farmers' dealings with the LMB in particular provided egregious examples of such costs. That bank's procedures involved numerous steps and a plethora of conditions, with minor variations over taluks. These steps and conditions were related in detail by LMB officials in five different branches during tour 2, and there is no need to repeat them here. As for cultivators' experiences in attempting to navigate their way through this maze, suffice it to mention the general altercation with the local member of parliament in village 5 in tour 1 and the individual sagas related to us in villages 5, 11, and 12 in tour 2.

Those and other accounts of households' trials and tribulations in their dealings with public sources of credit provided a compelling reason to supplement the ongoing survey work with an inquiry into borrowers' transaction costs, broadly defined, with public and private sources alike. Chung (1993, ch. III) analyzes the resulting data, albeit without making any adjustments for different sampling probabilities. The total cost of closing a contract comprised four components: documentation and application fees, transport and incidentals, "other costs" (including bribes), and opportunity costs of the borrower's time (estimated on the basis of the agricultural wage and the number of trips needed to complete the transaction). The average total cost of a transaction with public sources was Rs 73.7, with the four components equal to Rs 39.5, Rs 7.3, Rs 12.4, and Rs 14.5, respectively; the standard deviation of "other costs" was large, at Rs 38.4.

The corresponding total for private sources was Rs 5.7, with the respective components equal to Rs 0.1, Rs 0.9, Rs 0.1, and Rs 4.6. When expressed in relation to the size of the loan and annualized by the maturity period, the effective rates of interest were 16.0 and 6.9 percent, respectively.

As expected, the contractual interest rates on institutional loans clustered closely about the 12 percent mark. Those on private loans, in contrast, varied enormously around an average of 34 percent: 20.4 percent on average for cash loans and 69.7 percent for loans in kind. The latter were overwhelmingly in-kind rates on food grains destined for consumption, with some cases of seed loans. Confining the comparison by source to cash loans, the effective annualized costs of credit from public and private sources were therefore 28.0 and 27.3 percent, respectively. Wealthier households in good standing with private lenders were evidently able to get offers every bit as good as those from public sources. Poor households were naturally in a much weaker position; for they would have had slim chances of getting a loan from institutions for any purpose and hence correspondingly remote opportunities for smoothing consumption through such borrowing.

NOTES

1. For a thorough survey of rural financial markets, see Conning and Udry (2007).
2. In the literature, see, for example, Bardhan (1983).
3. For reference in what follows, the villages are numbered in the above order, with two in each taluk and two taluks each in Nalgonda and Chittoor Districts.
4. These figures and those in tables 4.2 and 4.3 are ratio estimates; see Srinivasan and Sussangkarn (1984) for the details.
5. Unlike for tables 4.1–4.3, ratio estimates are not available.

REFERENCES

Bardhan, P. K. 1983. "Labor Tying in a Poor Agrarian Economy: A Theoretical and Empirical Analysis." *Quarterly Journal of Economics* 98 (3): 501–14.

Bardhan, P. K., ed. 1989. *The Economic Theory of Agrarian Institutions.* Oxford: Clarendon Press.

Bell, C., and T. N. Srinivasan. 1985. "An Anatomy of Transactions in Rural Credit Markets in Andhra Pradesh, Bihar, and Punjab." RPO671-89 Working Paper 8, Development Research Center, World Bank, Washington, DC.

Bell, C., and T. N Srinivasan. 1989. "Interlinked Transactions in Rural Markets: An Empirical Study of Andhra Pradesh, Bihar, and Punjab." *Oxford Bulletin of Economics and Statistics* 51 (February): 73–84.

Chung, I. 1993. "Roles of Borrower Transaction Costs and Rationing Constraints on Market Choice and the Effective Demand for Credit." PhD thesis, Vanderbilt University.

Conning, J., and C. Udry. 2007. "Rural Financial Markets in Developing Countries." In *Handbook of Agricultural Economics*, vol. 3, edited by R. Evenson and P. Pingali. Amsterdam: North-Holland.

Hoff, K., A. Braverman, and J. Stiglitz. 1993. *The Economics of Rural Organization: Theory, Practice, and Policy.* New York: Oxford University Press.

Otsuka, K., H. Chuma, and Y. Hayami. 1992. "Land and Labor Contracts in Agrarian Economies: Theories and Facts." *Journal of Economic Literature* 30 (4): 1965–2018.

Singh, N. 1989. "Theories of Sharecropping." In *The Economic Theory of Agrarian Institutions*, edited by P. K. Bardhan, 31–72. Oxford: Clarendon Press.

Srinivasan, T. N., and C. Sussangkarn. 1984. "Sampling Scheme and Estimation." RPO671-89 Working Paper 4, Development Research Center, World Bank, Washington, DC.

Townsend, R. M. 1994. "Risk and Insurance in Village India." *Econometrica* 62 (3): 539–91.

Walker, T. S., and J. G. Ryan. 1990. *Village and Household Economies in India's Semi-Arid Tropics.* Baltimore, MD: Johns Hopkins University Press.

5 Labor

Choosing between attached farm servant (AFS) and casual labor contracts was a decision of central importance, especially for labor households. It involved not only the bearing of risks but also access to credit. The first step in analyzing households' choices is to describe the incidence of such contracts, their terms, and households' expressed motives for entering into them.

In the 14 sample villages, about 27 percent of all households gave agricultural labor as their primary occupation, but only 11 percent of such labor households fell into the AFS category (see table 4.2). Yet households with one male worker—all AFSs were male—and at least one other worker of either sex could, in principle, combine an AFS contract with casual labor. In fact, the proportion of all the working members of agricultural labor households who were engaged as AFSs was much higher than 11 percent. The villages ranged in size from about 170 to 540 households, a very high proportion of which depended on agricultural labor—according to the focus groups in tour 1, between one-third and well over half. In the eight villages in West Godavari, Nalgonda, and Mahbubnagar Districts, these respondents put the number of AFSs at between about 50 to 100 or more; in Kurnool District, the estimates ran up to 30 to 40; in the four villages in Chittoor District, from none to 20 or 30. Taken together, these numbers of AFSs are about fourfold larger than the 137 households reported in the census round as having AFS as their primary occupation. This finding is confirmed by the number of AFSs reported in that round. In village 1, 74 households hired one AFS, and 12 households hired two or more AFSs. In villages 2 through 8, the respective numbers were as follows: 45 and 8, 42 and 11, 14 and 4, 14 and 14, 16 and 13, 30 and 21, and 16 and 9 (Bell and Srinivasan 1985).[1] Most agricultural labor households were combining wage contracts.

The much lower incidence of AFS contracts in villages 9 through 14 calls for some commentary. The guarded response that there were "some" AFSs in village 10, coupled with the claim that they were paid daily, like casual laborers, suggests a concern that such contracts might violate laws prohibiting debt bondage. Since the census round was canvassed at the start, when the enumerators were still getting a feel for conditions in their villages, they might easily have misclassified some of the workers who were paid daily, not all of whom were necessarily casual laborers. No such speculation is needed for villages 13 and 14 in Chittoor Taluk: Chittoor Town apparently offered adult males good job opportunities as laborers. In village 13, the only AFSs engaged were some boys who tended livestock. They must have been indentured by their fathers, who doubtless pocketed the cash paid up-front.

The terms of the AFS contracts, as reported by the focus group respondents in tour 1 and summarized in table 5.1, varied a good deal over villages—as to be expected in light of the variations in the natural environment and infrastructure. What they had in common were the motives for accepting such contracts. It is no surprise that security of employment and income were important, but obtaining a substantial advance of wages, which is effectively credit, and, even more, an additional sum as an explicit loan from the employer appeared to be more important still. The contractual advances, invariably taken at the start, were large but without interest. Additional amounts were clearly desired—and in some measure obtained—as loans, usually at an interest rate of 1.5–2.0 percent a month (simple). All of this points to a desire to smooth consumption not just seasonally, but also over years. This conjecture is confirmed by the strikingly large average loans obtained by AFSs in the kharif season of 1980, as reported in the survey round itself (recall the estimates in table 4.1).

What induced some households to seek such substantial amounts? The respondents in village 7 in tour 1 specifically mentioned the need to finance marriages and ceremonies. The same motive was at work in the International Crops Research Institute for the Semi-Arid Tropics (ICRISAT) village of Aurepalle, which is about 10 kilometers from village 8. Binswanger et al. (1984) report a typical outlay of Rs 1,000. A session with respondents from sample households

TABLE 5.1 **Attached farm servant (AFS) contracts during the kharif season, by village, 1980**

VILLAGE	NUMBER OF AFSs	PAYMENT IN CASH (Rs)[a]	PAYMENT IN KIND (grain)	MOTIVE FOR ACCEPTING AFS CONTRACT
1	50		Monthly[b]	Advance, loan
2	—			
3	200		1,650 kg[a] [50]	Loan
4	—			Security
5	100	400 [100]	25 kg monthly	Security
6	—		48 kg monthly	Loan
7	70		48 kg monthly[b]	Loan
8	50	300–600[c]	3 meals	Advance
9	30–40	800–1,200 [50]		Loan
10	"Some"	1,100–1,800[d]		Security, loan
11	—			
12	20–30		450 kg, 3 meals[b]	Security, loan
13	10[e]	30 [100]	3 meals	Loan
14	"None"			
Aurepalle[f]	50		54 kg monthly[b]	Loan

Source: Based on focus group interviews detailed in chapter 2.
Note: — = not available. Village 2 was not visited; details are missing in villages 4 and 11. kg = kilogram.
a. Annual amount, proportion paid in advance in brackets. Paddy support price, Rs 105 per quintal.
b. Plus blanket annually.
c. Alternatively, 72 kilograms monthly, no daily meals.
d. Paid daily.
e. Children, to tend livestock.
f. An ICRISAT (International Crops Research Institute for the Semi-Arid Tropics) village, about 10 kilometers from village 8.

in village 5 during tour 2 yielded a vivid example. An employer had three AFSs, who had taken loans of Rs 500, Rs 200, and Rs 2,000, respectively. The first two workers were relatives. The father of the third joined in at the close of the discussion and related that he had indentured one son—for 12 years—in order to marry off his eldest. Nature also had a hand in these decisions. An adult male engaged as an AFS happened to be among the respondents from the sample households interviewed in villages 11 and 12 in tour 2. These villages had been hit hard by successive droughts in 1979–80 and 1980–81, and respondents from both villages gave this hardship as the reason for their decision, their own fields having yielded poor crops in succession. (Another respondent declared that such an engagement in the family would be unacceptable as a matter of principle, but perhaps his family was not in such dire straits.) Thus marriage customs and Mother Nature, singly or—worse still—in concert, led to indebtedness on such a scale that contracts would usually run for a few years, as respondents in both tours readily declared. By way of confirmation, the survey round yielded an estimated average total borrowing by AFS households that borrowed of Rs 1,902 in the kharif season of 1980–81 (see table 4.1), a sum at least twice as large as an AFS's annual wages.

The need for a substantial sum of cash also impelled many males to take up AFS contracts, not only in the other ICRISAT villages (Walker and Ryan 1990, ch. 5), but also in the very different setting of some Haryana villages in the late 1980s (Jodhkar 2012). Two decades later, further mechanization and improved chances of getting nonfarm employment in that relatively prosperous state had reduced their numbers, but by no means to the point of insignificance. Village "insiders," moreover, had been replaced by "outsiders," albeit always relatives of insiders, who would vouch for them where ultimate repayment of the advance was concerned.[2]

The alternative of employment as a casual worker received rather patchy attention in the tour discussions, since the details were to be canvassed in the household survey itself. Table 5.2 provides a summary, whereby it should be recalled that the respondents in tour 1 were overwhelmingly employers of labor. The variation across villages is striking, not only in level, but also in form. Piece-rate contracts, usually in kilos of grain per acre, were the rule for the main operations, except in Chittoor District, where a daily rate paid in cash and a meal or two was the norm. A direct comparison of piece rates with AFS rates yields little, since casual employment was far from steady and there was surely some degree of selection into gangs.[3]

SELECTED LITERATURE

Certain features of the contracting described above find no place in the earlier literature on the choice between casual and AFS contracts, which is concisely surveyed by Rosenzweig (1988, 736–38). One line of inquiry is concerned with risk bearing in a two-season, one-period framework. The cultivators' choices of inputs in season 1 combine with nature and labor in season 2 to produce output (Bardhan 1983). Like the harvest itself, the harvest wage is stochastic. A landless, risk-averse household may well choose to engage a family member or two as an AFS, if big cultivators choose to offer such contracts. Events leading to indebtedness or a contractual relationship over a run of periods, however, are ruled out by assumption, as is the riskiness of earnings in season 1.

TABLE 5.2 **Casual wage rates during the kharif season, by operation and village, 1980**

| VILLAGE | OPERATION | | | OTHER (Rs + NUMBER OF MEALS PROVIDED) |
	PLANTING	HARVESTING	THRESHING	
1	—	—	—	—
2	—			
3	Contract	100 kg per acre	135 kg per acre	Cash[a]
4	60 kg per acre	Contract	2 kg per 8-hour day	1.5 + 0
5	—	—	—	3–4 kg per day
6	4 kg per day	4 kg per day	4 kg per day	Cash[a]
7	120 kg per acre	120 kg per acre	Individual[b]	—
8	75 kg per acre	75 kg per acre	Daily	—
9	Contract	Contract	Contract	2.50 + 0
10	Contract	Contract	Contract	3.0–4.0[c] + 0
11				3.0[d] + 2
12				2.0[e] + 2
13				4.50[f] + 1
14		6 kg per day		5.0[g] + 2

Source: Based on focus group interviews detailed in chapter 2.
Note: — = not available. Village 2 was not visited, so all details are missing in the village. kg = kilogram.
a. Weeding.
b. 3/80th of the output if by tractor.
c. Amount in peak season; Rs 2.5–Rs 3.0 in off-peak season. Women paid about Re 1 less than men.
d. All operations, 8:00 a.m.–4:30 p.m.; cash component a bit higher at harvest time.
e. All operations, six-hour day, no seasonal fluctuation.
f. All operations, five-hour day, no seasonal fluctuation. Women paid Rs 1.5 less than men.
g. All operations, eight-hour day, no seasonal fluctuation.

An alternative is to assume that workers' efforts are prohibitively costly to monitor in the first of a two-season period (Eswaran and Kotwal 1985). There are neither risks of any kind nor borrowing. Shirking can be inferred without error from output, and shirkers are consigned for ever after to the casual labor market. Permanent workers (that is, AFSs) are better off than workers with casual contracts, since otherwise the threat of being fired would carry no sting. Yet as Rosenzweig (1988) notes, there is neither movement of workers between the two contracts nor a rule for assigning them to one or the other at the outset. Dutta, Ray, and Sengupta (1989) pursue this line of inquiry in an infinite-horizon setting, now with the worker facing the risk that the contract will not be renewed, the probability of which depends on his efforts. As in Eswaran and Kotwal (1985), there is no borrowing. It seems fair to say that these formulations of the choices open to individual agents bear little relation to the central concerns expressed by households in the travelogues and ICRISAT's intensively studied villages.

Pal (1996), in her detailed empirical study of three ICRISAT villages (among them Aurepalle, with fresh data collected in 1991–92), emphasizes the importance of possessing some land and access to credit, as well as caste, in determining choices on the supply side. The picture is revealing in some ways, but the duration of AFS contracts and its possible causes are neglected. The observed choices are, moreover, treated not as the household's allocation of family workers, but as individual decisions, in which the demographic structure of the household to which the individual belongs is denied any role. The decision is analyzed using a probit model, without formal theoretical underpinnings.

Borrowing and attachment raise the related matter of debt bondage, for households that seek to smooth consumption by borrowing and are endowed only with labor may fall into a debt trap. Srinivasan (1980) establishes that a landlord need not be deterred from adopting yield-improving innovations when a sharecropper provides him with labor services at less than the latter's opportunity cost in exchange for consumption credit. Srinivasan (1989) returns to this topic, now introducing the possibility for the sharecropper to borrow from a credit institution as an alternative to the landlord. In the event that the sharecropper fails to meet his repayment obligations in full, the institution appropriates his total income and denies him any credit in the future. Both the institution and the landlord are able to enforce exclusive credit contracts, and if one denies the sharecropper credit, the other is assumed to do likewise.

Moral hazard in cultivation is ruled out by fixing the input of labor on a plot of given size, leaving the sharecropper with a residual to employ elsewhere. (His total income therefore includes a random component, so the terms of this contract do not correspond to those of an AFS contract.) In view of all of the complications, it is not surprising that the response of borrowing to changes in nonagricultural income and the rate of interest is not wholly unambiguous. Having examined the various factors at work, Srinivasan concludes, "[T]he optimal amount borrowed can be presumed to have a 'normal' response, that is, *decreasing* when the interest rate goes up and *increasing* when income (or wealth) goes up" (Srinivasan 1989, 213, emphasis in the original).

Genicot (2002) argues that the landlord is unlikely to deny a bonded contract to a borrower who has defaulted on an institutional loan. She proceeds to introduce this option, while also simplifying the structure in a way that can be regarded as rather drastic: all risk is banished.[4] Unattached individual workers earn zero in season 1 and w_2 for sure in season 2, so that, in the absence of savings or storage opportunities, they must borrow. If they are in good standing, they can do so from institutions. If they default, they are shut out of the credit market for good, leaving them with the sole alternative of an attached contract in perpetuity with a landlord who provides them with a fixed level of consumption in each season. The institutions are fully aware of this and set the terms of their loans accordingly. The landlord moves first in a Stackelberg game, offering a contract to all workers, regardless of their standing with the institutions; the institutions then offer a set of loan contracts; and finally the workers choose between these alternatives.

The game possesses two equilibria. In one, institutions offer no loans and all workers are bonded. In the other, the landlord employs only casual workers. Genicot argues that the latter is improbable, since the landlord possesses collateral, which should enable him to borrow at a rate close to the institutions' cost of funds. The former equilibrium, however, is heavily at odds with labor households' actual choices in rural Andhra Pradesh. The AFS contracts involved substantial credit and reportedly did not endure for many years; households that chose only casual labor not only had extremely limited access to institutional credit, but also fared little better with private sources. The riskiness of income was a weighty consideration.

There follows an attempt to extend the theory of contractual choices in the rural labor market, with two salient features of contracting in practice at the forefront—namely, the possibility of combining AFS and casual work, whereby engaging at least one member as an AFS enables the household to borrow on a scale greatly exceeding that open to households choosing to supply only casual labor. It builds on Bell and Srinivasan (1985), who employ a two-season, one-period framework in which all labor households can borrow at some parametric rate, rollovers and defaults are ruled out, the casual wage rate in season 1 is certain, and preferences are defined over total (discounted) income accruing during the entire period. As in that paper, what follows also covers the demand side, with cultivating households having the choice between engaging workers on an AFS or a casual basis, whereby inputs of labor in the second season are chosen only after the state of nature and the casual wage rate have been revealed.

A preliminary remark is warranted on the subject of who, exactly, makes the allocative decisions in labor households. The so-called unitary model dominates in the literature. The members' preferences are assumed to be aggregated in some way so as to yield a collective, quasi-individual expression thereof. The head of a peasant household is usually assumed to act as a dictator, perhaps constrained by social norms governing the sharing of income or consumption. That model is adopted in the next four sections (on labor households' choices, rolling over loans, employers, and equilibrium), with an egalitarian sharing rule. It is followed by the analysis of a model of intrahousehold bargaining.

LABOR HOUSEHOLDS: CHOOSING CONTRACTS AND CREDIT

A household comprises m members, n (≥ 2) of whom are workers. Each period τ comprises two seasons ($t = 1,2$). A casual laborer's earnings (the product of the daily wage and the number of days worked) are random variables in both: let the variate W_t denote earnings in season t and $w_t \in [w_t^1, w_t^2]$ denote a specific realization thereof. Such earnings are higher, on average, in the harvest season: $E[W_1] < E[W_2]$, where E denotes the expectation operator. There may be extraordinary and unavoidable expenditures in season 1, such as those on marriage. Let the net burden of such expenditures on normal consumption be denoted by b, which is, or becomes, known at the beginning of each period.

Suppose the household lacks the endowments necessary to engage in cultivation. Its choices are limited to deciding how many of its members to engage as AFSs, $s \in \{0,...,n\}$, and how much to borrow in season 1, k, whereby at least one member must be engaged as an AFS if borrowing is to be possible. An AFS earns the fixed wage w_0 in each season. In keeping with the practice reported in chapters 2 and 3, s and k must be chosen at the very beginning of season 1, before w_1 is revealed.

Consider, to begin with, the one-period setting with unlimited liability. All income net of b and loan repayments $(1 + r)k$ is consumed in the season in which it accrues—that is, savings are ruled out. Consumption per capita in season t is denoted by the variate C_t, where

$$C_1 = [sw_0 + (n - s)W_1 + k - b]/m, \tag{5.1}$$

and

$$C_2 = [sw_0 + (n - s)W_2 - (1 + r)k]/m. \tag{5.2}$$

Let the family's preference functional with respect to the two-season lotteries induced by the choice of (k,s) be represented by

$$V(k, s) = E[u(C_1)] + \beta E[u(C_2)] \equiv E[u_1] + \beta E[u_2], \tag{5.3}$$

where u is an increasing, strictly concave, and thrice-differentiable function, and $\beta(<1)$ is the interseasonal discount factor. The first-order condition (f.o.c.) with respect to (w.r.t.) k is, provided $s \geq 1$,

$$E[u_1'] - \beta(1+r)E[u_2'] \leq 0, \, k \geq 0. \qquad (5.4)$$

Where the choice of s is concerned, one result follows immediately from the requirement that consumption be positive in both seasons. If $b \geq nw_1^1$, then $s \geq 1$, for in that event, the household must borrow.

Recall that, in practice, family size and composition, together with the restriction that only males are engaged as AFSs, normally yield just two possibilities: $s = 0$ or $s = 1$. Although s takes one of these two values, it is still permissible to examine the corresponding f.o.c. at each value in order to analyze the effects of $b \, (< w_1^1)$ and other parametric variables of the household's decision problem.

If the male engages in casual work $(s = 0)$,

$$\frac{\partial V(0,0)}{\partial s} = \left\{ E[u'(nW_1 - b) \cdot (w_0 - W_1)] + \beta E[u'(nW_2) \cdot (w_0 - W_2)] \right\} / m^2.$$

Differentiating w.r.t. b,

$$\frac{\partial^2 V(0,0)}{\partial b \partial s} = -E[u''(nW_1 - b) \cdot (w_0 - W_1)] / m^2. \qquad (5.5)$$

It is now necessary to specify the structure of earnings, which emerges from all households' decisions, including those of cultivators. Let the superscript h denote household h. If for all h the annual, discounted AFS wage, $(1 + \beta^h)w_0$, is at least as large as the corresponding expected earnings of a casual laborer, $E[W_1] + \beta^h E[W_2]$, then no household will supply casual labor, for households are risk averse. The following condition is therefore a natural one:

$$(1 + \beta^h)w_0 < E[W_1] + \beta^h E[W_2], \quad \forall h, \qquad (5.6)$$

which must hold for at least one labor household if any casual labor is to be supplied. Whether w_0 exceeds or falls short of $E[W_1]$ in equilibrium is still open.

In practice, $w_0 \geq E[W_1]$ is often observed. Proposition 5.1 is then immediate and intuitive.

Proposition 5.1: If $w_0 \geq E[W_1]$, then taking up an AFS contract will become more attractive, though not necessarily optimal, when the "burden" b increases.

Proof: To offset any increase in the "sure thing" loss b, earning w_0 as an AFS yields a "sure thing" increase in income in season 1 that is no smaller than the average income yielded by the lottery earnings W_1 received as a casual laborer. For any given k, neither choice has an effect on the corresponding income received in season 2, there being no opportunities to borrow when $s = 0$. ∎

There remains the less attractive possibility, $w_0 < E[W_1]$, which cannot be ruled out. If the household is somewhat risk averse, then by continuity, the foregoing result will also hold if w_0 is sufficiently close to $E[W_1]$. Suppose, therefore, that the difference is quite substantial.

It is instructive to consider the case where u is quadratic, so that u'' is constant. Since $w_0 < E[W_1]$, $\partial^2 V(0,0) / \partial b \partial s < 0$: choosing $s = 0$ becomes more attractive relative to $s = 1$ as b increases. This finding is strongly counterintuitive. Quadratic utility implies increasing absolute risk aversion, which not only runs against virtually all evidence, but also entails that an increase in the "sure thing" loss of b will induce the household to take up a riskier position. It is therefore natural to impose the condition that the Arrow-Pratt measure of absolute risk aversion, $-u''/u'$, be nonincreasing.

Inspection of equation (5.5) reveals that the family's demographic composition is important. It is seen from the right-hand side (r.h.s.) that the sign of $\partial^2 V$ $(0,0) / \partial b \partial s$ depends, in particular, on how strongly u'' (< 0) is increasing—that is, on the size of u''' (> 0), over the interval $[w_1^1, w_1^2]$; for this works to counterbalance the market condition $w_0 < E[W_1]$ through the negative covariance term.

The choice $s = 1$ makes taking credit possible. Suppose $k^0 > 0$, so that the first part of condition (5.4) holds as an equality. Differentiating totally, holding $s = 1$ and m constant, and collecting terms yields

$$\{E[u_1''] + (1+r)^2 \beta E[u_2'']\} \cdot dk = E[u_1''] \cdot db + \{(1+r)\beta E[u_2''] - E[u_1'']\} s \cdot dw_0$$
$$+ \{(1+r)\beta E[u_2'' \cdot W_2] - E[u_1'' \cdot W_1]\} \cdot dn.$$

The desired amount of credit is increasing in b, but less than one-for-one, in keeping with intuition: $\partial k^0 / \partial b = E[u_1''] / \{E[u_1''] + (1+r)^2 \beta E[u_2'']\} \in (0,1)$. The effect of a change in b on s when k is in play is

$$\frac{\partial^2 V(0,1)}{\partial b \partial s} = -E[u_1''(s=1) \cdot (w_0 - W_1)] \cdot (1 - \partial k^0 / \partial b)$$
$$-(1+r)^2 \beta E[u_2''(s=1) \cdot (w_0 - W_2)] \cdot \partial k^0 / \partial b. \tag{5.7}$$

In order to compare the cross-derivative in equation (5.5) with its counterpart in equation (5.7), consider the limiting case of constant absolute risk aversion: $u = 1 - (1/\gamma)e^{-\gamma c}$, where γ is the coefficient thereof. Since $u'' = -\gamma u'$, the r.h.s. of equation (5.5) specializes to

$$(\gamma/m)\{E[u'(nW_1 - b)/m] \cdot E[w_0 - W_1] + \text{cov}(u', w_0 - W_1)\},$$

where the covariance term is positive. The whole expression is positive if $w_0 \geq E[W_1]$. The same holds if $w_0 < E[W_1]$ and sufficiently close to $E[W_1]$. The expression is negative otherwise.

Turning to the alternative choice $s = 1$, and hence to equation (5.7), if $w_0 \geq E[W_1]$, then $-E[u_1''(s=1) \cdot (w_0 - W_1)] > 0$. The sign of $-E[u_2''(s=1) \cdot (w_0 - W_1)]$ is ambiguous, however; for $w_0 < E[W_2]$, and the associated covariance term $\text{cov}(u', w_0 - W_2)$ is positive.

Suppose, therefore, that there are just two states in season 2, with probabilities p_2 and $1 - p_2$, respectively. Then, noting equation (5.2),

$$-E[u_2''(s=1) \cdot (w_0 - W_2)] = [p_2 \cdot (w_0 - w_2^1)e^{-\gamma(w_0 + (n-1)w_2^1 - (1+r)k)/m}$$
$$+ (1 - p_2) \cdot (w_0 - w_2^2)e^{-\gamma(w_0 + (n-1)w_2^2 - (1+r)k)/m}]\gamma/m,$$

which is positive or negative according as

$$\frac{p_2 \cdot (w_0 - w_2^1)}{(1-p_2) \cdot (w_2^2 - w_0)} \overset{>}{<} e^{-\gamma(n-1)(w_2^2 - w_2^1)/m}. \tag{5.8}$$

The probabilities of the two states, the associated spread in earnings, $[w_2^1, w_2^2]$, and the market condition $w_0 < p_2 w_2^1 + (1 - p_2)w_2^2$ are features of the household's environment. The household's taste for risk bearing, γ, and its demographic composition (m, n) are its particular characteristics, which appear only on the r.h.s.

The latter is decreasing in γ, n, and the spread $[w_2^1, w_2^2]$, and is increasing in family size, m, holding n constant—that is, it is increasing in the number of dependents given n. The amount borrowed, k, has dropped out. This follows from the fact that, with constant absolute risk aversion, changes in the level of the "sure thing" have no effect on the household's willingness to take up a riskier position.

If w_0 is at most as large as w_2^1—namely, the level of earnings from casual labor in the bad state, then $-E[u_2''(s=1) \cdot (w_0 - W_2)] < 0$, and, by continuity, this will also hold for all distributions of W_2 such that $w_0 > w_2^1$, with w_0 sufficiently close to w_2^1. It is seen from equation (5.7) that the sign of $\partial^2 V(0,1) / \partial b \partial s$ is then ambiguous. If the response of borrowing to an increase in b is close to one-for-one and the rate of interest is high, $s = 0$ will become more attractive relative to $s = 1$, though not necessarily optimal. Otherwise, an increase in b will make both $s = 1$ more attractive relative to $s = 0$ and $s = 2$ relative to $s = 1$. These results yield sufficient conditions for that effect to hold. Proposition 5.2 follows at once.

Proposition 5.2: Let the market condition (5.6) hold, but with $w_0 < E[W_1]$, and let absolute risk aversion be constant. Then, as expenditure b increases, engaging one family member as an AFS ($s = 1$) becomes more attractive to labor household h than engaging none ($s = 0$) if the distribution of earnings in season 2 satisfies the following condition:

$$\frac{p_2 \cdot (w_0 - w_2^1)}{(1 - p_2) \cdot (w_2^2 - w_0)} \geq \exp[-\gamma^h (n-1)(w_2^2 - w_2^1)/m].$$

Remark: Only part of the smoothing is accomplished by taking additional credit.

ROLLING OVER LOANS

In order to examine the possibility of rolling over a loan and so necessarily extending an AFS contract, it will suffice to consider two periods. If the debt is not retired in the first period, whatever debt is still outstanding must be settled in full in season 2 of the second period. The argument proceeds by backward induction.

Let the burden $b(< w_1^1)$ occur only in period 1; the environment is otherwise stationary, with all variates independent and identically distributed (i.i.d). If it has borrowed in season 1 of period 1, the household must make a decision in season 2—namely, on learning the realization $w_2(1)$, it must decide whether to repay the due amount $(1 + r)k$ at once or to roll over the debt, in part or in whole. For simplicity, let the whole be rolled over, so that $(1 + r)^2 k$ must be paid with certainty in season 2 of period 2. Let $V^0(0)$ denote the value of V at the household's optimum when it is unencumbered by current debt and any burden b. If it repays in season 2 of period 1, then it will obtain $V^0(0)$ in period 2. If it rolls over the debt, there will be no further choices, and per capita consumption in seasons 1 and 2 in period 2 will be given by the variates

$$C_1(2) = [sw_0 + (n - s)W_1(2)]/m,$$

and

$$C_2(2) = [sw_0 + (n - s)W_2(2) - (1 + r)^2 k]/m.$$

Let $V(s, k; \tau = 2)$ denote the value placed on the ensuing lottery. Given the realization $w_2(1)$, the household will be indifferent between these two courses of action if, and only if,

$$u[(sw_0 + (n-s)w_2(1) - (1+r)k)/m] + \delta V^0(0)$$
$$= u[(sw_0 + (n-s)w_2(1))/m] + \delta V(s,k;\tau = 2), \quad (5.9)$$

where δ is the interperiod discount factor. Recalling that $s \in \{0,1\}$ and that borrowing is possible only with an AFS contract, condition (5.9) becomes

$$u[(w_0 + (n-1)w_2(1))/m] - u[(w_0 + (n-1)w_2(1) - (1+r)k)/m]$$
$$= \delta[V^0(0) - V(1,k;\tau = 2)]. \quad (5.10)$$

Since u is strictly concave, it follows that, for any given (k, n, m, w_0), there is a unique value of $\zeta(1) \equiv (n-1)w_2(1)$ such that condition (5.10) holds. Denoting this value by ζ^*, the probability that the debt will be rolled over, as assessed by the household at the start of season 1, is $\pi \equiv \text{prob}[(n-1)W_2(1) < \zeta^*]$.

At the start of season 1, the household chooses $s \in \{0,1\}$ and k, knowing that the rollover decision in season 2 will be governed by (5.10). If the household chooses $(s = 0, k = 0)$, it will obtain $\Omega(0,0) = V(0,0;b) + \delta V^0(0)$. If it chooses $s = 1$, together with some k, it will obtain

$$\Omega(1,k) = E[u(w_0 + (n-1)W_1(1) + k - b)/m)]$$
$$+ \pi(k)\beta\{E[u((w_0 + (n-1)W_2(1))/m)] + \delta V(1,k;\tau = 2)\} \quad (5.11)$$
$$+ [1 - \pi(k)]\beta\{E[u((w_0 + (n-1)W_2(2) - (1+r)^2 k)/m)] + \delta V^0(0)\}$$

Let $k^0 = \arg\max_k \Omega(1,k)$. An AFS contract is chosen if, and only if, $\Omega(1,k^0) > \Omega(0,0)$. Under the conditions derived above in the one-period problem, $s = 0$ becomes less attractive as b increases. Changes in b affect $\Omega(0,0)$ exactly like $V(0,0;b)$. If $s = 1$, there is always the option of repaying for certain in period 1, in which case, the result from the one-period problem would hold, but the household is unable to commit to this strategy.

By choosing to borrow in the two-period setting, the household necessarily introduces the option of rolling over the loan, rationally recognizing that condition (5.10) will govern its actions when the time comes. An increase in b makes a larger loan attractive to relieve the pressure on consumption in season 1 of period 1, but it may also increase the probability of a rollover, with the attendant austerity enforced by repaying a still larger sum in season 2 of period 2. If the realized value $\zeta(2)$ is sufficiently low, the household will request a second rollover, thus continuing the relationship.

Such a continuation is rendered more likely by the assumption that outstanding debts are rolled over in full, if rolled over at all. In fact, a household always has the option of tightening its collective belt somewhat more in the present season 2 to pay off part of its debt and thus reduce the size of its obligation in season 2 of the next period, which makes a further rollover less probable. This refinement complicates matters.

Partial repayment

Exercising the option of making a partial repayment not only works against perpetual debt bondage, but also makes choosing an AFS contract, and hence the opportunity to borrow, more attractive in the first place.

The first assumption is that b is so large that borrowing, and hence choosing $s = 1$, is unavoidable. In light of the tales in chapters 2 and 3, this assumption is not so much restrictive as fitting. Let R denote the level of repayment at the close of season 2 of the first period, where, viewed at the start of that period, R is a random variable, depending as it does on the casual wage rate in season 2. Equation (5.11) becomes

$$\Omega(1,k) = E\Big[u\big((w_0 + (n-1)W_1(1) + k - b)/m\big)\Big]$$
$$+ \beta E\Big[u\big((w_0 + (n-1)W_2(1) - R)/m\big)\Big] + \delta E\Big[u\big((w_0 + (n-1)W_1(2))/m\big)\Big]$$
$$+ \delta\beta E\Big[u\big((w_0 + (n-1)W_2(2) - (1+r)^2 k + (1+r)R)/m\big)\Big] \qquad (5.12)$$

The repayment decision is taken only when $w_2(1)$ has been revealed. The argument proceeds by backward induction. Let

$$\Lambda[R,k,w_2(1)] = u[((w_0 + (n-1)w_2(1) - R))/m] + \delta E[u((w_0 + (n-1)W_1(2))/m))]$$
$$+ \delta\beta E[u((w_0 + (n-1)W_2(2) - (1+r)^2 k + (1+r)R)/m)], \qquad (5.13)$$

where, at this juncture, R is not random. The associated f.o.c., contingent on the realization $w_2(1)$, is

$$\frac{\partial\Lambda}{\partial R} = -u'[(w_0 + (n-1)w_2(1) - R)/m]$$
$$+ \delta\beta(1+r)E\Big[u'\big((w_0 + (n-1)W_2(2) - (1+r)^2 k + (1+r)R)/m\big)\Big] \le 0, \; R \ge 0. \qquad (5.14)$$

Since u is strictly concave, this yields the optimal choice of R as a function of $w_2(1)$, the terms of the contract, and tastes: $R^0 = R^0[w_2(1), w_2, k, r; \cdot]$. In order to make further progress, some restrictive assumptions are imposed.

An example

Let W_1 and W_2 be independent variates, both also serially independent, and suppose there are just two states in each season, with the realizations w_1^1 and w_2^1 having the probabilities p_1 and p_2, respectively. Where risk bearing is concerned, let $u = \ln c_t$. The family's demographic structure is defined by $n = 2$, with one male. Then condition (5.14) specializes to

$$-\frac{1}{w_0 + w_2 - R}$$
$$+ (1+r)\delta\beta\left(\frac{p_2}{w_0 + w_2^1 - (1+r)^2 k + (1+r)R} + \frac{1-p_2}{w_0 + w_2^2 - (1+r)^2 k + (1+r)R}\right) \le 0,$$
$$R \ge 0, \; w_2 = w_2^1, w_2^2.$$

If some repayment is made $[R^0(w_2) > 0]$, (5.14) becomes a quadratic equation in $R^0(w_2)$, which can be solved in closed form and substituted into equation (5.12). The associated f.o.c. w.r.t. k then yields the optimal level of borrowing for any given b.

It will be useful to construct a robust numerical example. Let $w_0 = 5$, $w_1^1 = 4$, $w_1^2 = 6$, $w_2^1 = 6$, $w_2^2 = 8.775$, $p_1 = p_2 = 0.5$. Thus $w_0 = E[W_1] < E[W_2]$. Let the rate of interest $r = 0.2$, and the discount factors $\beta = 0.95$ and $\delta = 0.9$. The level of the outlay b is 12.06, which not only greatly exceeds the joint casual earnings in the bad state in season 1 $(2w_1^1 = 8)$, but also is about 80 percent of the earnings of a casual laborer when the good state is realized in both seasons $(6 + 8.775)$. Since $u = \ln c_t$, borrowing is unavoidable. It can be verified that if $k = 8$, then

$R^0(w_2 = 6) = 4.81$ and $R^0(w_2 = 8.775) = 6.065$ and that, given $b = 12.06$, the choice $k = 8$ indeed maximizes $\Omega(1,k)$, taking into account the dependence of repayment on the realized value of $W_2(1)$: $dR^0(w_2)/dk > 0$.

In this example, therefore, the loan meets two-thirds of the outlay b, and the half-yearly wage as an AFS, $w_0 = 5$, is paid in advance. Together, they more than cover b, leaving a small, but useful, residual to supplement the female's casual earnings in season 1. The amount that is repaid in season 2 when the bad state occurs, 4.81, is half of the amount due at that time ($8 \cdot 1.2 = 9.6$). The residual 4.79 plus interest—that is, 5.478—is then, by assumption, repaid in full at the close of season 2 in the next period. In view of $w_0 = 5$ and the distribution of W_2, this repayment is burdensome, but manageable. When the good state occurs in season 2 of period 1, the amount repaid is correspondingly somewhat larger—namely, 6.065—which is 63 percent of the amount due. The amount repaid in season 2 of period 2 is then 4.242, which is smaller even than w_0.

Although debt bondage has been ruled out by the assumption that the debt must be wholly repaid within two periods, it is clear that the above run of events is far removed from such a danger anyway. The example is also rather robust, in the sense that substantial variations in the functional forms and parameter values would leave the qualitative conclusions unchanged. Heavier special outlays will surely induce more borrowing; but even if b is larger than the maximal annual earnings of a casual laborer, smoothing through (contingent) partial repayments in the first period will do much to ward off the necessity of a second rollover at the close of the second period.

EMPLOYERS

The demand for labor is a derived demand from production activities. The land is plowed and the crop is sown and tended in the first season, and the resulting output is harvested in the second season. Let inputs of labor, l_1, and a composite of draft power, seeds, fertilizers, and the like, x_1, be applied to a holding of area a. These inputs establish a young crop, or "saplings," of size $z_1 = h(l_1, x_1, a)$, where all three inputs are necessary in production. Rainfall and growing conditions thereafter are represented by the variate Θ, and these events combine with what is now the intermediate input z_1 and thereafter harvest labor to yield output. With the realization $\Theta = \theta$ and inputs of harvest labor, l_2, the realized level of output is $y_2 = f(z_1, l_2, \theta)$, whereby increasing values of the index θ indicate progressively more favorable states of nature. It is plausible that favorable states can compensate, at least in part, for lackadaisical husbandry, as expressed by low values of z_1.

A cultivating household has n working adults and a holding of area a. At the very start of each period, it must decide how many AFSs, if any, to engage, a decision it must make before the wage rate in each season and the realized value of Θ are known. Suppose, for simplicity, that it finances its need for working capital out of its own funds carried over from the previous period and that its preferences are defined over the total income accruing during the whole period, with a seasonal discount rate of δ. The interest rate on the loans given to AFSs is rather modest, and such usury income is also discounted at the rate δ, so it can be neglected.

In the two-season, one-period setting, all AFS contracts are wound up at the end of each period, and a fresh choice of s AFS is made at the start of the next.

Having chosen s and then l_1 and x_1 to establish the crop, the level of total income at that juncture, when θ and the harvest wage rate, and hence also the input of harvest labor, have yet to be revealed, is the variate

$$Y_2^l(l_1,x_1)=f(z_1,L_2,\Theta)-[w_0 s+x_1+w_1(l_1-(n+s))](1+\delta)-[w_0 s+W_2(L_2-(n+s))],$$

where $l_1-(n+s)$ and $L_2-(n+s)$ are the inputs of casual labor in seasons 1 and 2, respectively.[5] Suppose, further, that inputs of harvest labor are proportional to output: $L_2=cq(z_1,\Theta)$. Then we have the simpler form

$$Y_2^l(l_1,x_1)=(1-cW_2)q(z_1,\Theta)-[w_0 s+x_1+w_1(l_1-(n+s))](1+\delta)-[w_0 s-W_2(n+s)].$$
$$(5.15)$$

Having chosen $s(\geq 0)$ AFS, the household observes the spot wage for casual laborers in season 1 and chooses l_1 and x_1. Its decision problem is

$$\max_{(l_1,x_1|s,w_1)} E[u(Y_2^l)] \text{ s.t. } l_1\geq n+s, x_1\geq 0, \qquad (5.16)$$

where the expectation is formed when making these decisions in season 1. The associated f.o.c. are

$$E\left[u'(Y_2^l)\cdot\left((1-cW_2)\cdot\frac{\partial q}{\partial z_1}\cdot\frac{\partial z_1}{\partial l_1}-(1+\delta)w_1\right)\right]\leq 0, l_1\geq n+s \qquad (5.17)$$

and

$$E\left[u'(Y_2^l)\cdot\left((1-cW_2)\cdot\frac{\partial q}{\partial z_1}\cdot\frac{\partial z_1}{\partial x_1}-(1+\delta)\right)\right]\leq 0, x_1\geq 0. \qquad (5.18)$$

Since all inputs are necessary in production, the optimum must involve $x_1^0>0$ if the household engages in cultivation. This is ensured if the technologies represented by h and q are sufficiently productive, where the derivative $\partial q(z,\Theta)/\partial z_1$ is a random variable when viewed at the close of season 1.

Let $l_1^0(w_1,s)$ and $x_1^0(w_1,s)$ solve problem (5.16). For each choice of s at the outset and then each realized value of the wage in season 1, there is an optimal input bundle. For any choice of $s\in\{0,1,2,...\}$, the value of the ensuing lottery, as assessed before the wage is revealed, is $V^l(s)=E[u(Y_2^l(l_1^0,x_1^0))]$, where, at this juncture, the expectation also involves the variate W_1. The household maximizes $V^l(s)$ by choice of s.

The household's decision problem is formidably complicated. It is instructive to examine the special case wherein the household is risk neutral, so that condition (5.17) specializes to

$$E\left[(1-cW_2)\cdot\frac{\partial q}{\partial z_1}\cdot\frac{\partial z_1}{\partial l_1}\right]-(1+\delta)w_1\leq 0, l_1\geq n+s,$$

where

$$E\left[(1-cW_2)\cdot\frac{\partial q}{\partial z_1}\cdot\frac{\partial z_1}{\partial l_1}\right]=\{(1-cE[W_2])\cdot E[\partial q/\partial z_1]+\mathrm{cov}(1-cW_2,\partial q/\partial z_1)\}\cdot\frac{\partial z_1}{\partial l_1}.$$

It is highly plausible that the harvest wage rate is positively correlated with the marginal product of the intermediate input z_1, since the latter is high when the rains and growing conditions are good. Given as much, the covariance term is negative, and if casual labor is hired, then

$$\{(1-cE[W_2])\cdot E[\partial q/\partial z_1]\}\cdot \frac{\partial z_1}{\partial l_1} > (1+\delta)w_1.$$

Now suppose that the household were to engage only AFSs. Then ignoring for the moment that s is an integer, the marginal cost of labor would be w_0 in both seasons and condition (5.17) would specialize to

$$\{(1-cw_0)\cdot E[\partial q/\partial z_1]\}\cdot \frac{\partial z_1}{\partial l_1} = (1+\delta)w_0,$$

where the term $E[\partial q/\partial z_1]\cdot \partial z_1/\partial l_1$ is the expected marginal product of inputs of labor in season 1. Since the households supplying AFSs are surely risk averse, $(1+\beta)w_0 < E[W_1]+\beta E[W_2]$, where $E[W_1] < E[W_2]$. It is seen that cultivation in season 1 is more labor intensive, on average, than when any casual labor is employed. It is clear from condition (5.18) that the same also holds for all other inputs.

If rollovers are permitted, the structure must be extended correspondingly by employing backward induction. There is little to be gained by pursuing this additional complication on the demand side of the labor market.

EQUILIBRIUM

A brief discussion of the labor market is now in order. By assumption, the village comprises landless households, which choose between AFS and casual labor contracts, and landowning households, which cultivate with family and hired labor. This sharp separation is maintained by the assumption that there is no tenancy.

Given the AFS wage w_0 and the joint distribution G of the casual wage rates W_1 and W_2, those households desiring to supply labor and currently without AFS contracts simply choose between engaging one family worker and none. Augmented by the number of AFSs still encumbered by debts incurred in connection with such contracts in earlier periods, the current choices of households free to make them yield the current supply of AFS workers and hence also a residual supply of casual workers. Cultivating households, likewise facing (w_0, G), but also having a rich set of opportunities in cultivation, may make offers to supplement any AFS presently encumbered by debts from previous periods. Summing over all cultivating households yields the market demand for AFSs, and some cultivating households may supply casual workers in one or both seasons. If the labor market is to clear, not only w_0 but also the distribution function $G(w_1, w_2)$ must be such as to bring that about—that is, the AFS wage rate and the distribution function of casual wage rates are mutually and simultaneously determined. In principle, both are endogenous. If, for some reason or other, w_0 or the casual wage rate in the slack season were fixed, then the form of the distribution function $G(w_1, w_2)$ would have to bear much or all of the burden of adjustment for the labor market as a whole to clear.

In any given period, such an equilibrium need not be unique. The configuration itself will also tend to vary from period to period, although w_0 may be rather sticky. First, it could happen that relatively many, or rather few, households incur the unavoidable expenditures denoted by b, which also could arise from the need to settle outstanding debts to third parties. Second, and arguably more important, common shocks like droughts, which can pitch poorer households into indebtedness, may occur. When debts can be rolled over, these shocks will have effects on the structure of wage rates that may endure for several periods.

INTRAHOUSEHOLD BARGAINING

The unitary model does not seem especially objectionable where sharing the burden of risks is concerned. Working as an AFS, however, is objectionable in itself, and the individual so engaged cannot displace onto other members of the family the disagreeable experience of being at another man's beck and call at all times of the day and night. This awkward fact has been ignored in previous sections. Yet consider the tales related in chapter 3. The son who was indentured for 12 years to finance his brother's marriage must have felt a strong grievance and may have been able to extract some concession from their father. In another village, a father released a son from an AFS contract to allow the boy some time of his own by working instead as a casual laborer, and it is quite possible that the son gave him something in return. The possibility that the choice between casual and AFS contracts involves intrahousehold bargaining is a real one.

The following formulation is developed from the unitary model presented earlier and is kept avowedly simple. Readers interested in certain subtle aspects of comparisons of collective and unitary models are referred to the detailed discussion in Browning, Chiappori, and Lechene (2006). Gersbach and Haller (2017) provide a comprehensive, albeit largely abstract, treatment of the problem in general equilibrium.

Consider the one-period setting with unlimited liability. The family comprises one male worker, his working spouse, and $m - 2$ dependents. Given the restriction that only males are engaged as AFSs, there are just two possibilities where labor contracts are concerned: $s = 0$ or $s = 1$. All income net of b and loan repayments $(1 + r)k$ is consumed in the season in which it accrues—that is, savings are ruled out.

A social norm governs the consumption of nonworkers: each obtains the fraction q of total consumption in each season. The aggregate amount available to the two workers in season t is denoted by the variate Z_t, where

$$Z_1 = [sw_0 + (2-s)W_1 + k - b][1 - (m-2)q], \tag{5.19}$$

$$Z_2 = [sw_0 + (2-s)W_2 - (1+r)k][1 - (m-2)q], \tag{5.20}$$

and $k = 0$ if $s = 0$. The husband's share of Z_t is denoted by $\lambda_t^M (= 1 - \lambda_t^F)$, which is the subject of negotiation between them.

Let the cooperative outcome of each of the games defined by the choices $s = 0$ and $s = 1$ be the solution of the corresponding Nash bargaining problem. Both husband and wife know the outcomes of these games. Given the strong patriarchy that rules in village life, let the male choose which of the two will be played—that is, whether or not to engage himself as an AFS. This assumption is all the more plausible in view of the fact that he is the one who will directly suffer the indignity of being an AFS. He will swallow that bitter draft if the resulting agreement with his spouse offers him sufficient compensation to outweigh the utility he would obtain from the alternative game with $s = 0$; otherwise, he will choose the latter.

Extending the model to cover the nonpecuniary drawbacks of being an AFS, let the preference functionals with respect to the two-season lotteries induced by the choice of (k, s) be represented by

$$V^j(k,s) = E[u^j(\lambda_1^j Z_1)] + \beta E[u^j(\lambda_2^j Z_2)] - \eta^j(s), \quad j = M, F, \tag{5.21}$$

where u^j is an increasing, strictly concave, and twice-differentiable function and $\eta^j(s)$ is the disutility of the status involved in choosing s. In the event that they do not reach an agreement, let the values of the couple's respective utilities be v^j, where it may be safely assumed that $v^M > v^F$.

Suppose that the husband chooses to work as a casual laborer ($s = k = 0$). Then the product of their respective gains from cooperation is

$$\Gamma(0,0) \equiv [V^M(0,0) - v^M] \cdot [V^F(0,0) - v^F]. \tag{5.22}$$

The shares λ_t^j solve the following problem:

$$\max_{(\lambda_1^j, \lambda_2^j)} \Gamma(0,0), \quad \text{subject to } \lambda_t^M + \lambda_t^F = 1, \tag{5.23}$$

$$V^M(0,0) = E[u^M(\lambda_1^M(2W_1 - b)\xi)] + \beta E[u^M(\lambda_2^M(2W_2)\xi)] - \eta^M(0), \tag{5.24}$$

$$V^F(0,0) = E[u^F(\lambda_1^F(2W_1 - b)\xi)] + \beta E[u^F(\lambda_2^F(2W_2)\xi)] - \eta^F(0), \tag{5.25}$$

where $\xi \equiv 1 - (m - 2)q$. In view of $\lambda_t^M + \lambda_t^F = 1$, define $\lambda_t \equiv \lambda_t^M$ and let $(\lambda_1^*(0,0), \lambda_2^*(0,0))$ solve the above problem, thus yielding the male $V^M(\lambda_1^*(0,0), \lambda_2^*(0,0))$.

The alternative is for the male to be engaged as an AFS ($s = 1$), with the level of k also to be bargained over. In this alternative,

$$\Gamma(1,k) \equiv [V^M(1,k) - v^M] \cdot [V^F(1,k) - v^F]. \tag{5.26}$$

The shares λ_t^j and k solve the following problem:

$$\max_{(\lambda_1^j, \lambda_2^j, k)} \Gamma(1,k), \quad \text{subject to } \lambda_t^M + \lambda_t^F = 1, \tag{5.27}$$

$$V^M(1,k) = E[u^M(\lambda_1^M(w_0 + W_1 + k - b)\xi)] + \beta E[u^M(\lambda_2^M(w_0 + W_2 - (1+r)k)\xi)] - \eta^M(1), \tag{5.28}$$

$$V^F(1,k) = E[u^F(\lambda_1^F(w_0 + W_1 + k - b)\xi)] + \beta E[u^F(\lambda_2^F(w_0 + W_2 - (1+r)k)\xi)] - \eta^F(0), \tag{5.29}$$

Defining $\lambda_t \equiv \lambda_t^M$ as before, let $(\lambda_1^*(1), \lambda_2^*(1), k^*)$ solve the above problem, thus yielding the male $V^M(\lambda_1^*(1), \lambda_2^*(1), k^*)$.

The male will choose an AFS contract if $V^M(\lambda_1^*(1), \lambda_2^*(1), k^*) > V^M(\lambda_1^*(0,0), \lambda_2^*(0,0))$ and will work as a casual labor otherwise.

The above formulation is quite general. Some assumptions are imposed to make it tractable. With the status of casual laborer as reference, let $\eta^M(0) = \eta^F(0) = 0$, and suppose that only the male suffers the odious burdens imposed by working as an AFS, so that $\eta^M(1) > 0$ and $\eta^F(1) = 0$. Let the husband and wife have the same utility function u. Thus which of the games will be played depends not on differences in their taste for risk bearing, but rather on the difference between the values of their disagreement utilities, v^M and v^F, and the size of $\eta^M(1)$. If the husband chooses to work as a casual laborer, the assumption that both have the same u implies that the upper frontier of the set of all allocations in the space of V^M and V^F is symmetric about the 45-degree line through the origin. Hence, $v^M > v^F$ implies that the agreement point is such that $V^M > V^F$. If, instead, he chooses to engage as an AFS, then the frontier will be symmetric about the 45-degree line through the point $[-\eta^M(1), 0]$. Hence, he will choose this alternative only if the gains from the opportunity to borrow are sufficiently large and shared in such a way as to compensate him for the costs entailed by that status.

Where tastes for risk bearing are concerned, let $u_t^j = (\lambda_t^j z_t)^{1-\rho}/(1-\rho)$, where ρ is the coefficient of relative risk aversion. (If $\rho = 1$, then $u_t^j = \ln \lambda_t^j z_t$ and the following expressions must be modified accordingly.) Suppose the husband chooses casual labor. Then equations (5.24) and (5.25) specialize to, respectively,

$$V^M(0,0) = (1-\rho)^{-1}\xi^{1-\rho}\{\lambda_1^{1-\rho}E[(2W_1-b)^{1-\rho}] + \beta\lambda_2^{1-\rho}E[(2W_2)^{1-\rho}]\} \tag{5.30}$$

and

$$V^F(0,0) = (1-\rho)^{-1}\xi^{1-\rho}\{(1-\lambda_1)^{1-\rho}E[(2W_1-b)^{1-\rho}] + \beta(1-\lambda_2)^{1-\rho}E[(2W_2)^{1-\rho}]\} \tag{5.31}$$

It is seen from equation (5.22) that the f.o.c. associated with problem (5.23) – (5.25) may be written in the form

$$\left(\frac{\lambda_t}{1-\lambda_t}\right)^{\rho} = \frac{V^F(0,0)-v^F}{V^M(0,0)-v^M} \equiv \frac{\Delta V^F(0,0)}{\Delta V^M(0,0)}, t=1,2, \tag{5.32}$$

where $\Delta i(0,0)$ denotes j's gain in the cooperative outcome. Hence, $\lambda_1^*(0,0) = \lambda_2^*(0,0)$: the male's share is the same in both seasons, although its exact level is still to be determined.

A further characterization of the cooperative outcome is obtained by noting that equations (5.30) and (5.31) yield

$$\frac{V^F(0,0)}{V^M(0,0)} = \left(\frac{1-\lambda^*(0,0)}{\lambda^*(0,0)}\right)^{1-\rho}.$$

Substituting from equation (5.32) and rearranging yields

$$\frac{\Delta V^F(0,0)/V^F(0,0)}{\Delta V^M(0,0)/V^M(0,0)} = \frac{\lambda^*(0,0)}{1-\lambda^*(0,0)}. \tag{5.33}$$

The ratio of the proportional gains from cooperation is equal to the inverse of the ratio of the respective shares.

If, instead, the husband chooses to work as an AFS, then equations (5.28) and (5.29) specialize to, respectively,

$$V^M(1,k) = (1-\rho)^{-1}\xi^{1-\rho}\{\lambda_1^{1-\rho}E[(w_0+W_1+k-b)^{1-\rho}]$$
$$+ \beta\lambda_2^{1-\rho}E[(w_0+W_2-(1+r)k)^{1-\rho}]\} - (1+\beta)\eta^M(1), \tag{5.34}$$

and

$$V^F(1,k) = (1-\rho)^{-1}\xi^{1-\rho}\{(1-\lambda_1)^{1-\rho}E[(w_0+W_1+k-b)^{1-\rho}]$$
$$+\beta(1-\lambda_2)^{1-\rho}E[(w_0+W_2-(1+r)k)^{1-\rho}]\}. \tag{5.35}$$

It is seen from problem (5.27) – (5.29) that the form of equation (5.32) also holds here:

$$\left(\frac{\lambda_t}{1-\lambda_t}\right)^\rho = \frac{V^F(1,k)-v^F}{V^M(1,k)-v^M} \equiv \frac{\Delta V^F(1,k)}{\Delta V^M(1,k)}, t=1,2, \tag{5.36}$$

so that $\lambda_1^*(1) = \lambda_2^*(1)$, although its exact level is still to be determined, along with the outcome k^*. The f.o.c. w.r.t. to k supplies the required additional condition to solve for $(\lambda_1^*(1),\lambda_2^*(1),k^*)$:

$$\frac{\partial V^M(1,k)}{\partial k}\cdot\Delta V^F(1,k)+\frac{\partial V^F(1,k)}{\partial k}\cdot\Delta V^M(1,k)=0,$$

where

$$\frac{\partial V^j(1,k)}{\partial k}=(1/k)\{(\lambda_1^j\xi)^{1-\rho}\cdot E[(w_0+W_1+k-b)^{-\rho}]$$
$$+\beta(\lambda_2^j\xi)^{1-\rho}\cdot E[(w_0+W_2-(1+r)k)^{-\rho}]\}, j=M,F.$$

Recalling that $\lambda_t^M+\lambda_t^F=1$ and $\lambda_1^*(1)=\lambda_2^*(1)$, it is seen that the f.o.c. can hold if, and only if, k satisfies

$$E[(w_0+W_1+k-b)^{-\rho}]=(1+r)\beta E[(w_0+W_2-(1+r)k)^{-\rho}]. \tag{5.37}$$

This is a pure (Pareto-) efficiency condition, as required by one of the Nash axioms. In the present game, it is independent of the outcome $\lambda_1^*(1)=\lambda_2^*(1)$, whereas those shares depend on k^*. With k^* thus determined, the upper frontier of the set of all allocations in the space of V^M and V^F remains symmetric about the 45-degree line through the point $[-\eta^M(1),0]$, but now shifts relative to the frontier with $k=0$ such that each of V^M and V^F increases by the same amount when the other is held constant. The size of that shift is equal to

$$(1-\rho)^{-1}\xi^{1-\rho}\{E[(w_0+W_1+k^*-b)^{1-\rho}]+\beta E[(w_0+W_2-(1+r)k^*)^{1-\rho}]$$
$$-E[(w_0+W_1-b)^{1-\rho}]-\beta E[(w_0+W_2)^{1-\rho}]\}, \rho\neq 1.$$

The foregoing results are summarized in proposition 5.3.

Proposition 5.3: If, under the social norm granting each dependent the same, fixed share of aggregate consumption in each season, the husband and wife have the same coefficient of relative risk aversion, then the Nash bargaining game between them yields the following outcomes:

(i)   Their shares in the family's aggregate consumption will be the same in both seasons, regardless of whether the husband chooses to engage himself as an AFS.

(ii) In the event that he so chooses and that he alone bears the nonpecuniary costs associated with that status, the amount borrowed will satisfy the efficiency condition (5.37), which is independent of the shares in the cooperative outcome.

To make further progress, specific assumptions must be made about the joint distribution of the variates W_t. The following numerical example draws on the example given earlier, but now in a one-period setting.

A numerical example: As in the example in the section entitled "Rolling over Loans", let W_1 and W_2 be independent variates and suppose there are just two states in each season, with the realizations w_1^1 and w_2^1 having the probabilities p_1 and p_2, respectively. Where risk bearing is concerned, let $\rho = 1$—that is, $u_t^j = \ln \lambda^j z_t^j$.

If $s = 0$, then

$$E[\ln(2W_1 - b)] = p_1 \ln(2w_1^1 - b) + (1 - p_1)\ln(2w_2^1 - b),$$

and

$$E[\ln(2W_2)] = p_2 \ln(2w_2^1) + (1 - p_2)\ln(2w_2^2).$$

Substituting these expressions into equation (5.32) yields an equation in λ_t, which can be solved for any given constellation of the parameters

$$(b, w_1^1, w_1^2, w_2^1, w_2^2, p_1, p_2, v^M, v^F, \beta, m, q).$$

The solution yields, inter alia, the value of the male's utility $V^M(\lambda_1^*(0,0), \lambda_2^*(0,0))$.

Consider the constellation of parameter values when $b = 0$:

$$(0, 4, 6, 6, 8.775, 0.5, 0.5, 1, 0.8, 0.95, 5, 0.1).$$

The outcome is the share $\lambda_t^*(0,0) = 0.7$, which yields $V^M(\lambda_1^*(0,0), \lambda_2^*(0,0)) = 2.8896$.

Now suppose, instead, that the heavy expenditure $b = 6$ arises. Observe that $b = 6 < 2w_1^1 = 8$, so that, while consumption in season 1 is always positive, severe austerity rules half the time. The male is unable to impose the whole of this burden onto his spouse, although his share does rise: $\lambda_t^*(0,0) = 0.766$, which yields him the lower value $V^M(\lambda_1^*(0,0), \lambda_2^*(0,0)) = 2.5697$.

Smoothing through borrowing will be attractive—if the terms are right. Let the offer under an AFS contract be $w_0 = 5$ and $r = 0.2$. Although $w_0 = E[W_1]$, there is also the drawback represented by $\eta^M(1)$: let its value be 0.1. The opportunity to choose k yields

$$E[\ln(w_0 + W_1 + k - b)] = p_1 \ln(w_0 + w_1^1 + k - b) + (1 - p_1)\ln(w_0 + w_1^2 + k - b),$$

and

$$E[\ln(w_0 + W_2 - (1+r)k)] = p_2 \ln(w_0 + w_2^1 - (1+r)k) + (1 - p_2)\ln(w_0 + w_2^2 - (1+r)k),$$

which are then substituted into equations (5.34) and (5.35) to complete the specification of problem (5.27) – (5.29).

In virtue of proposition 5.3, the solution can be obtained recursively. The f.o.c. (5.37) yields $k^* = 3.3$, a little more than half of b. Substituting into equation (5.36), we obtain $\lambda_t^*(1) = 0.761$ and $V^M(1, k^*) = 2.662$, which exceeds $V^M(\lambda_1^*(0,0), \lambda_2^*(0,0)) = 2.5697$. On balance, therefore, the male prefers to engage himself as an AFS, something he would decline to do if $b = 0$. In the latter event, $k^* = 0.4$, which yields marginal gains from smoothing against the loss of $\eta^M(1) = 0.1$ utils.

It is enlightening to express this net advantage in money-metric terms. Suppose the male were to receive the sum w^e with certainty in both seasons. If he chooses casual labor, this is equivalent to receiving the "sure thing" w^e, such that

$(1+\beta) \ln w^e = 2.5697$—that is, $w^e = 3.735$. The value of the equivalent when he chooses the AFS contract is about 5 percent higher at $w^e = 3.916$, which includes a full allowance for the nonpecuniary costs entailed by that status.

NOTES

1. In villages 9 to 14, the numbers were judged too small to be used in the econometric investigation.
2. A somewhat looser arrangement for plowmen was very common in Bihari villages, at least in earlier times. They were engaged for 10 months a year and plowed only in the mornings. In one village not far from Patna, almost one-quarter of all households had AFS contracts in 1981, but not one could be found in 2009 (Datta et al. 2014). Tractors and, increasingly, power tillers had displaced both bullocks and plowmen in the 1990s.
3. The contract system also posed problems for the enumerators when dealing with wage labor and earnings; it is not at all clear that they employed a uniform convention.
4. As Srinivasan notes in his introduction, "Analysing such a switch does not appear to be tractable" (Srinivasan 1989, 220). In that stochastic setting, a glance at the four-page appendix should remove all doubt.
5. If family members and AFSs cannot be hired out to other farmers as casual laborers, the r.h.s. must be reformulated so as to impose the nonnegativity conditions $l_1 \geq (n + s)$ and $L_2 \geq (n + s)$. These conditions are unlikely to bind in practice, as argued below.

REFERENCES

Bardhan, P. K. 1983. "Labor Tying in a Poor Agrarian Economy: A Theoretical and Empirical Analysis." *Quarterly Journal of Economics* 98 (3): 501–14.

Bell, C., and T. N. Srinivasan. 1985. "The Demand for Attached Farm Servants in Andhra Pradesh, Bihar, and Punjab." RPO671-89 Working Paper 11, Development Research Center, World Bank, Washington, DC.

Binswanger, H. P., V. S. Doherty, T. Balaramaiah, M. J. Bhende, V. B. Kshirsagar, V. B. Rao, and P. S. S. Raju. 1984. "Common Features and Contrasts in Labor Relations in the Semiarid Tropics of India." In *Contractual Arrangements, Employment, and Wages in Rural Labor Markets in Asia*, edited by H. P. Binswanger and M. R. Rosenzweig. New Haven: Yale University Press.

Browning, M., P.-A. Chiappori, and V. Lechene. 2006. "Collective and Unitary Models: A Clarification." *Review of Economics of the Household* 4 (March): 5–14.

Datta, A., G. Rodgers, J. Rodgers, and B. Singh. 2014. "Contrasts in Development in Bihar: A Tale of Two Villages." *Journal of Development Studies* 50 (9): 1197–208.

Dutta, B., D. Ray, and K. Sengupta. 1989. "Contracts with Eviction in Infinitely Repeated Principal-Agent Relationships." In *The Economic Theory of Agrarian Institutions*, edited by P. K. Bardhan, 93–121. Oxford: Clarendon Press.

Eswaran, M., and A. Kotwal. 1985. "A Theory of Contractual Structure in Agriculture." *American Economic Review* 75 (3): 352–67.

Genicot, G. 2002. "Bonded Labor and Serfdom: A Paradox of Voluntary Choice." *Journal of Development Economics* 67 (1): 101–27.

Gersbach, H., and H. Haller. 2017. *Groups and Markets: General Equilibrium with Multi-Member Households*. Cham: Springer.

Jodhkar, S. S. 2012. "Agrarian Changes in the Times of (Neo-Liberal) 'Crises': Revisiting Attached Labour in Haryana." *Economic and Political Weekly* 47 (26–27): 5–13.

Pal, S. 1996. "Casual and Regular Contracts: Workers' Self-Selection in the Rural Labour Markets in India." *Journal of Development Studies* 33 (1): 99–116.

Rosenzweig, M. 1988. "Labor Markets in Low-Income Countries." In *Handbook of Development Economics*, edited by H. B. Chenery and T. N. Srinivasan. Amsterdam: North-Holland.

Srinivasan, T. N. 1980. "Bonded Labour Contracts and Incentives to Adopt Yield Raising Innovations in 'Semifeudal' Agriculture." *Indian Economic Review* 14 (2): 165–69.

Srinivasan, T. N. 1989. "On Choice among Creditors and Bonded Labour Contracts." In *The Economic Theory of Agrarian Institutions*, edited by P. K. Bardhan, 203–20. Oxford: Clarendon Press.

Walker, T. S., and J. G. Ryan. 1990. *Village and Household Economies in India's Semi-Arid Tropics.* Baltimore, MD: Johns Hopkins University Press.

6 Tenancy and Wells

The choice between fixed-rent and sharecropping leases is a classic and central topic in studies of rural economic organization; for the parties to the contract must balance the provision of incentives with the sharing of risks. Irrigated plots offer different cultivation possibilities from dryland ones, although whether cultivation under irrigated conditions is inherently less risky may well depend on the source of irrigation. Thus the terms of a tenancy contract will depend not only on whether the plot in question is irrigated, but, if so, how it is irrigated.

Investments in wells have a prominent place in the accounts in chapter 3. In the decades that followed, the great extension of well irrigation was a salient feature of agricultural development in Andhra Pradesh. Here, it must be emphasized that percolation wells do not provide assured irrigation, since they depend on recharge from the rains. If, as is normal, the crop has to be chosen before the well's storage profile over the course of the coming season is clear, the well provides an option that, if exercised, introduces an additional risk into cultivation. This risk plays a central role in the decision problems analyzed in this chapter. Its burdens fall more rarely on farmers whose fields depend on irrigation by a deep tube well or a canal. Those sources are subject, respectively, to the vagaries of power supply and the workings of the canal system and the officials who manage its operations.

Such investments also involve dealings with bureaucracy, with various forms of subsidies at stake. Wells and tenancy are potentially linked, too; for when assessing the profitability of investing in a well, the owner should also entertain the option of leasing out the plots it commands as an alternative to cultivating them himself. These themes are pursued in this chapter, in the context of investing in a percolation well.

A potentially important, related alternative can be ruled out. In principle, taking on a tenancy is an alternative to working as an attached farm servant (AFS) or a casual laborer (Otsuka, Chuma, and Hayami 1993). In practice, there were formidable obstacles, including the legislation passed in June 1980, whose deterrent effects were already apparent in the discussions in tour 1 a few months later. These obstacles justify the sharp separation between chapter 5 and what follows.

THE INCIDENCE AND FORMS OF TENANCY

According to the initial census round, which was conducted a month or so after tour 1, the incidence of tenancy was not particularly low: about 10 percent of all cultivating households were either owner-tenants or pure tenants (see table 4.2). A process of adjustment was doubtless under way. The single respondent in village 1, a powerful man in his community, estimated that about one-sixth of its land was leased out, but many owners were not renewing their leases. Similar proportions were reported by the focus groups in village 4 and Aurepalle. The answers elsewhere were distinctly guarded. "Some" or "little" tenancy or a "few" tenants were the expressions used in villages 3, 5–9, and 11; the respondents in villages 10 and 12–14 claimed that there was no tenancy at all.[1] For all that, the respondents described in some detail key aspects of contracting in the market for tenancies, where it reportedly existed. Much of the following account may therefore be interpreted as relating to the state of affairs before the new legislation was passed.

There were essentially two forms of lease—sharecropping and fixed rents payable in arrears, almost invariably in kind. Both were found in villages 1, 4, 5, 9, and Aurepalle. Sharecropping ruled alone in villages 6, 7, and 8; fixed rents did so in villages 3 and 11.

An interesting—and rather puzzling—feature of the arrangements in village 1 was the dependence of the contract on the season, despite the fact that virtually the whole area was under assured irrigation by canal: fixed rents ruled in kharif and sharecropping in rabi. All of the village land was under double cropping, and paddy was overwhelmingly the main crop in both seasons. There is more sunlight in rabi, which promotes yields and hence the derived demand for inputs, but it is difficult to believe that this effect could be very large. Thus, although tenants' ample supplies of family labor and bullock draft power reduced the need to finance working capital, it is hard to see why conditions in rabi should have induced a switch to share contracts—unless cultivation in that season was inherently more risky. Under the combined conditions of assured irrigation, more sunlight, and less rain, that seems implausible. As things stand, the puzzle remains.

Fixed-rent contracts in village 1 were also widely subject to a contingency. If the crop turned out to be very poor, the payment could be commuted to a 50 percent share. The decision lay with the landlord, presumably informed by the general growing conditions ruling in that season. Such a commutation was reportedly uncommon in village 3. In village 9, where cotton was the main crop, payments were in cash; the commutation then took the form of a rollover until the following year. The closest to the "English" contract of a fixed cash payment wholly in advance were the leases in village 4, under which half of the amount was due in advance. All of these contracts were therefore subject, in some degree or other, to moral hazard; but in view of the (mal)functioning of credit markets, to say nothing of tenants' aversion to risk, the "English" system offered no mutually acceptable solution.

To mitigate this problem, landlords sought tenants qualified in particular ways. First, in all but village 3, owning draft animals was essential. The market for draft-power services did not function well, if at all, in some villages. In others, where the market was fairly active, especially in villages with tractors, the tenant still needed to finance the hiring, thus adding to the pressure on his limited working capital. Second, he had to have a good reputation, as a cultivator and as a reliable person (villages 1–5 and 9). In village 4, only such a person would be granted a sharecropping contract, in keeping with the sharper incentive problems sharecropping poses. Third, a line of credit was needed (villages 1, 3, 8, and 11), which indicates that landlords were not always able—or willing—to finance their tenants in an interlinked contract. Indeed, with the exception of village 1, it was claimed that there were no conditions requiring a tenant's family to supply labor to the landlord's own operations; nor was there anywhere a requirement that the tenant's crop, if marketed, be sold to his landlord. Lastly, there was no condition that the tenant lease land from only one landlord, even if the tenant possessed no land of his own. For the great majority who did, such an "exclusivity" condition, whose comparative prominence in the theoretical literature is unwarranted by actual practice, would have been an empty one anyway.

As for the terms of sharecropping contracts, there were only two exceptions to the ubiquitous 50:50 sharing of output—namely, two-thirds in the tenant's favor in village 7 and 60:40 in the landlord's favor on fertile black soils in village 9. Outlays on chemical fertilizers and pesticides were shared in the same proportion as output, with their levels negotiated in villages 5, 7, 8, and 9, thus embroiling the landlord in further monitoring efforts—unless the tenant happened to be utterly trustworthy. Much more easily monitored and enforced are the crops and varieties to be grown, which were the subject of negotiation in villages 1, 7, and 8.

The levels of fixed rents naturally varied with the soil, irrigation, location, and the like. In village 3, they ranged between Rs 300 and Rs 400 an acre. In village 11, the only leases were of irrigated land owned by absentees, who were in consequence unable to monitor cultivation at all closely; the common rate was 300 kilograms of paddy per acre.

Some illuminating examples emerged in discussions with two traders and the respondents from a few of the sample households in tour 2. One trader did much business in village 10. He also owned land, though perhaps elsewhere, which he leased under the following terms. He provided credit for the cultivation of commercial crops in the usual way, with the natural requirement that the whole output be marketed through him. He then deducted a special fee, in addition to interest, principal, and commission fees, out of the proceeds of sale. The special fee was the rent, payable in arrears, unrecorded, and thus safe from the prying eyes of the authorities. He would roll over all payments if circumstances warranted. The tenants were rotated among his plots, so as to avoid the legal provisions that would grant them security of tenure.

The second trader was in business in Chittoor Town. He owned 10 acres of land on which he had installed five or six tenants, whom he rotated every two or three years for the same reasons as the first trader. All of them also had land of their own. Under the terms of these sharecropping contracts, output was split 60:40 in his favor; he paid for electricity (for pumping) and fertilizers; they supplied bullocks and labor. His choice of sharecropping stemmed from the balance of reward and risk. He claimed that no farmer would have offered more than Rs 1,500 an acre on fixed-rent terms, but the share contract yielded him Rs 2,000 an acre (presumably a long-run average).

These accounts also cast some doubt on the claims in tour 1 that there was no tenancy in villages 10, 13, and 14. Tour 2 yielded a direct contradiction of that claim in village 12. Two respondents in the sample related how they were locked in a dispute over the sharecropping sublease of a plot that had been leased from a third party under the terms of a usufructuary mortgage. The subtenant was also leasing 0.18 acre of irrigated land from a widow. It seems that she preferred to have someone other than a relative as a tenant—to be sure of getting the rent. The contract was oral and had run for two years. The rent was 80 kilograms of paddy (440 kilograms an acre). She paid the land revenue, the receipt for which secured her ownership rights. He had wanted to pay the rent in cash, but she had insisted on kind. Sharecropping was ruled out; for she was unable to supervise cultivation (especially harvesting) and, despite the risks, he preferred to get the whole return from his investment as residual claimant under a fixed-rent arrangement. A laborer in village 8 provided an obverse example. He had obtained some land under a special redistribution program a few years earlier, but after cultivating it for a while, he found it better to lease out the plot at the rate of 240 kilograms an acre.

Nothing in the foregoing account occasions any great surprise in light of the vast literature on tenancy contracts. Yet there emerged an interesting twist, which deserves closer attention. Sharecropping was prevalent on land irrigated by percolation wells, whereas fixed-rent contracts normally ruled on dryland: this pattern prevailed in villages 5–8 and in Aurepalle, and it was confirmed by the second respondent in village 12, although his own landlord's circumstances dictated otherwise. Irrigation suggests lower levels of risk, thus favoring fixed-rent leases. Percolation wells, however, depend on recharge from current rains. If the monsoon is poor, there will be little or no water for irrigation and hence no cultivation of paddy or, worse still, a failed crop after an attempted start. Other crops grown on dryland are more robust to this hazard, but must be sown on time. The pattern is therefore less paradoxical than it appears to be at first sight. This twist motivates the formal treatment that follows, with the important accompanying remark that Shaban (1987) provides convincing evidence that cultivation under sharecropping contracts in International Crops Research Institute for the Semi-Arid Tropics (ICRISAT) villages exhibited "Marshallian" inefficiency.[2]

WELL IRRIGATION AND THE CHOICE OF LEASE

A landlord and a tenant seek agreement on the terms under which a plot will be leased. If sharecropping is chosen, the tenant will bear all costs and receive the fraction $\alpha \in (0,1)$ of the total output. The alternative is a fixed rent payable in arrears and in kind in the amount β, whatever be the level of output. These alternatives are labeled the α- and β-contracts, respectively. The choice must be made at the start of the period ($t = 0$), before the rains begin. It is assumed that the landlord resides in the village or its near locality. For if he is an absentee and lacks reliable agents, he will have great difficulty ensuring that the tenant does not hide some of the output, while relating at harvest time some story or other about the crop turning out worse than expected. This particular hazard would almost surely rule out sharecropping in favor of fixed rent.

In the first stage of the cultivation cycle, the tenant must prepare the land for sowing. Somewhat later, early in the monsoon period (at $t = 1$), he observes the rainfall to date, r_1, and must decide between sowing a dryland crop like sorghum, millets, or castor and establishing a nursery for paddy seedlings. These actions involve not only further plowing, but also inputs of seed, possibly fertilizers, and care, each aggregate of which is denoted by x_1^d and x_1^p, respectively. For simplicity, the associated financing of these inputs is assumed to be available without interest.[3]

The rains that follow this cultivation decision supplement any earlier recharging. Their amount is denoted by the variate R_2, and realized values thereof by r_2. If the rains are sufficiently poor, it will not be worthwhile transplanting the paddy crop at $t = 2$ (about 30 days after establishing the nursery at $t = 1$), and it will be too late to plant a dryland crop, so there will be no output. Transplanting and subsequently irrigating and weeding paddy involves choosing inputs denoted by x_2^p. The argument proceeds by backward induction.

Suppose sharecropping had been chosen at the start of the cycle. If, having established a nursery at $t = 1$ and observed r_2, the tenant proceeds to transplant the paddy seedlings at $t = 2$, the resulting output will depend on the earlier choice of x_1^p, the realized level of rainfall, $r_1 + r_2$, the current decision x_2^p, and the realization θ of the variate Θ, which represents growing conditions and other environmental shocks up to the harvest, but is not observed when x_2^p must be chosen. Let $y^p = f^p(x_1^p, x_2^p; r_1 + r_2, \theta)$ denote the level of output when $\Theta = \theta$, where f^p is increasing and differentiable in its arguments.

The tenant will surely have other sources of income, very likely including own cultivation. Let them yield in total an amount denoted by the variate Y^a, whose value is also not revealed until after $t = 2$. At that moment of decision, the tenant's total income is given by the variate

$$Y_2^p(\alpha) = \alpha y^p(\Theta) - x_1^p - x_2^p + Y^a, \tag{6.1}$$

where the various inputs (including any interest charges) are measured in units of output (the numéraire).

Let the tenant's preferences over lotteries be represented by the von Neumann–Morgenstern utility function u, which is increasing, strictly concave, and twice-differentiable. His decision problem is to choose x_2^p so as to maximize $E[u(Y_2^p(\alpha))]$, whose associated first-order condition is $E[u'(Y_2^p(\alpha)) \cdot (\alpha f_2^p - 1)] \leq 0$, $x_2^p \geq 0$, whereby moral hazard arises from $\alpha < 1$. Under the foregoing assumptions, this problem has a unique solution, denoted by $x_2^{p,0}(\alpha; x_1^p, r_1 + r_2; H(\theta, y^a))$, where H is the joint cumulative distribution function (CDF) of Θ and Y^a. The associated value of $E[u(Y_2^p(\alpha))]$ is denoted by $V_2^{p,0}(\alpha, x_1^p, r_1 + r_2; \cdot)$.

It may well happen that transplanting the seedlings is unprofitable. Although f^p is strictly concave in its arguments, it is implausible that, under these circumstances, the lower Inada condition holds with respect to x_2^p. It follows that if total rainfall $r_1 + r_2$ is sufficiently small, then $x_2^{p,0}(\alpha; \cdot) = 0$, the investment in cultivation is written off, and the tenant will obtain $V_2^{p,a} \equiv E[u(Y^a - x_1^p)]$. Let $x_2^{p,0}(\alpha; \cdot) = 0$ for all $r_1 + r_2 \leq r^{min}(\alpha)$.

At the previous stage, the tenant must decide between planting millets and establishing a paddy nursery. Continuing with the latter, the probability that the rains will suffice to make transplanting attractive at $t = 2$, as assessed at $t = 1$, is the probability that, conditional on $R_1 = r_1$, the realized value of $r_1 + R_2$ will be such that $x_2^{p,0}(\alpha; \cdot) > 0$. Denote it by $\pi_2(\alpha; x_1^p, r_1) = 1 - G(r^{min}(\alpha) - r_1; r_1)$, where G is the joint CDF of R_1 and R_2. Suppose, for simplicity, that x_1^p is fixed. Then the value yielded by choosing paddy, conditional on $R_1 = r_1$, is

$$V_1^{p,0}(\alpha; r_1) = \pi_2(\alpha; x_1^p, r_1) V_2^{p,0}(\alpha; x_2^p > 0) + [1 - \pi_2(\alpha; x_1^p, r_1)] V_2^{p,a}.$$

The alternative is to sow the plot to millets, a decision that must be made before r_2 is revealed. Analogously to y^p, this yields the level of output $y^d = f^d(x_1^d, x_2^d; r_1 + r_2, \theta)$.

Let x_1^d be fixed, with inputs at $t = 2$ chosen by the tenant. The tenant's total income is given by the variate

$$Y_2^d = \alpha y^d(r_1 + R_2, \Theta) - x_1^d - x_2^d + Y^a. \tag{6.2}$$

The associated first-order condition (f.o.c.) is $E[u'(Y_2^d) \cdot (\alpha f_2^d - 1)] \leq 0, x_2^d \geq 0$, whose unique solution is $x_2^{d,0}(\alpha; \cdot)$, yielding $V_2^{d,0}(\alpha; r_1)$. At this juncture, given r_1, the tenant will be indifferent between sowing millets and establishing a paddy nursery if, and only if, $V_2^{d,0}(\alpha; r_1) = V_2^{p,0}(\alpha; r_1)$. Let $r_1^*(\alpha)$ satisfy this condition. Then the probability that the tenant will choose paddy at $t = 1$, as assessed at $t = 0$, is

$$\pi_1^*(\alpha) = \int_{r_1^*(\alpha)}^{r_1^2} \int_{r_2^1}^{r_2^2} g(r_1, r_2) dr_2 dr_1.$$

Now, the level of rainfall leading up to $t = 1$ is not known at $t = 0$. At that juncture, both $V_1^{d,0}(\alpha)$ and $V_1^{p,0}(\alpha)$ are random variables, depending as they do on the variate R_1. Thus at the very start of the cycle, the sharecropping contract yields the tenant the value

$$V_0^0(\alpha) = \pi_1^*(\alpha) E[V_1^{p,0}(\alpha, R_1)] + [1 - \pi_1^*(\alpha)] E[V_1^{d,0}(\alpha, R_1)].$$

The analysis of the fixed-rent contract proceeds in exactly the same way, now with $\alpha = 1$ and the fixed rental payment of β units of output at harvest. It is assumed that the tenant is always able and willing to deliver the latter. Thus equations (6.1) and (6.2) become, respectively,

$$Y_2^p = y^p(\Theta) - x_1^p - x_2^p - \beta + Y^a, \tag{6.3}$$

and

$$Y_1^d = y^d(r_1 + R_2, \Theta) - x_1^d - x_2^d - \beta + Y^a. \tag{6.4}$$

Proceeding as before, these yield the associated value of the preference functional at $t = 0$:

$$V_0^0(\beta) = \pi_1^*(\beta) E[V_1^{p,0}(\beta, R_1)] + [1 - \pi_1^*(\beta)] E[V_1^{d,0}(\beta, R_1)].$$

The tenant chooses a sharecropping or a fixed-rent lease according as $V_0^0(\alpha) \gtrless V_0^0(\beta)$.

The landlord makes analogous calculations. His income from a fixed-rent lease is $\beta + Y^{a,l}$, which is wholly independent of the tenant's calculations and doings, and yields $V_0^l(\beta) = E[u^l(\beta + Y^{a,l})]$.

Sharecropping brings with it all sorts of complications. There is not only the matter of moral hazard in the use of inputs, but also the uncertainty surrounding which crop will be cultivated—if, as assumed above, the two parties are unable to commit themselves to paddy from the start. If the tenant is free to choose, and at $t = 1$ establishes a paddy nursery, the landlord's income will be

$$Y_2^{p,l}(\alpha) = \begin{cases} (1-\alpha)y^p(\Theta) + Y^{a,l} & \text{if transplanting is undertaken,} \\ Y^{a,l} & \text{otherwise.} \end{cases}$$

Now suppose the landlord is so well informed about the tenant's calculations that he can arrive at $x_2^{p,0}(\alpha; x_1^p, r_1 + r_2; H(\theta, y^a))$ and $\pi_2(\alpha; x_1^p, r_1)$. Then, at $t = 1$,

$$V_1^{p,l}(\alpha; r_1) = \pi_2(\alpha; x_1^p, r_1)V_2^{p,l}(\alpha; x_2^p > 0) + [1 - \pi_2(\alpha; x_1^p, r_1)]E[u^l(Y^{a,l})].$$

If, instead, the tenant chooses millets, the landlord will obtain the (random) income $\alpha f^d(\Theta) + Y^{a,l}$ and hence $V_1^{d,l}(\alpha; r_1) = E[u^l(\alpha f^d(\Theta) + Y^{a,l})]$.

This well-informed landlord will also be able to arrive at $\pi_1^*(\alpha)$. Hence, analogous to $V_0^0(\alpha)$, he obtains the value of his preference functional at the start:

$$V_0^l(\alpha) = \pi_1^*(\alpha)E[V_1^{p,l}(\alpha, R_1)] + [1 - \pi_1^*(\alpha)]E[V_1^{d,l}(\alpha, R_1)],$$

which he compares with $V_0^l(\beta)$ and so arrives at his preferred contract.

If, given (α, β), the two parties desire the same contract, all is well and good: their endowments and tastes for risk bearing are then sufficiently well matched under those terms and the prevailing environmental conditions. If they disagree, the question arises as to whether there is any scope for negotiation. Where α is concerned, there seems to have been little flexibility in practice, for the ubiquitous 50:50 sharing rule has something of the character of a social norm. The fixed rent β may, however, be somewhat negotiable, for in a rural community wherein various markets are imperfect or simply absent and the number of potential tenants is limited, it is implausible that a value of β would emerge from a Walrasian auction market, whose level all parties would take as parametrically given. In support of this conjecture, there is the remark by the commission agent in Chittoor to the effect that, whereas the sharecropping arrangement yielded him Rs 2,000 an acre (presumably, on average), no farmer would have offered more than Rs 1,500 an acre on fixed-rent terms.

The whole decision problem, though formidably complicated, raises other issues worthy of discussion. In semiarid zones like Rayalaseema and Telangana, growing paddy, a semiaquatic plant, on dryland is simply ruled out, whereas millets and castor are hardy and drought-resistant, although they, too, can benefit from irrigation. On land irrigated by wells, cultivating paddy becomes an option, but it does not have to be exercised at the start of the season, when the contract is closed. This option turns out to be double-edged; for the additional stage of establishing a nursery, with its associated investment, must be undertaken before the prospects of transplanting a successful crop are fully clear. In the above variant, the tenant is free to choose which crop to cultivate at $t = 1$, when early rainfall, r_1, is revealed. He therefore enjoys an option value, whose effect is to reduce risk ex ante at $t = 0$, thus making a fixed-rent lease more attractive, all else being equal. If, in contrast, the parties can enter into a binding commitment that paddy will be grown come what may, then the case for sharecropping becomes stronger. The absentee owners of wetland in village 11, unable as they were to monitor cultivation, had a strong incentive to insist on fixed-rent arrangements, with paddy as the crop to be cultivated. Confronted with poorer, risk-averse potential tenants, they would have had to settle for correspondingly fewer bags of paddy.

Another aspect of the contracting problem is that, although both parties share the same environment, as represented by the rainfall variates R_1 and R_2 and growing conditions Θ, they need not share the same prior distributions thereof. If the tenant is free to choose the crop at $t = 1$, the landlord's income will depend on the tenant's decisions under both forms of lease, decisions that depend, in turn, on the tenant's prior distribution functions G and H. Yet how these outcomes enter into the landlord's preference functional V^l depends on the landlord's prior distributions. Such differences therefore enter into the process in which contracting partners are matched.

For all intents and purposes, the option value associated with choosing the crop only at $t = 1$, and the risk it mitigates, arises more rarely under canal irrigation or on unirrigated plots. The option plays a central role in the decision of whether to invest in a percolation well, which is the subject of the next section. That decision is explored in detail below by means of a numerical example, which provides the basis for a similar exploration of the choice of lease under well irrigation, in which most of the other chief factors in play also feature. The aim is to establish a pair of related, robust examples, whereby going through the calculations provides a more immediate and intuitive grasp of what is involved in both decisions.

DIGGING WELLS AND DEALING WITH OFFICIALDOM

Digging new wells and repairing old ones loomed large in cultivators' recent fixed investments, and financing them largely out of current income and savings was impossible for all but a few of the very richest villagers. This meant the need to deal with officialdom, not only in the form of the state-owned Land Mortgage Bank (LMB), which was the chief lender for such purposes, but also officials in various layers of the state bureaucracy, as required by the LMB's procedures.

Assessing the profitability of investment

An investment in a percolation well involves hazards beyond surmounting the hurdles to financing it and the possibility that the trial pit will fail to strike water. The decision whether to grow paddy depends on the rains. Although the option can be exercised on the basis of partial information, an additional stochastic element enters into the resulting net payoff. The above structure lends itself to an analysis of this important complication.

Let the proposed well command the area a of the household's landholding, all of which it owns and cultivates (implying $\alpha = 1$). In order to finance its continued operation, the household must service the original loan, carry out regular desilting, maintain the pump, and eventually replace the pump itself. Let it do all of this in perpetuity; for simplicity, let the resulting annual expenditure be constant, at β^i, whose outlay is unavoidable whatever the household's current income. The investment will convert the payoff Y_1^d of dryland cultivation on the entire holding to the combination of (a) the corresponding payoff on a acres fewer and (b) a lottery on a acres, on which paddy and dryland crops will be grown with the ex ante probabilities $\pi_1^*(\beta^i)$ and $1 - \pi_1^*(\beta^i)$, respectively. Suppose, for simplicity, that the technique of cultivation on dryland plots is fixed and scalable. Then, from equations (6.3) and (6.4), the investment yields the resulting *difference* in the payoff for the realization of early rainfall $R_1 = r_1$ as the variate

$$Y_1^w(r_1) = [y_2^p(\Theta; a) - (x_1^p + x_2^p)) - a(y^d(r_1 + R_2, \Theta) - x_1^d - x_2^d)] - \beta^i.$$

The expected value thereof, at the very start of the cycle, is $\pi_1^*(\beta^i) \cdot E[Y_1^w(R_1)]$, where the additional hazard is represented by the fact that paddy may not be grown: $\pi_1^*(\beta^i) < 1$, but the outlay β^i must be made whatever happens.

A risk-neutral household will undertake the investment if, and only if, the expected value $\pi_1^*(\beta^i) \cdot E[Y_1^w(R_1)]$ is positive, but a risk-averse one will demand something more attractive, whereby both terms of the product will also depend on its preferences over lotteries. The obvious candidate is to reduce β^i by means of a subsidy, but that is exactly where much of the trouble begins in practice.

The Land Ceiling Act may, perhaps quite unintentionally, have made investment in wells more attractive, to big farmers at least. If the legal ceilings for irrigated and unirrigated land do not fully reflect the profitability of the former, then converting the latter into the former is yet another—perfectly legal—way to circumvent the act's intent, and this discrepancy will weigh in the decision even if enforcement is patchy and uncertain. Walker and Ryan (1990, 163) place pure profitability over the threat of enforcement, but without addressing the possible influence of separate ceilings.

A numerical example

A numerical example, albeit a rather stylized one, can provide a more tangible grasp of how the various factors enter into the decisions analyzed above, which have much in common. It will become clear at the close of the calculations that the following example is a fairly robust one.

No well

Suppose a family possesses an unirrigated holding. If it leases the land to others and hires out its other productive resources, let it obtain the perfectly certain income y^a. If it decides to cultivate, it must plow the land before the rains come— that is, before it knows the realization $R_1 = r_1$. This operation costs c. On learning r_1, it must decide whether to continue cultivation by planting a crop such as sorghum or to stop, thus writing off c. It will also have passed up some outside opportunities during this part of the season, so that if it abandons cultivation at this juncture and employs its resources elsewhere, it can no longer obtain y^a in full. Let the amount in question be denoted by y^b. Planting and subsequent operations cost x_1^d; only afterward do the realizations of the variates R_2 and Θ become known. For simplicity, let no further inputs be required.

Output depends on rainfall, growing conditions, and x_1^d. At the time of decision, when r_1 is known, let output on the plots in question be given by the variate

$$y^d(r_1, R_2, \Theta) = \Theta \cdot Q(r_1, R_2) \cdot (x_1^d)^{1/3},$$

where Q is an index of rainfall quality. Now, even in the semiarid tropics, there can be too much rainfall. Thus let Q take the quadratic form $Q = a(r_1 + R_2) - (r_1 + R_2)^2$, so that Q is maximal for all realizations such that $(r_1 + r_2) = a/2$.[4] Having decided to continue, the family's income over the whole cycle is the variate $Y^d(r_1)$ $= y^d(r_1, R_1, \Theta) - x_1^d - c + y^a$. Let the technique of cultivation be fixed, with the normalization $x_1^d = 1$ (If any part of the outlay on working capital $c + 1$ must be financed, let the loan be interest free and repaid without fail at the end of the cycle.)

Let the variates R_1, R_2, and Θ be independent, each taking just two values, the smaller ones with probabilities p_1, p_2, and p_θ, respectively. There are thus eight possible states ex ante at the start of the cycle and four after r_1 is revealed. Let

$$R_1 = (0.2, 0.75; p_1 = 1/3); R_2 = (1, 2; p_2 = 1/4); \Theta = (0.20, 0.28; p_\theta = 1/3),$$

with the remaining parameters taking the values $a = 6$, $c = 0.2$, $y^a = 0.6$, and $y^b = 0.5$. Observe that the functional form of the index Q takes a maximum at $a/2 = 3$, which just exceeds the maximum attained by Q—namely, when $r_1 + R_2 = 0.75 + 2$.

In the event that the early rains are poor ($R_1 = 0.2$), the decision to plant induces the following lottery:

$$Y^d(0.2) = \begin{cases} 0.20 \cdot 5.76 - 1 - 0.2 = -0.0480 & \text{with prob. } 1/4 \cdot 1/3 = 1/12, \\ 0.28 \cdot 5.76 - 1 - 0.2 = 0.4128 & \text{with prob. } 1/4 \cdot 2/3 = 1/6, \\ 0.20 \cdot 8.36 - 1 - 0.2 = 0.4720 & \text{with prob. } 3/4 \cdot 1/3 = 1/4, \\ 0.28 \cdot 8.36 - 1 - 0.2 = 1.1408 & \text{with prob. } 3/4 \cdot 2/3 = 1/2. \end{cases} \tag{6.5}$$

The expected value thereof is clearly positive, at 0.7532. The corresponding value in the event that the early rains are good ($R_1 = 0.75$) is greater still, since the realized value of Q is increasing in r_1 for both values of R_2. The alternative is not to cultivate, which yields $y^a = 0.6$ with certainty. Hence, cultivation is profitable ex ante at the start of the cycle, and a risk-neutral family will begin to plow without further ado.

A risk-averse family will tend to focus much of its attention on the worst outcome—namely, poor rains followed later by adverse growing conditions. Let its preferences over lotteries be represented by the von Neumann–Morgenstern utility function $u = \ln y^d$. In the state in question, $u = \ln(-0.0480)$ is not defined, which should be interpreted to mean that the distress that the state causes is so acute that the family will simply cut its losses when the early rains are poor. Would it continue with planting if the early rains were good ($R_1 = 0.75$)? To do so would induce the lottery

$$Y^d(0.75) = \begin{cases} 0.20 \cdot 7.4375 - 1 - 0.2 = 0.2875 & \text{with prob. } 1/4 \cdot 1/3 = 1/12, \\ 0.28 \cdot 7.4375 - 1 - 0.2 = 0.8825 & \text{with prob. } 1/4 \cdot 2/3 = 1/6, \\ 0.20 \cdot 8.9375 - 1 - 0.2 = 0.5875 & \text{with prob. } 3/4 \cdot 1/3 = 1/4, \\ 0.28 \cdot 8.9375 - 1 - 0.2 = 1.3025 & \text{with prob. } 3/4 \cdot 2/3 = 1/2. \end{cases} \tag{6.6}$$

The expected utility thereof is $Eu[Y^d(0.75)] = -0.1256$ utils, which exceeds that of stopping, namely, $u(0.5 - 0.2) = -1.204$ utils.

There remains the decision of whether to cultivate at all. Since the option not to continue when r_1 has been revealed will be exercised if, and only if, the early rains are poor, the expected utility of the ex ante compound lottery induced by the decision to plow is

$$p_1 u(0.5 - 0.2) + (1 - p_1) Eu[Y^d(0.75)] = -(1/3) \cdot 1.204 - (2/3) \cdot 0.1256 = -0.4850,$$

which exceeds that of the alternative of leasing and hiring out—namely, $\ln(0.6) = -0.5185$. The certainty equivalent income yields a more transparent comparison: cultivation generates $\exp(-0.4850) = 0.6157 > y^a$. In the above configuration, therefore, the family will always engage in cultivation, but in the event of poor early rains, it will not proceed to plant a crop, thus writing off the investment in plowing.

Investment in a well

Let the proposed well command the entire holding. This introduces the option of growing paddy, to be exercised only when r_1 has been revealed. It will also improve the yield of sorghum, making that option more attractive should paddy look risky in the event of poor early rains. Against these advantages, there are not only the capital costs of the well, in the form of the perpetual payment β^i, but also those of pumping water, denoted by b.

By storing water, the well improves the production technology by effectively enhancing the rainfall index. For sorghum, let a increase to 7 and let $b = 0.1$. Then ignoring the perpetual charge β^i for the present, planting sorghum in the event that the early rains are poor induces the lottery

$$Y^d(0.2) = \begin{cases} 0.20 \cdot 6.96 - 1 - 0.2 - 0.1 = 0.0920 & \text{with prob. } 1/4 \cdot 1/3 = 1/12, \\ 0.28 \cdot 6.96 - 1 - 0.2 - 0.1 = 0.6488 & \text{with prob. } 1/4 \cdot 2/3 = 1/6, \\ 0.20 \cdot 10.56 - 1 - 0.2 - 0.1 = 0.8120 & \text{with prob. } 3/4 \cdot 1/3 = 1/4, \\ 0.28 \cdot 10.56 - 1 - 0.2 - 0.1 = 1.6568 & \text{with prob. } 3/4 \cdot 2/3 = 1/2. \end{cases} \tag{6.7}$$

This yields $E[u(Y^d(0.2))] = -0.0706$, which exceeds that yielded by stopping.

Paddy is a semiaquatic plant, which argues for a threshold effect where the rainfall index is concerned. Retaining the quadratic form, let $Q = a(r_1 + R_2) - (r_1 + R_2)^2 - d$, where d is positive. At the same time, paddy is more responsive to moisture than sorghum. Let $a = 8$ and $d = 3$. Then Q takes the following values:

$$Q(0.2, 1) = 6.36; \; Q(0.2, 2) = 11.96; \; Q(0.75, 1) = 9.6875; \; Q(0.75, 2) = 14.1875.$$

A further consideration is that cultivating paddy involves heavier use of inputs. For simplicity, let the whole bundle of inputs after plowing be applied immediately after r_1 has been revealed, with x_1^p fixed, at 1.2.

In the event that the early rains are poor and the following worst state occurs, the resulting income will be $0.20 \cdot 6.36 \cdot 1.2^{1/3} - 1.2 - 0.2 - 0.1 = -0.1483$, and u is not defined. Hence, if the early rains are poor, sorghum will be grown. If, on the contrary, the early rains are good, it is easily checked that the payoff structure of paddy stochastically dominates that of sorghum, so that paddy will be cultivated. To be precise,

$$Y^p(0.75) = \begin{cases} 0.20 \cdot 9.6875 \cdot 1.2^{1/3} - 1.2 - 0.2 - 0.1 = 0.5589 & \text{with prob. } 1/4 \cdot 1/3 = 1/12, \\ 0.28 \cdot 9.6875 \cdot 1.2^{1/3} - 1.2 - 0.2 - 0.1 = 1.3825 & \text{with prob. } 1/4 \cdot 2/3 = 1/6, \\ 0.20 \cdot 14.1875 \cdot 1.2^{1/3} - 1.2 - 0.2 - 0.1 = 1.5153 & \text{with prob. } 3/4 \cdot 1/3 = 1/4, \\ 0.28 \cdot 14.1875 \cdot 1.2^{1/3} - 1.2 - 0.2 - 0.1 = 2.7214 & \text{with prob. } 3/4 \cdot 2/3 = 1/2. \end{cases}$$

$$\tag{6.8}$$

This yields $E[u(Y^d(0.2))] = 0.6100$. Excluding the perpetual cost of the well, β^i, the expected utility of the ex ante compound lottery induced by the decision to plow is

$$-(1/3) \cdot 0.0706 + (2/3) \cdot 0.6100 = 0.3831,$$

whose certainty-equivalent income is 1.4668, which compares favorably to that of unirrigated cultivation—namely, 0.6157.

The central question of whether investment in the well is attractive remains. It is clearly so if β^i is sufficiently close to zero, but such a generous subsidy can be ruled out. It is seen from the lottery (6.7) that, strictly speaking, any $\beta^i \geq 0.092$ will make even the option of irrigated sorghum unacceptable. One could argue, however, that historical experience yields every expectation that the government would declare a temporary moratorium on repayments in the worst of all cases, with the due amount β^i to be paid off in subsequent, more "normal" periods. In the foregoing setting, such a moratorium would be declared, on average, once every 36 years ($p_1 \cdot p_2 \cdot p_\theta = 1/3 \cdot 1/4 \cdot 1/3$). That being so, it is fairly readily checked from lotteries (6.7) and (6.8) that investment in the well would be attractive for values of β^i not exceeding about 0.53—that is, about 35 percent of the value of working capital invested in paddy cultivation ($c + x_1^P + b$).

Subsidies and bribes

The value of the perpetual outlay β^i such that the investment in the well is barely attractive can be thought of as the farmer's willingness to pay for it, which is denoted by $\beta^{i,*}$. The components that comprise β^i—the amortized costs of digging the well, installing the pump, and then maintaining them, with a suitable allowance for the terms under which the whole is financed—are also subject to public policy. The interest rates on formal loans are regulated, as are the upper limits on their size, and subsidies on pumps are commonplace, for small and marginal farmers at least. If these interventions yield a β^i less than the farmer's willingness to pay, the various officials involved, from the bank manager down to the village patwari (village accountant and land records keeper) and the lineman who connects the pump to the grid, are well placed to demand a cut, as the tales in chapters 2 and 3 reveal so vividly.

Their power to extract payments for services rendered—otherwise called bribes—depends on, inter alia, their ability to assess $\beta^{i,*}$ and their place in the sequence of steps needed to bring the well to working completion, there being various opportunities to hold up the process along the way. Indeed, the bank's employees are likely to coordinate their actions, with rules for sharing the proceeds. A farmer's decision to apply for a loan signals that his $\beta^{i,*}$ exceeds whatever β^i he expects to come out of the process, including any payments of bribes. The patwari, who is well acquainted with the farmer's abilities and circumstances, and the loan officer, who examines the loan application, are first in the queue, and both are fully aware of any special subsidies that apply. Matters then play out, culminating occasionally in a failed trial pit, but usually in a line connection and final inspection.

There is no space to go into the intricacies of this game here. Suffice it to say that the farmer has the clear outside option of continuing with dryland cultivation, and his aversion to risk implies that paying the sure thing of a bribe up-front is especially costly when weighed against the stochastic stream of net income subsequently yielded by the well. For their part, bank officials are often under pressure to meet loan disbursement targets, a fact of which farmers may be aware. Reputation is also a consideration when the game is repeated over the course of time. Although each game involves one particular farmer, some details of its final outcome are likely to get into circulation, particularly if the farmer thinks the officials have been unduly rapacious.

TENANCY AND WELLS: A NUMERICAL EXAMPLE

The choice of rental contract on well-irrigated land is now revisited, based on the numerical example in the section entitled "Digging Wells and Dealing with Officialdom" and a further simplification of the structure in the section entitled "Well Irrigation and the Choice of Lease." The aim is to find a robust constellation of parameters such that sharecropping will be preferred to fixed rents.

Tenants in the villages studied almost always possessed holdings of their own, whose cultivation constituted their outside option. Let y^a denote the tenant's certainty-equivalent value thereof. If he accepts the lease, there will be some diversion of the household's resources to the tenancy, thus reducing the yield of its own holding. Let $y^{a,t}$ ($< y^a$) denote the resulting certainty-equivalent value. The landlord is assumed to be risk neutral.

The tenancy in question is the irrigated holding analyzed earlier. The simplifying assumption is that paddy can be cultivated only when the early rains are sufficient to establish the nursery and then puddle the plots for transplanting. Hence, if $R_1 = 0.2$, sorghum will be grown. The terms of the sharecropping contract stipulate that the output be divided 50:50 ($\alpha = 0.5$) and that the costs of certified seeds, fertilizers, pesticides, and pumping be divided likewise. Cultivating irrigated sorghum involves only pumping; the excess of x_1^p over x_1^d—that is, 0.2—arises from the need for certified seeds, fertilizers, and pesticides in paddy cultivation. Suppose further, contrary to the evidence in Shaban (1987), that there is no Marshallian inefficiency. Thus x_1^d and x_1^p remain fixed as before and, by assumption, no further inputs are required. Under a fixed-rent contract, the tenant bears all costs as residual claimant.

If the rains in season 1 are poor, the tenant will plant sorghum. The net revenue yielded by the tenancy is denoted by the variate $Z^d(0.2)$, which is distributed as follows:

$$Z^d(0.2) = \begin{cases} 0.20 \cdot 6.96 - 1 - 0.2 - 0.1 - 0.1 = -0.008 & \text{with prob. } 1/4 \cdot 1/3 = 1/12, \\ 0.28 \cdot 6.96 - 1 - 0.2 - 0.1 - 0.1 = 0.5488 & \text{with prob. } 1/4 \cdot 2/3 = 1/6, \\ 0.20 \cdot 10.56 - 1 - 0.2 - 0.1 - 0.1 = 0.7120 & \text{with prob. } 3/4 \cdot 1/3 = 1/4, \\ 0.28 \cdot 10.56 - 1 - 0.2 - 0.1 - 0.1 = 1.5568 & \text{with prob. } 3/4 \cdot 2/3 = 1/2. \end{cases}$$

The tenant's own holding will surely be rather different. Let it yield a somewhat higher certainty-equivalent income, say, $y^a = 0.75$, with $y^{a,t} = 0.7$. It is seen that the tenant will never accept a fixed rent (β) exceeding about 0.69, however attractive paddy cultivation might be when $R_1 = 0.75$.

Under the terms of the sharecropping contract, the tenant would obtain the corresponding part of $Z^d(0.2)$ plus the income from own cultivation. The latter is almost surely positively correlated with the family's net income from the tenancy, so that adding the certainty-equivalent $y^{a,t}$ to the latter will understate the riskiness of total income and hence the attractiveness of sharecropping. The said addition yields the payoff vector (0.0460, 0.3244, 0.4060, 0.8284) and hence the expected utility $E[u(^d; 0.2)] = -0.7637$. This is far inferior to the utility yielded by the outside option, $u(y^a) = \ln 0.75 = -0.2877$, but it occurs with probability 1/3, and paddy cultivation might still be attractive if the rains turn out to be good. For his part, the landlord would obtain (0.6460, 0.9244, 1.0060, 1.4284), whose expected value of 1.1736 comfortably exceeds a fixed rent of 0.69.[5] In practice, moral hazard was operative. That being so, the tenant would do a bit better, and the landlord a bit worse, than these calculations indicate. We return to this point at the close of this section.

In the event that the early rains are good, paddy cultivation will come into consideration, and the expected value of output will exceed that under sorghum. The risk-neutral landlord will therefore prefer sharecropping independently of the level of early rainfall, so the only remaining question is whether the tenant will accept this contract. Under the lottery (6.8), the tenant's payoff vector is (-0.3205, 0.0910, 0.1576, 0.7607). Augmented by $y^{a,t} = 0.7$, this yields $E[u(^p; 0.75)]$ = -0.2337. The landlord obtains the vector (0.8795, 1.2912, 1.3576, 1.9607), whose expected value is a fulsome 1.6082.

At the very start of the season, when the realization of R_1 is still unknown, the sharecropping contract offers the tenant, ex ante, $1/3 \cdot E[u(^d; 0.2)] + 2/3 \cdot E[u(^p; 0.75)] = -0.2075$, which exceeds that yielded by the outside option of own cultivation—namely, $u(y^d) = -0.2877$. Thus the contract is acceptable to him, and the landlord is surely content with the expected rental income of $1/3 \cdot 1.1736 + 2/3 \cdot 1.6082 = 1.4434$, as opposed to a fixed rent of at most 0.69.

Three remarks are in order. First, the effects of moral hazard on resource allocation have been ruled out by assumption, so that the sharecropping contract will surely be acceptable to the tenant when moral hazard is operative. As for the landlord, any losses on that account will be dwarfed by his payoffs whichever crop is cultivated. Second, the yields under sorghum cultivation, which will be chosen when the early rains are poor, can be increased substantially—and with them the maximal sum β the tenant is willing to pay as fixed rent—without endangering the landlord's preference for a 50:50 sharecropping contract. Third, the landlord's payoffs are such that the assumption that he (or she) is risk neutral can also be relaxed somewhat without overturning this contractual preference. The example therefore emerges as fairly robust. In this connection, it should be recalled once more that the trader in Chittoor Town put the (expected) rental income on his share tenancies at Rs 2,000 per acre, as against possible bids of at most Rs 1,500 per acre for a fixed-rate lease.

NOTES

1. These responses for villages 11 and 12 are rather at odds with Olsen's (1993, 84) finding that about 10–15 percent of cultivated land was rented in two Rayalaseema villages in 1986–87.
2. The estimated difference between the levels of output per acre on owned and sharecropped plots cultivated by farmers having both kinds was 16.3 percent, after controlling for irrigation, soil quality, and plot value. The corresponding differences for inputs of male, female, and bullock labor supplied by the family were 20.8, 46.7, and 16.6 percent, respectively (Shaban 1987, 905).
3. In practice, tenants usually face far less favorable terms, which makes fixed rents payable in advance less attractive. In this connection, Das, de Janvry, and Sadoulet (2019) report the results of introducing randomized access into a credit program for landless workers and marginal farmers in the very different setting of Bangladesh. The findings relate to the rabi season, in which the main crop is irrigated paddy. Among borrowers (participants), there was no change in the average number of share contracts, but the average number of fixed-rent contracts increased by 0.9 and the associated area increased by 147 percent.
4. In fact, shortfalls are much more damaging than excesses of the same size. See Lahiri and Roy (1985) for an estimate of an asymmetric all-India index for paddy production. Accordingly, the numerical values chosen in this example keep the maximal realized value of Q just short of the optimum.
5. If, in the event of the worst outcome, the landlord were to commute the fixed payment into a share rent, the tenant would pay the even larger sum of 0.6960.

REFERENCES

Das, N., A. de Janvry, and E. Sadoulet. 2019. "Credit and Land Contracting: A Test of the Theory of Sharecropping." *American Journal of Agricultural Economics* 101 (4): 1098–114.

Lahiri, A., and P. Roy. 1985. "Rainfall and Supply Response: A Study of Rice in India." *Journal of Development Economics* 18 (2-3): 315–34.

Olsen, W. 1993. "Competition and Power in Rural Markets: A Case Study from Andhra Pradesh." *IDS Bulletin* 24 (3): 83–89.

Otsuka, K., H. Chuma, and Y. Hayami. 1993. "Permanent Labour and Land Tenancy Contracts in Agrarian Economies: An Integrated Analysis." *Economica [New Series]* 60 (237): 57–77.

Shaban, R. A. 1987. "Testing between Competing Models of Sharecropping." *Journal of Political Economy* 95 (5): 893–920.

Walker, T. S., and J. G. Ryan. 1990. *Village and Household Economies in India's Semi-Arid Tropics.* Baltimore, MD: Johns Hopkins University Press.

7 Finance and Marketing

Traders and commission agents are deeply involved in the financing of cultivation, as are cooperative and state-owned sugar mills. How they combine the terms under which they finance their clients with those concerning contractual delivery of the resulting output is an important question, yet a fully satisfactory explanation of what they are observed to do is still lacking. That is reason enough to address the question once more. In doing so, there arises a further question—namely, how does competition from a cooperative mill influence contracts between private parties? The final product cane sugar provides a prime example.

Private traders, whether dealing on own account or acting as commission agents for farmers, have a clear interest in securing business in advance. Sugar mills need to secure deliveries of cane. Both do so by using credit for cultivation as a carrot, under the condition that their clients' output be sold to or through them. This tying condition, often imposed as part of an exclusive contract, was a salient feature of the marketing of commercial crops.

How the traders' system works is nicely exemplified by the accounts of the two agents mentioned in chapter 6. The first dealt in cotton and groundnut, and his establishment included quite a large general store in Kurnool District.[1] He had about 2,000 clients, three-quarters of whom had been dealing with him for 10 years or more. His system of operations is described in detail in tour 1.

The second trader, who had about 500 clients, not only gave a specific account of his own operations in tour 2, but also sketched the general situation in Chittoor District. About 45,000 acres were under sugarcane. The two factories had a joint requirement of about 15,000 acres. Most of the 250 or so registered dealers traded in groundnut as well as jaggery. They were financing cultivation in Chittoor and Vyalpad Taluks to the tune of Rs 30 million to Rs 40 million a year, which dwarfed public sector lending.

In this connection, the cooperative mill was, in effect, a dealer in its own right, imposing its own contractual obligations on its shareholders. About one-fifth of this trader's clients were shareholders, and there was some tension here. He accepted new clients who were shareholders only if their current areas under cane were sufficient to meet both obligations. He himself owned 12 shares.

What was not delivered to the mill, his tenants converted into jaggery in their backyards.

A senior official of the cooperative sugar mill provided an account of its operations, which are set out in tour 2. Competition for cane at that time was sharp, the price of jaggery being high relative to the regulated price of cane at the mill.

To complete—if not confuse—this many-sided picture, respondents in villages 13 and 14 related, in both tours, their own stories of dealings with commission agents and the mill.

Two particular questions arise from these various accounts. First, given the tying of credit to delivery, what determined the choice of interest rate, commission rate, and quantity in private contracts between cultivators and agents? According to the household surveys, instances of interest-free contracts cropped up quite frequently in Punjab, but not in Andhra Pradesh.[2] Second, how did the presence of the cooperative mill, as a third party in many cases, influence private decisions in the marketing of sugarcane? These questions are taken up formally in this chapter, although it should be emphasized that the setting matters. The following examples in the wider literature illustrate the range of variations.

SELECTED LITERATURE

Sugarcane cultivation in Taiwan in the Japanese colonial period is the subject of a study by Koo, Huang, and Kan (2012). Mills advanced fertilizer loans to farmers, some of whom had wetland and hence the option of growing paddy. There were no commission agents. The authors argue that the mills practiced perfectly discriminating monopoly, fixing the delivery price and the interest rate separately for the two types of farmer. To analyze the system, they extend the model of Gangopadhyay and Sengupta (1987), but retain the assumptions that there is neither risk in production nor any chance of default. These assumptions will not serve when dealing with matters in Chittoor District, as related by all parties concerned in chapters 2 and 3.

Fisheries are particularly interesting—and quite different from cultivation—because a boat's revenue tends to be very volatile, day-to-day and month-to-month. If fixed interest payments are due at regular intervals, the owner(s) must maintain a substantial float to finance household consumption and current operations and to meet any debt obligations when they fall due. A trader-lender who takes part of the catch as first claimant secures business and enjoys debt seniority, while also easing his clients' financial transactions, a service for which he may be able to extract a charge through the terms of the contracts. Such an arrangement does not sit easily with a fixed loan maturity, and when loans are eventually wound up, the vessel's owner seeks out another lender, hoping for similar or better terms.

The Chilika Lagoon fishery in the eastern Indian state of Orissa is one such example, and it offers a sharp contrast to sugarcane cultivation in colonial Taiwan. Formal credit is rather limited, trader-lenders are active, seasonal catches are highly variable, and fishermen are poor and risk averse. Using her own primary data for the period 2009–11, Riekhof (2019) establishes that the share contracts between fishermen and such lenders were exclusive where delivery was concerned, had no accompanying explicit interest charges, were unsecured, and contained a substantial insurance premium as part of the implicit interest charge. The latter arose in the form of a discount on the spot price when the catch was sold and averaged a stiff 49 percent per year. Additional, standard loans were not ruled out, but were little cheaper.

Kerala's ring seine fishery, whose boats and crews are much larger, has a good deal in common with the Chilika fishery where financing and marketing are concerned. According to a survey of eight coastal districts conducted in 2017 (Parappurathu et al. 2019), the sources of credit spanned the entire spectrum, from commercial and cooperative banks, Matsyafed (a fishermen's cooperative), commission agents, private lenders, other informal lenders, all the way to friends and relatives. Whereas 69 and 60 percent, respectively, of all vessels had outstanding loans with commission agents and Matsyafed, the corresponding proportions for the commercial and cooperative banks were only 16 and 9 percent, respectively. Commission agents charged between 4 and 10 percent of the value of the catch, but no interest; Matsyafed charged 3–6 percent of the catch and interest at rates between 4 and 13 percent per year. The banks charged annual rates of 11–15 percent, while other private sources charged 18–60 percent.

The absence of explicit, fixed interest payments in contracts involving trader-lenders calls for further comment. A notable study of two fishing villages in Kerala (Platteau and Abraham 1987) reveals, incidentally, a religious cause for their absence—namely, the observance of Sharia Law, which prohibits them. The authors remark in a footnote that most of the Muslim commission agents in one village had been driven out in communal rioting in the early 1970s.

In his study of Chambar Town and its surrounding villages in Sind, Pakistan, in 1980–81, Aleem (1990, 332–33) reminds readers of this prohibition, also in a footnote. What is then all the more puzzling is the wholesale use of the terms "interest charges" and "interest rates" throughout the remainder of the article. The qualifying adjective "implicit" indicates what is meant, but such terminology is misleading. Fixed interest payments, with or without unlimited liability, are one thing; share payments on the basis of revenue or output are something else—namely, returns to a form of equity, which are not to be confused with interest. The calculations needed to transform share payments into a numerical interest rate are simple enough, but, as argued in the following section, interpreting the results runs into difficulties. The results should be viewed as conditionally descriptive rather than analytical. At all events, it would be far better to view interest and commission charges as special cases of what should be termed "payment for the services of capital," but the use of (implicit) "interest rates" in connection with what are share payments seems to be deeply ingrained.

CONTRACTUAL TERMS

Let the crop involved be like paddy or groundnut, which, unlike sugarcane, cannot be processed by households for subsequent commercial sale.

A risk-averse, cultivating household has an endowment of productive resources. If it wishes to augment these with inputs such as fertilizers, pesticides, electricity, and the like, it must borrow to finance them. The output yielded by the endowment and bought-in inputs x is denoted by the variate $Q = f(x,\Theta)$, where f is strictly concave in x. When cultivation decisions are made, the crop price at harvest is unknown. Denoting it by the variate P, the gross value of output is $Z = PQ$. If the household does not borrow, its income will be $Y(0) = Z(0) = P \cdot f(0,\Theta)$, which yields $V^a = E[u(Y(0))]$. Let the environment be stationary, with P_t and Θ_t each i.i.d. (independent and identically distributed). If the household never borrows, it will obtain the stationary stream $\{V^a, ...,\}$, whose value is denoted by $\Omega^a = V^a/(1 - \delta)$, where δ is its discount factor. Thus Ω^a is the value of the household's outside option.

The alternative, if the household is creditworthy at $t = 1$, is to borrow the amount x_1 (these inputs are the numéraire good), bearing the interest factor ρ, together with the commission rate $1 - \alpha$ charged on Z_1. At the end of the crop cycle, the household must decide between meeting its contractual obligations to pay the amount $\rho x_1 + (1 - \alpha)z_1$, thus remaining creditworthy, and defaulting, with the consequence of being shut out of the credit market for good. It will be indifferent between these courses of action if, and only if, the realization z_1 is such that

$$u(\alpha z_1 - \rho x_1) + \delta \Omega^c = u(z_1) + \delta \Omega^a, \tag{7.1}$$

where Ω^c is the continuation value of remaining creditworthy and borrowing x_1. Since u is increasing and strictly concave, this condition will be satisfied by a unique value of z_1, which is also the same in all periods in a stationary environment. Let it be denoted by $z^d(x_1, \alpha, \rho, \delta)$, so that the probability of default, as assessed at the start of cultivation, is $\pi = \text{prob}(Z < z^d)$, and the subscript $t(=1)$ can be dropped without ambiguity. Hence,

$$\Omega^c = \left\{ E[u(Z(x) | Z < z^d)] + \pi \delta \Omega^a \right\} + \left\{ E[u(\alpha Z(x) - \rho x | Z \geq z^d)] + (1 - \pi) \delta \Omega^c \right\},$$

or

$$\Omega^c = [V(x) + \pi \delta \Omega^a]/[1 - (1 - \pi)\delta], \tag{7.2}$$

where $V(x) = E[u(Z(x)|Z < z^d)] + E[u(\alpha Z(x) - \rho x | Z \geq z^d)]$.[3] The size of the penalty for defaulting is therefore

$$\Delta \Omega \equiv \Omega^c - \Omega^a = [V(x) - (1 - \delta)\Omega^a]/[1 - (1 - \pi)\delta].$$

Since Ω^a is independent of x, it follows from condition (7.1) that Ω^c is increasing in x. More generally, π depends on the terms of the contract, thereby introducing the possibility of moral hazard.[4]

Commission agents are assumed to be risk neutral, with access to loanable funds at the parametric interest factor $\bar{\rho}$. They are also assumed to be fully informed about the details of condition (7.1). The structure of competition among them certainly matters to households.

Suppose, to begin with, that each trader has a fixed "territory," so that the system is a set of exclusive monopolies: each cultivator always faces the same trader. As related in the above accounts, the trader sets the size of the loan and hence x and the cumulative distribution function of $Z_t(x_t)$, which is denoted by $G(z(x))$, with support $[z^1(x), z^2(x)]$. Indeed, he is in position to choose all terms of the contract (α, ρ, x), noting that these terms affect the chances of a default. This latter consideration limits his power to extract a surplus from the household; for if, in a stationary environment, the household is offered a loan, it can always do better by taking it, defaulting at the end of the period, and getting V^a forever after than by not taking it and getting just V^a in the current period. Although G is fixed by x, moral hazard arises from the cultivator's option to default and sell the output directly in the open market, albeit with painful future consequences, as measured by $\Delta \Omega$.

That option is not, however, the only factor limiting the trader's power. When he has a fixed territory, defaults shrink his pool of clients, and hence his lifetime expected profits; for in choosing (α, ρ, x), he must take into account not only the potential loss arising from a default in the current period, but also the loss of opportunities to extract a surplus from a defaulting client in the future. These considerations might well induce him to consider allowing clients to roll over loans if growing conditions have been generally adverse. For simplicity, this strengthening of the household's bargaining power is neglected, so that the trader's decision problem boils down to maximizing the expected profit, $E[Y^t]$, yielded by each contract in the current period.[5] Formally stated, his decision problem is

$$\max_{(\alpha, \rho, x)} E[(1-\alpha)Z(x) + \rho x \,|\, Z \geq z^d] - \bar{\rho}x. \tag{7.3}$$

The first-order conditions (f.o.c.) with respect to (w.r.t.) α and ρ are, assuming an interior solution,

$$-E[Z(x)\,|\,Z \geq z^d] - [(1-\alpha)z^d + \rho x]G'(z^d)\frac{\partial z^d}{\partial \alpha} = 0 \tag{7.4}$$

and

$$(1-\pi(z^d))x - [(1-\alpha)z^d + \rho x]G'(z^d)\frac{\partial z^d}{\partial \rho} = 0. \tag{7.5}$$

Differentiating condition (7.1) totally and noting equation (7.2) to obtain the derivatives $\partial \pi / \partial \alpha$ and $\partial \pi / \partial \rho$, the f.o.c. imply that (see the annex to this chapter)

$$\frac{E[Z(x)\,|\,Z \geq z^d]}{(1-\pi(z^d))z^d} = \frac{(1-\delta+\delta\pi)u'(\alpha z^d - \rho x) + \delta E[u'(\alpha Z - \rho x \,|\, Z \geq z^d) \cdot Z]/z^d}{(1-\delta+\delta\pi)u'(\alpha z^d - \rho x) + \delta E[u'(\alpha Z - \rho x \,|\, Z \geq z^d)]}.$$

The left-hand side (l.h.s.) is the ratio of the expected value of the total value of the delivery when the contract is fulfilled to the value of the trigger amount, z^d, multiplied by the probability that delivery will occur. The right-hand side (r.h.s.) comprises analogous terms involving the household's expected marginal utility when it fulfills the contract, with both numerator and denominator augmented by its realized marginal utility at the trigger value when it does likewise, adjusted by discounting and the probability of default.

Proposition 7.1: The optimum contract involves a positive probability of default, with an interest-free loan ($\rho = 1$).

Proof: Suppose the probability of default is zero—that is, $z^d < z^1(x)$. Since $E[Z(x)] > z^1(x)$ and u is strictly concave, there is a contradiction; for the l.h.s. of equation (7.6) then exceeds the r.h.s. Hence, in keeping with the empirical account of things, the probability of default is positive.

In practice, however, it is also rather small. This again leads to a contradiction; for if $\pi(z^d)$ is small, $E[Z(x)\,|\,Z \geq z^d]$ must surely substantially exceed z^d and the negative covariation of u' and Z, conditional on $Z \geq z^d$, remains when $z^d(x)$ is sufficiently close to $z^1(x)$. It is seen from equations (7.4) and (7.5) that this contradiction stems from the profitability of reducing ρ in order to increase the commission rate $1 - \alpha$, thereby shifting risk from the risk-averse household to the risk-neutral trader, even though incentives are at work through the former's option to default. The practical limit is an interest-free loan—namely, $\rho = 1$. ∎

Remark: Moral hazard is actually at work, since $\pi(z^d)$ is positive and z^d depends on the terms of the contract. The lender's choice $\rho = 1$ is part of his optimal choice of contract in view of this fact.

How sensitive are these results to the lack of competition among traders? Suppose, at the other extreme, that there is a system of contestable monopolies, in which competition is so sharp as to reduce expected profits to zero. This variant is adopted by Bell, Srinivasan, and Udry (1997) in their investigation of loans and tying in Punjab, but they assume that commission agents charge only interest. In contrast, and in keeping with the respondents' rule of thumb, let the trader fix x, but now offer the household a menu of combinations of (α, ρ) yielding $E[Y^t] = 0$. Let

$$S(x) \equiv \{(\alpha, \rho) : E[(1-\alpha)Z(x) + \rho x \mid Z \geq z^d] - \bar{\rho}x = 0\}.$$

The household's decision problem is

$$\max_{(\alpha, \rho)} \Omega^c \quad \text{s.t. } (7.1), (\alpha, \rho) \in S(x). \tag{7.7}$$

Proposition 7.1 continues to hold for the same reason as under exclusive monopolies. Indeed, it holds for any configuration of relative bargaining strengths (for the proof of this claim, see the annex to this chapter). The intuition for this result is that, once agreement is reached on x, the remaining task is to allocate the resulting risks represented by the distribution $G(x)$. Since the Nash solution to the bargaining problem is Pareto-efficient, the risks will be borne, as far as the contractual parameters permit, by the risk-neutral trader.

The chief conclusion to be drawn from the analysis of these two variants of competition is that traders must be risk averse too, if the actual practice involving both interest and commission charges is to arise as an optimum within the above framework.

To close this section, it remains to examine the variant wherein the trader discounts the price. If the discount applies as a percentage, it is equivalent to a share of the revenue, since $(1-\alpha)Z$ may be written as $(1-\alpha)P \cdot Q$. The only contractual alternative is that the discount is fixed as a monetary amount, say d per kilo or quintal.[6] As a consequence, for any given level of output, the proportion of the gross revenue paid to the trader is decreasing in the spot price, in contrast to the constant proportion $(1 - \alpha)$. This indicates that, under certain conditions, this form of discount may be attractive to a risk-averse peasant farmer or fisherman.

Suppose his output can take n distinct values; let them be arranged in ascending order: $q_1 < q_2 \dots < q_n$. The spot price depends on market conditions—in particular, the output of all other producers. Suppose, therefore, that the common component of the random shocks affecting the level of individual outputs is sufficiently strong that the spot price is nondecreasing when arranged in the same order as the numbering of outputs: $p_1 \geq p_2 \dots \geq p_n$, where $p_1 > p_n$ so that there is some variability in price. On some days, a few vessels may do well when all others have poor catches, but this will tend to get evened out over the course of a whole season, whereby some seasons will be generally good, others average, and others poor. The same argument holds for peasant producers: some may enjoy the good fortune of getting a bumper crop when the general harvest is poor, but all consider such a stroke of good luck to be such a rare event that it does not enter into their reckoning. The final assumption where outputs and prices are concerned is that market demand, including the effects of price support policies, is sufficiently elastic that individual levels of revenue are increasing in individual levels of output: $p_1q_1 < p_2q_2 ... < p_nq_n$.

Turning to the determination of d, in keeping with proposition 7.1, let there be no interest charges. In the above scheme, a risk-neutral trader will be indifferent between the share of revenue $(1 - \alpha)$ and d per unit of output if, and only if, $(1 - \alpha) \cdot E[Z] = d \cdot EQ$ and both contractual terms induce the same probability of default. Suppose he offers these alternative terms. The producer's income is αZ with revenue sharing and $Z - d \cdot Q = Z - (1 - \alpha)(E[Z]/[EQ]) \cdot Q$ with price discounting. Now, in virtue of the above assumptions on the ordered vectors $(q_1,...,q_n)$ and $(p_1,...,p_n)$, it follows that the payment to the trader is larger under price discounting than under revenue sharing when output and revenue are maximal and the spot price is lowest; the converse holds when output and revenue are lowest and the spot price is highest. There is, moreover, a single crossing point, so that the (algebraic) size of the difference is rising in the level of the producer's revenue. By construction, the producer obtains the same level of expected income under both alternatives; but since u is strictly concave and the proportional payment is increasing with revenue under price discounting, that alternative will be the producer's preferred option. If the negotiations over d leave him with some advantage, there will also be the indirect effect of reducing the probability of default.

By continuity, this argument will also hold if there are sufficiently few and small departures from weak monotonicity in the ordered price vector $(p_1,...,p_n)$ in relation to the ordered individual output vector $(q_1,...,q_n)$. These departures permit occasional instances in which a few vessels do fairly well when most do relatively badly; and, conversely, also when a few do rather poorly and most have relatively good landings.

Finally, where accounting is concerned, the producer's total payment to the trader is the random variable $d \cdot Q$, which is made in exchange for the services of the loan x. It is commonly called the "(implicit) interest charge," and it yields the (random) seasonal rate $d \cdot Q/x$. Surveys record the individual draws q_i over the whole sample, whereby x_i surely varies and d_i may do so. The sample averages and other summary statistics therefore conflate stochastic variation in output with variation in contractual terms, which rules out interpreting them in terms of risk bearing in any straightforward way. The same applies, mutatis mutandis, to the random quantity $(1 - \alpha)Z$ under revenue sharing.

A COMPETING COOPERATIVE SUGAR MILL

The household is a member of the cooperative. If it decides to grow cane, it must deliver the quantity q^m or incur a penalty. For its part, the mill arranges fixed financing in the amount x^m, with interest factor ρ^m. The bank that provides the loans is treated as a passive party, but it requires each loan to be secured by the borrower's land. The price net of transport charges, p^m, is also fixed at the beginning of the season. In a stationary setting in which this is also the household's only financing option when growing sugarcane, let the contract (p^m, q^m, x^m, ρ^m) yield the household the continuation value Ω^m, whereby the option of defaulting on delivery and repayment is fully considered.

The household also has the option of processing some or all of the crop into jaggery, which it can sell in the marketing center or to retailers. This it can do without incurring a penalty if its harvest exceeds q^m. Let a denote the conversion rate of cane into jaggery and c the household's unit cost of conversion. If the spot price of jaggery just after the harvest is p^j, the household will obtain the net revenue $p^j/a - c$ for each unit of cane so processed and sold as jaggery.

Now suppose the trader is active and, plausibly, fully informed about the household's dealings with the mill. If the household is a client in good standing, the trader can make the offer (α, ρ^t, x^t), conditional on the future delivery of at least q^t units of jaggery. At the time of offer, the price of jaggery is unknown; it is denoted by the variate P^j. If the household defaults on the contract to the mill, but remains in good standing with the trader, then in future it will find itself in the same position as the household in the section entitled "Contractual Terms." The trader will offer the corresponding contract, which will differ from that when the household continues to deal with the mill. Let it yield the value Ω^t.

When the crop is harvested, the household learns p^j as well as output q and has an array of options, including default on one or both contracts. The following assumptions reduce the possibilities to just two regimes.

Assumption 1: If total output covers contractual deliveries ($q \geq q^m + aq^t$), the household delivers q^m to the mill, converts the rest into jaggery, and sells all of it through the trader.

Both contracts are fulfilled, thus keeping the household in good standing with both other parties. If the price of jaggery is especially high or low, there will be the temptation to default on the delivery of cane or jaggery, respectively. The assumption implies that the associated penalties are too great for this to be attractive when $q \geq q^m + aq^t$.

Assumption 2: If $q < q^m + aq^t$, the household delivers the entire output either to the mill or, after processing, to the trader, depending on which course of action is better, taking into account that default entails ruling out future dealings with that party. It is also assumed that $q \geq \max(q^m, aq^t)$, so that at least one contract can be fulfilled.

Taking the two regimes in turn, in regime 1, the household realizes the income

$$y = p^m q^m + (\alpha p^j/a - c)(q - q^m) - (\rho^m x^m + \rho^t x^t),$$

and remains in overall good standing at the start of the next period. In regime 2,

$$y = \begin{cases} p^m q - \rho^m x^m & \text{if it delivers to the mill,} \\ (\alpha p^j/a - c)q - (\rho^m x^m + \rho^t x^t) & \text{if it delivers to the trader,} \end{cases}$$

whereby it is assumed that, with the household's land serving as collateral in such contracts, the loan to the mill's captive bank is always repaid. The trader's loan is unsecured, with only the penalty of being shut out in the future deterring the household from default if the jaggery price is sufficiently unfavorable. The household will be indifferent between these two courses of action if, and only if,

$$u(p^m q - \rho^m x^m) + \delta\Omega^m = u[(\alpha p^j/a - c)q - (\rho^m x^m + \rho^t x^t)] + \delta\Omega^t. \quad (7.8)$$

Given (a, c, q), the contractual parameters and the parametric alternatives Ω^m and Ω^t, there exists a unique value of p^j such that condition (7.8) holds. It is denoted by p^*.

The next assumption is purely technical and is made in the interest of simplicity.

Assumption 3: The variate Θ takes just two values, with associated probabilities π^1 and $(1 - \pi^1)$, whereby $\theta^1 < \theta^2$. The variates Θ and P^j are also independent.

The following restriction is also imposed.

Assumption 4: Let regime 2 come into force only in the bad state $\Theta = \theta^1$. That is,

$$\max(q^m, aq^t) < f(x^m + x^t, \theta^1) < q^m + aq^t \leq f(x^m + x^t, \theta^2).$$

With these assumptions, q in condition (7.8) may be replaced by $f(x^m + x^t, \theta^1)$, thus yielding the response of the trigger value p^* to changes in the contractual terms.

The order of moves in this game is therefore as follows. The terms offered by the cooperative are determined in advance by outside policy makers. This institution therefore moves first, and members in good standing decide whether to grow cane. Commission agents observe both these terms and farmers' decisions and then make their own exclusive offers under assumptions 1 and 2. After the harvest, the farmer decides how to allocate output between the mill and the agent with whom he has a contract, also in accordance with assumptions 1 and 2.

Of particular interest are the trader's terms. It is seen that

$$\frac{\partial p^*}{\partial \alpha} = -\frac{p^*}{\alpha}, \quad \frac{\partial p^*}{\partial \rho^t} = \frac{ax^t}{\alpha f(x^m + x^t, \theta^1)}. \tag{7.9}$$

The elasticity of p^* w.r.t. α is -1. A small rearrangement yields the elasticity w.r.t. ρ^t as the ratio of the value of the inputs financed by the trader (including interest thereon) to the value of the household's share of output, a ratio that, even in the bad state, is unlikely to exceed 1. This stronger sensitivity to α indicates that the trader's optimum may well involve setting $\rho^t = 1$, as in the section entitled "Contractual Terms."

His contract is always fulfilled, unless the bad state occurs and the realized jaggery price fails to exceed p^*, in which event the household defaults and he loses his loan. By assumption 3, the probability that $P^j < p^*$ is $\pi^* \equiv \int_{p^{j1}}^{p^*} dG(p^j)$, where the support of G is $[p^{j1}, p^{j2}]$. Hence, his contract yields the expected profit

$$E[Y^t] = (1 - \pi^1)E[(1 - \alpha)P^j(f(x^m + x^t, \theta^2) - q^m)/a] \tag{7.10}$$
$$+ \pi^1 E[(1 - \alpha)P^j f(x^m + x^t, \theta^1)/a \mid P^j \geq p^*] + [(1 - \pi^1 \pi^*)\rho^t - \bar{\rho}]x^t.$$

His optimum has the same character as that in the section entitled "Contractual terms", provided an additional condition is met. It is proved in the annex that the following condition must hold at any interior optimum:

$$(1 - \pi^1) \cdot \frac{f(x^m + x^t, \theta^2) - q^m}{f(x^m + x^t, \theta^1)} \cdot E[P^j] + \pi^1 E[P^j \mid P^j \geq p^*] = (1 - \pi^1 \pi^*)p^*, \tag{7.11}$$

where $f(x^m + x^t, \theta^2) - q^m$ and $f(x^m + x^t, \theta^1)$ are the quantities of cane processed into jaggery in the good and bad states, respectively. The l.h.s. is the expected value of a unit of jaggery, adjusting for the probability that it will be delivered; the r.h.s. is the probability that jaggery will be delivered multiplied by the trigger price.

Proposition 7.2: If $f(x^m + x^t, \theta^2) - q^m \geq f(x^m + x^t, \theta^1)$, then

(i) The trader's optimum always involves a positive probability that the household will default on the contract with him.

(ii) The loan will be interest free ($\rho^t = 1$).

Proof: If $p^* \leq p^{j1}$, then $\pi^* = 0$ and $E[P^j|P^j \geq p^*] = E[P^j] > p^*$. Hence, condition (7.11) will be violated if $f(x^m + x^t, \theta^2) - q^m \geq f(x^m + x^t, \theta^1)$. Since the l.h.s. exceeds the r.h.s. for all p^* sufficiently close to p^{j1}, the optimum will involve a positive probability of default, with $\rho^t = 1$. ∎

The sufficient condition $f(x^m + x^t, \theta^2) - q^m \geq f(x^m + x^t, \theta^1)$ can be weakened somewhat. If p^* is close to p^{j1}, then $E[P^j|P^j \geq p^*] > p^*$, and it is highly plausible that, in practice, $E(P^j)$ will exceed p^* by a substantial margin. Thus, even if deliveries of jaggery in the good state fall a bit short of those in the bad state, condition (7.11) will still hold.

There remains the matter of how the presence of the cooperative, as a third player, affects the household and the trader. The household is certainly better off if $\Omega^m > \Omega^t$, since the latter exceeds Ω^a, which is yielded by the alternative of neither growing cane nor borrowing. An exclusive contract with the mill then offers the household an improved outside option when dealing with the trader.

This competitive pressure does not, however, necessarily make the trader worse off; for the finance provided through the cooperative increases the output of cane in both states, and hence the potential supply of jaggery, on which he would earn a commission. By offering sweeter terms so as to exploit this possibility, he may be able to gain sufficient compensation for the necessity of making concessions in some form. By proposition 7.2, $\rho^t = 1$ remains optimal for changes that do not grossly violate the condition $f(x^m + x^t, \theta^2) - q^m \geq f(x^m + x^t, \theta^1)$. Recalling equation (7.10) and using the envelope theorem, we have

$$\partial E[Y^t]/\partial x^m = (1-\alpha)[(1-\pi^1)f'(x^m + x^t, \theta^2)E[P^j]/a + \pi^1 f'(x^m + x^t, \theta^1)E[P^j|P^j \geq p^*]/a] - \pi^1 x^t \partial \pi^*/\partial x^m. \tag{7.12}$$

The expression in brackets is the expected value of the marginal monetary return to finance. It is positive, which implies greater expected profits from commission fees, albeit with α close to 1. The potential drawback is the effect on the trigger price p^*: if p^* increases, the probability that the household will default and switch permanently to contracting with the cooperative will rise. The trader would lose the loan x^t.

Differentiating equation (7.8) totally and noting that $Q = f(x^m + x^t, \Theta)$, we obtain

$$\frac{\partial p^*}{\partial x^m} =$$

$$\frac{u'(\cdot^m)(p^m f'(x^m + x^t, \theta^1) - \rho^m) - u'(\cdot^t)[(\alpha p^*/a - c)f'(x^m + x^t, \theta^1) - \rho^m] + \delta\frac{\partial \Omega^m}{\partial x^m}}{u'(\cdot^t)(\alpha/a)f(x^m + x^t, \theta^1)},$$

where $u(\cdot^m) = u(p^m f(x^m + x^t, \theta^1) - \rho^m x^m)$, $u(\cdot^t) = u[(\alpha p^*/a - c)f(x^m + x^t, \theta^1) - (\rho^m x^m + x^t)]$, and $(\alpha p^*/a - c)$ is the household's net price of cane when transformed into jaggery at the trigger price p^*. It is seen that the numerator on the r.h.s. is positive or negative according as

$$u'(\cdot^m)(p^m f'(x^m + x^t, \theta^1) - \rho^m) + \delta\frac{\partial \Omega^m}{\partial x^m} \gtrless u'(\cdot^t)[(\alpha p^*/a - c)f'(x^m + x^t, \theta^1) - \rho^m].$$

Suppose $\Omega^m > \Omega^t$. It then follows from condition (7.8) that $u(\cdot^t) > u(\cdot^m)$, so that $u'(\cdot^t) < u'(\cdot^m)$. Suppose also that Ω^m is increasing in x^m, as will hold when the household has unsatisfied notional demand for credit at the regulated rate ρ^m, as surely holds in practice. Yet if $p^m f'(x^m + x^t, \theta^1) < \rho^m < (\alpha p^*/a - c)f'(x^m + x^t, \theta^1)$, the r.h.s. will be positive, whereas the sign of the l.h.s. will be ambiguous. If, further, the regulated price of cane for crushing at the mill, p^m, is sufficiently lower than $(\alpha p^*/a - c)$, then p^* will respond rather little to changes in x^m and may even be decreasing in x^m.

To complete this examination of equation (7.12), note that $\partial\pi^*/\partial x^m = (\partial p^*/\partial x^m) \cdot G'(p^*)$, where $G'(p^*)$ is the density at the trigger price. If this, too, is rather small, a policy of easing the supply of regulated credit to the cooperative's members will indeed lead to an improvement in traders' expected profits, even if p^* is (weakly) increasing in x^m. If $\Omega^m < \Omega^t$, such an outcome will occur under less restrictive conditions, since then $u'(\cdot^t) > u'(\cdot^m)$.

In a system of contestable monopolies, it remains the case that the mill's presence makes households better off if $\Omega^m > \Omega^t$. Traders' expected profits will be zero, mill or no mill, but the terms of the private contracts, other than $\rho^t = 1$, will respond to an increase in x^m. Equation (7.10) may be written

$$E[Y^t] = (1-\alpha)A(x^m, x^t; \theta^1, \theta^2, \pi^1; G; \cdot) + ((1-\pi^1\pi^*) - \overline{\rho})x^t = 0:$$

the expected losses on lending $(1 - \pi^1\pi^* - \overline{\rho} < 0)$ are exactly balanced by the expected income from commission fees. In the event that x^m increases, suppose the household lowers x^t by the same amount, thus keeping $x^m + x^t$ constant. Then, if π^* does not change, neither will A, and losses from lending will fall, so that the condition $E[Y^t] = 0$ will require a reduced commission rate $(1 - \alpha)$. Now, the trigger price p^*, and hence π^*, is decreasing in α. An increase in α will therefore reduce losses from lending, and it will also increase A, both ceteris paribus. It follows that an increase in x^m will lead to a reduction in the commission rate, though in view of the strict concavity of f, it will not induce a full one-for-one reduction in x^t.

These conclusions will also hold if the interest factor ρ^t sticks not at 1, but at some level less than $\overline{\rho}/(1 - \pi^1\pi^*)$; for there must be expected losses on lending to balance the necessarily positive expected income from commission fees.

A NUMERICAL EXAMPLE

As in chapters 5 and 6, it is useful to support and illustrate the theory by constructing a robust example, beginning here with the production technology. When the household decides to grow cane, the plots in question cannot be sown to other crops, but the holding is perfectly divisible. Let land and the inputs denoted by x be strict complements in cane cultivation. In view of the presence of fixed family factors such as management and husbandry skills, however, the state-contingent level of output of cane is not proportional to x. The output of cane yielded by x is denoted by the variate Θx^ξ, where $\xi < 1$. Producing it involves not only the cost of x plus any interest thereon, but also the opportunity cost γx units of perfectly certain income. Let the alternative crop require only family resources and be risk free.

The contract with the mill involves the guaranteed net price of cane, p^m, the minimum quantity to be delivered, q^m, the financing of x^m, and the interest factor ρ^m, whereby q^m is determined by the household's number of shares, with an administrative rule then yielding x^m. In the event that the household can deal only with the mill, its income will be $Y = \Theta x^\xi - (\rho^m + \gamma)x + y^a$, where y^a is the level of its income when it produces only the alternative crop, and the pledging of its land as collateral ensures that it will always repay the loan needed to cultivate cane.

Let the constellation of parameter values be as follows:

$$\theta^1 = 1,\ \theta^2 = 1.5,\ \pi^1 = 0.1,\ \xi = 0.8,\ \gamma = 0.7,\ p^m = 1.8,\ q^m = 0.425,\ x^m = 0.4,\ \rho^m = 1.1.$$

Output in the bad state is $1 \cdot 0.4^{0.8} = 0.4804 > q^m$. Thus the household is always able to fulfill its quota. Let $y^a = 0.5$. As a member of the cooperative, if it decides to grow cane, it must do so under the above terms. Its income will be the variate

$$Y = \begin{cases} 1.8 \cdot 0.4^{0.8} - (1.1 + 0.7) \cdot 0.4 + 0.5 = 0.6448 & \text{with prob. } 0.1, \\ 1.8 \cdot 1.5 \cdot 0.4^{0.8} - (1.1 + 0.7) \cdot 0.4 + 0.5 = 1.0772 & \text{with prob. } 0.9, \end{cases}$$

Let the household's preferences over one-period lotteries be represented by the von Neumann–Morgenstern utility function $u = \ln y$. The expected utility of the above lottery is 0.0230 utils, whose certainty-equivalent income of 1.023 exceeds that of growing the alternative crop, $y^a = 0.5$, by a substantial margin. It should be noted that the value of the marginal product of x in the bad state, $0.8 \cdot 1.8 \cdot 1 \cdot 0.4^{-0.2} = 1.730$, falls barely short of its certain marginal cost—namely, 1.8. Since $\theta^2 = 1.5$ and $1 - \pi^1 = 0.9$, it follows that the fixed offer $x^m = 0.4$ leaves the household heavily credit rationed.

Now consider an exclusive contract with a commission agent who, in view of the discussion following proposition 7.2, charges the commission rate $1 - \alpha$ on the value of sales of jaggery, but no interest on the loan ($\rho^t = 1$). In view of what farmers had to say in Chittoor Taluk, let the rate be 0.045. Let the price of jaggery, P^j, be the binomial variate taking the values (20, 30), each with probability 0.5; and let P^j and Θ be independent. The conversion rate of cane into jaggery is $a = 10$; the unit cost of conversion is $c = 0.2$. These values yield the household's net prices of jaggery at the farm gate, namely, (18, 28). There are also the transport costs of getting the product to market, which are assumed to be "iceberg" in nature, at 1.5 percent of the value of jaggery delivered. Let the agent offer an x^t such that the contractual delivery q^t is feasible in the bad state. Ruling out the possibility of default for the moment, the household's income is then

$$Y = \begin{cases} 0.94 \cdot (18/10) \cdot (x^t)^{0.8} - (1+0.7)x^t + 0.5 & \text{with prob. } 0.05, \\ 0.94 \cdot (28/10) \cdot (x^t)^{0.8} - (1+0.7)x^t + 0.5 & \text{with prob. } 0.05, \\ 0.94 \cdot (18/10) \cdot 1.5 \cdot (x^t)^{0.8} - (1+0.7)x^t + 0.5 & \text{with prob. } 0.45, \\ 0.94 \cdot (28/10) \cdot 1.5 \cdot (x^t)^{0.8} - (1+0.7)x^t + 0.5 & \text{with prob. } 0.45. \end{cases}$$

The commission agent's expected profit from this contract is, ruling out default, $0.045 \cdot E[P^j \cdot \Theta \cdot (x^t)^{0.8}] + (1 - \bar{\rho}^t)x^t$. The tales in chapters 2 and 3 suggest that the value $\bar{\rho}^t = 1.2$ is plausible. Now, let competition among agents be so sharp that expected profits are driven down to zero. This condition yields $x^t = 0.36$. Substituting this value into the above lottery for the household's income, the resulting expected utility is 0.2039 utils, whose certainty-equivalent income is 1.2261. This so greatly exceeds the alternative of defaulting on the loan of $x = 0.36$, attempting to sell independently, and being shut out of any dealings with all other agents for ever after, that the household is not only always able, but also very willing, to fulfill its obligations. Even so, it is also strongly credit rationed. For his part, the agent sets q^t notionally at $0.42 < 0.4^{0.8} = 0.442$, so that the contractual delivery can always be met.

To complete the story, consider a household currently in good standing with both the mill and commission agents. The mill's officials are in no position to verify how its members stand in the private market, so it simply makes the foregoing offer ($p^m = 1.8$, $x^m = 0.4$, $q^m = 0.425$, $\rho = 1.1$) to all qualified members. The agent is assumed to be fully aware of this and makes the household an offer of supplementary financing. Competition among agents keeps the commission rate unchanged at 0.045, but the condition that expected profits be zero will almost surely induce a value of x^t other than the value 0.36 that holds when the contract is exclusive. For under assumption 1, all output in excess of q^m is processed into jaggery when the household fulfills both contractual obligations, and under assumption 2, the whole of output is processed if the household defaults on those with the mill; and in both events, output depends on the level of total financing: $\Theta(x^m + x^t)^{0.8}$. It follows that the mill's offer favors the agent with a pecuniary externality.

Given the whole constellation of parameter values assumed above, an exclusive arrangement with the agent is better for the household than one with the mill. Hence, if the household is unable to meet its contractual deliveries to both the mill and the agent, it will default on the former, and by assumption, the agent is fully aware of this fact. Suppose output in the bad state is so low that a default must occur. The agent's expected profit is then

$$0.045 \cdot \{E[P^j \cdot \Theta \cdot (0.4 + x^t)^{0.8} - 0.425 | \Theta = 1.5] + E[P^j \cdot \Theta \cdot (0.4 + x^t)^{0.8} | \Theta = 1]\}$$
$$+ (1 - \bar{\rho}^t)x^t.$$

This expression is zero when $x^t = 0.375$, that is, a slight increase over the value 0.36 under an exclusive deal. Now, with this combined level of financing, output in the bad state is $(0.4 + 0.375)^{0.8} = 0.8155 < q^m + q^t = 0.425 + 0.42$, so that the household will indeed default on its contractual obligations to the mill when the bad state occurs, but not otherwise. That is to say, the mill faces a default rate of $\pi^1 = 0.1$.

For its part, the household will face the corresponding one-period lottery (the details are omitted), which yields an expected utility of 0.3469 utils, whose certainty-equivalent income of 1.4146 exceeds those obtained under the exclusive deals.

To sum up: in the above setting, the contractual preference of a household in good standing with both the mill and commission agents is, in descending order, a contract with both, then with the agent alone, then with the mill alone, and, finally, cultivation of the alternative crop. Moral hazard arises from the household's ability to choose which contract to honor when it is unable to honor both.

It is seen that the attractiveness of dealing with the agent in that setting stems from the favorable distribution of jaggery prices in comparison with the guaranteed mill price. With a distribution of P^j that does not stochastically dominate p^m, as above, defaulting to the agent instead of the mill when output does not suffice to cover both contractual deliveries can become the preferred option. The agent then offers a much less generous level of financing, since he will lose the loan itself with probability $\pi^1 = 0.1$. Proceeding as above, it can be shown that when P^j

takes the values (17, 27) instead of (20, 30), for example, it is the agent who will suffer the default. The details of the calculation are omitted.

In practice, the mill has other legal measures at its disposal to try to enforce contractual deliveries, as the accounts in chapters 2 and 3 reveal. In Andhra Pradesh in 1980, however, they were not always up to the task.

ANNEX 7A THE TERMS OF THE PRIVATE CONTRACT: PROOFS

Exclusive monopoly: The trader's optimum

Rearranging the f.o.c. and noting that $\pi(z^d) = \int_{z^1}^{z^d} dG(z)$, we obtain

$$\frac{\partial \pi / \partial \alpha}{\partial \pi / \partial \rho} = \frac{\partial z^d / \partial \alpha}{\partial z^d / \partial \rho} = -\frac{E[Z(x) | Z \geq z^d]}{(1 - \pi(z^d))z^d}. \tag{7A.1}$$

Total differentiation of the trigger condition (7.1) holding x constant yields

$$u'(\alpha z^d - \rho x) \cdot (\alpha dz^d + z^d d\alpha - x d\rho) + \delta[(\partial \Omega^c / \partial \alpha) d\alpha + (\partial \Omega^c / \partial \rho) d\rho] = u'(z^d) \cdot dz^d.$$

Hence,

$$\frac{\partial z^d}{\partial \alpha} = -\frac{u'(\alpha z^d - \rho x)z^d + \delta \partial \Omega^c / \partial \alpha}{\alpha u'(\alpha z^d - \rho x) - u'(z^d)} \quad \text{and} \quad \frac{\partial z^d}{\partial \rho} = \frac{u'(\alpha z^d - \rho x)x + \delta \partial \Omega^c / \partial \rho}{\alpha u'(\alpha z^d - \rho x) - u'(z^d)}.$$

From equation (7.2),

$$\partial \Omega^c / \partial \alpha = \frac{\partial V / \partial \alpha + \delta(\Omega^a - \Omega^c / (1 - \delta + \delta \pi)) \cdot (\partial \pi / \partial \alpha)}{(1 - \delta + \delta \pi)},$$

where $\partial \pi / \partial \alpha = G'(z^d) \cdot \partial z^d / \partial \alpha$ and

$$\partial V / \partial \alpha = [u'(z^d) - u'(\alpha z^d - \rho x)]G'(z^d)(\partial z^d / \partial \alpha) + E[u'(\alpha Z - \rho x | Z \geq z^d) \cdot Z].$$

Hence,

$$u'(\alpha z^d - \rho x)z^d + \delta \frac{\partial \Omega^c}{\partial \alpha}$$

$$= \frac{(1 - \delta + \delta \pi)u'(\alpha z^d - \rho x)z^d + \delta E[u'(\alpha Z - \rho x | Z \geq z^d) \cdot Z] + \Lambda \frac{\partial \pi}{\partial \alpha}}{1 - \delta + \delta \pi},$$

where $\Lambda \equiv [\delta(\Omega^a - \Omega^c / (1 - \delta + \delta \pi)) + u'(z^d)]G'(z^d)(\partial z^d / \partial \alpha)$. Likewise,

$$u'(\alpha z^d - \rho x)x + \delta \frac{\partial \Omega^c}{\partial \rho}$$

$$= \frac{(1 - \delta + \delta \pi)u'(\alpha z^d - \rho x)x + \delta E[u'(\alpha Z - \rho x | Z \geq z^d)] \cdot x + \Lambda \frac{\partial \pi}{\partial \rho}}{1 - \delta + \delta \pi}.$$

Substituting into $\partial z^d/\partial\alpha$ and $\partial z^d/\partial\rho$ and collecting terms involving π (equivalently, z^d), we obtain

$$\frac{\partial z^d/\partial\alpha}{\partial z^d/\partial\rho}=-\frac{(1-\delta+\delta\pi)u'(\alpha z^d-\rho x)z^d+\delta E[u'(\alpha Z-\rho x|Z\geq z^d)\cdot Z]}{(1-\delta+\delta\pi)u'(\alpha z^d-\rho x)x+\delta E[u'(\alpha Z-\rho x|Z\geq z^d)]\cdot x},$$

and hence, from equation (7A.1), condition (7.6):

$$\frac{(1-\delta+\delta\pi)u'(\alpha z^d-\rho x)z^d+\delta E[u'(\alpha Z-\rho x|Z\geq z^d)\cdot Z]}{(1-\delta+\delta\pi)u'(\alpha z^d-\rho x)+\delta E[u'(\alpha Z-\rho x|Z\geq z^d)]}=\frac{(1-\pi(z^d))E[Z(x)]}{\pi(z^d)}.$$

The general case: Bargaining

Given their respective bargaining strengths, the parties reach agreement on (x,α,ρ), yielding the trader the payoff $E[Y^{t,b}]$. Since the Nash solution is Pareto-efficient, (α,ρ) must solve problem (7.7), now under the condition that the trader obtain at least $E[Y^{t,b}]$.

The associated Lagrangian is

$$\Phi=\Omega^c+\lambda\{E[(1-\alpha)Z(x)+\rho x|Z\geq z^d]-\bar{\rho}x-E[Y^{t,b}]\}.$$

Assuming an interior solution and recalling equations (7.4) and (7.5), we obtain

$$\frac{\partial\Omega^c/\partial\alpha}{\partial\Omega^c/\partial\rho}=-\frac{E[Z(x)|Z\geq z^d]-[(1-\alpha)z^d+\rho x]G'(z^d)\frac{\partial z^d}{\partial\alpha}}{(1-\pi(z^d))x-[(1-\alpha)z^d+\rho x]G'(z^d)\frac{\partial z^d}{\partial\rho}}.$$

Suppose $\pi=0$. Then, from equation (7.2),

$$\frac{\partial\Omega^c/\partial\alpha}{\partial\Omega^c/\partial\rho}=\frac{\partial V/\partial\alpha}{\partial V/\partial\rho}=-\frac{E[u'\cdot Z]}{E[u'\cdot x]}.$$

The ratio of the derivatives of EY^t reduces to $-E[Z/x]$, so that an interior solution implies

$$\frac{E[u'\cdot Z]}{E[u'\cdot x]}=E[Z/x],$$

but since u is strictly concave, this cannot hold. It follows that the contract will involve a strictly positive probability of default, with $\rho=1$.

The trader's optimum in the presence of the cooperative

Assuming an interior solution, the f.o.c. w.r.t. α and ρ^t are, respectively,

$$\frac{\partial E[Y^t]}{\partial\alpha}=-\{(1-\pi^1)[f(x^m+x^t,\theta^2)+q^m]E[P^j/a]-\pi^1 f(x^m+x^t,\theta^1)E[P^j/a|P^j\geq p^*]\}$$

$$+\pi^1(1-\alpha)f(x^m+x^t,\theta^1)\frac{\partial E[P^j/a|P^j\geq p^*]}{\partial\alpha}-\pi^1\rho^t x^t\frac{\partial\pi^*}{\partial\alpha}$$

$$\equiv\Gamma_\alpha-\pi^1\rho^t x^t\frac{\partial\pi^*}{\partial\alpha}=0$$

and

$$\frac{\partial E[Y^t]}{\partial \rho^t} = \pi^1(1-\alpha)f(x^m + x^t, \theta^1)\frac{\partial E[P^j/a \mid P^j \geq p^*]}{\partial \rho^t} + (1 - \pi^1\pi^*)x^t - \pi^1\rho^t x^t \frac{\partial \pi^*}{\partial \rho^t}$$

$$\equiv \Gamma_{\rho^t} - \pi^1\rho^t x^t \frac{\partial \pi^*}{\partial \rho^t} = 0.$$

Noting that $\partial \pi^*/\partial \alpha = G'(p^*)\partial p^*/\partial \alpha$ and $\partial \pi^*/\partial \rho^t = G'(p^*)\partial p^*/\partial \rho^t$ and recalling decision problem (7.9), the f.o.c. imply

$$\frac{\partial \pi^*/\partial \alpha}{\partial \pi^*/\partial \rho^t} = \frac{-p^* f(x^m + x^t, \theta^1)}{ax^t} = \frac{\Gamma_\alpha}{\Gamma_{\rho^t}}.$$

Cross-multiplying, simplifying, and using $\partial E[P^j/a \mid P^j \geq p^*]/\partial \alpha = -p^* G'(p^*) \cdot \partial p^*/\partial \alpha$, we obtain equation (7.11).

NOTES

1. An educated, articulate, and well-informed man, he subscribed to *Finance and Development*.
2. Olsen (1993), however, reports such terms in connection with the marketing of groundnuts in a village in Rayalaseema.
3. The expectation relates here and in places below to an interval of the support of the variate in question. Thus if Z has the cumulative distribution function $G(z)$ with support $[z^1, z^2]$, then $E[u(Z(x)) \mid Z < z^d)] = \int_{z^1}^{z^d} u(z)dG(z)$, whereas simply $E[u(Z(x))] = \int_{z^1}^{z^2} u(z)dG(z)$ when there is no such restriction. This abuse of notation is committed in the interest of a more compact presentation.
4. The voluntary choice of default is not among the diverse variations of contractual possibilities under interlinking treated in Bell (1999), an essay contributed to the festschrift honoring Srinivasan, edited by Ranis and Raut (1999).
5. Drawing on Subbarao's (1978) account of the marketing of paddy in Andhra Pradesh, Zusman (1989) analyzes competition between a miller's agent, who buys at a fixed price, and a commission agent, who seeks out high-paying buyers, charging paddy producers a fee for his services. Paddy producers have fixed quantities to sell, but face a distribution of prices when dealing with the commission agent. The influence of the number of producers on the set of contracts in equilibrium is analyzed using a one-period Nash-Cournot game. There is, however, no lending.
6. Riekhof (2019) states that prices were discounted, but does not specify exactly in what form.

REFERENCES

Aleem, I. 1990. "Imperfect Information, Screening, and the Costs of Informal Lending: A Study of a Rural Credit Market in Pakistan." *World Bank Economic Review* 4 (3): 329–49.

Bell, C. 1999. "Explaining Interlinking." In *Trade, Growth, and Development: Essays in Honour of Professor T.N. Srinivasan*, edited by G. Ranis and L. Raut, 395–418. Amsterdam: North-Holland.

Bell, C., T. N. Srinivasan, and C. Udry. 1997. "Rationing, Spillover, and Interlinking in Credit Markets: The Case of Rural Punjab." *Oxford Economic Papers* 49 (October): 557–85.

Gangopadhyay, S., and K. Sengupta. 1987. "Small Farmers, Moneylenders, and Trading Activity." *Oxford Economic Papers* 39 (2): 333–42.

Koo, H., C. Huang, and K. Kan. 2012. "Interlinked Contracts: An Empirical Study." *Economica* 79 (314): 350–77.

Olsen, W. 1993. "Competition and Power in Rural Markets: A Case Study from Andhra Pradesh." *IDS Bulletin* 24 (3): 83–89.

Parappurathu, S., C. Ramachandrana, K. K. Baijua, and A. K. Xavier. 2019. "Formal Versus Informal: Insights into the Credit Transactions of Small-Scale Fishers along the South West Coast of India." *Marine Policy* 103 (May): 101–12.

Platteau, J.-P., and A. Abraham. 1987. "An Inquiry into Quasi-Credit Contracts: The Role of Reciprocal Credit and Interlinked Deals in Small-Scale Fishing Communities." *Journal of Development Studies* 23 (4): 362–90.

Ranis, G., and L. Raut, eds. 1999. *Trade, Growth, and Development: Essays in Honour of Professor T. N. Srinivasan*. Amsterdam: North-Holland.

Riekhof, M.-C. 2019. "The Insurance Premium in the Interest Rates of Interlinked Loans in a Small-Scale Fishery." *Environment and Development Economics* 24 (1): 87–112.

Subbarao, K. 1978. *Rice Marketing Systems in Andhra Pradesh*. New Delhi: Allied Publishers/ Institute of Economic Growth.

Zusman, P. 1989. "Peasants' Risk Aversion and the Choice of Marketing Intermediaries. A Bargaining Theory of Equilibrium Marketing Contracts." In *The Economic Theory of Agrarian Institutions*, edited by P. K. Bardhan, 297–316. Oxford: Clarendon Press.

8 Conclusions

A study of actual contracting should provide a description of the contractual forms encountered, their incidence and terms, and the environmental, cultural, and legal setting in which contracting takes place. It should also, if possible, go beyond description—essential though that is—by explaining why the parties chose as they did and how the terms of their contracts were determined. The present study of rural Andhra Pradesh in the drought-afflicted period of the early 1980s has revealed not only diverse contractual forms in the markets for labor, tenancies, and crops, but also their interplay with access to credit and its terms. The ensuing formal attempts to explain these alternative arrangements and the choices among them are partly inductive, drawing on what respondents had to say about their options and decisions as well as received theory.

Four topics have been treated in detail: first, the choice between employment as a casual laborer and as an attached farm servant; second, the choice between sharecropping and fixed rents paid in kind, with special reference to land irrigated by percolation wells; third, the closely related matter of loans, subsidies, and corruption in connection with the profitability of investments in wells; and fourth, the tying of loans for the cultivation of commercial crops to the arrangements for marketing them. Some of the findings and lessons are familiar; most involve the importance of villagers' outside options and access to credit.

A preliminary matter to be discussed are the interviews conducted in the two tours as a method of investigation. A trip to the field at the outset yields first-hand experience of the people and the setting to be studied. It is almost universally accepted that such experience is advantageous. What should be emphasized is its potential inductive value in thinking broadly about the research problem at hand. The particular opportunity such a trip offers to revise and refine the questionnaires to be used in the subsequent surveys is important, but rather derivative. A tour toward the close of the survey work enables a fuller exploitation of this potential value because the respondents will have become accustomed to answering and reflecting on questions about their activities. Most people like to talk about how they see things and at least some of their doings; and the researcher, however experienced, will likely meet with a surprise or two in what they have to say. Now, it is conceded that respondents might tell the researcher what they think he or she would like to hear, especially when the line of questioning concerns motives. Yet any reasons for them to mislead would also apply when answering the field enumerators as the latter are canvassing the questionnaires. At all events, the approaches and analyses in chapters 5, 6, and 7 arise from, and depend on, the tales in chapters 2 and 3 in an essential way, but not, in various respects, on the survey data themselves.

Turning now to specific topics, first, attached farm servants are no longer a salient feature of India's rural economy. This is due, in part, to the great improvements in wages and job prospects wrought by rapid growth and the structural transformation of the Indian economy over the past four decades. Such improvements yield smoother earnings over the course of a year, but they do not do away with the need to smooth consumption across years. Here, the development of the financial system and the growing creditworthiness of the poor come into play. Both were notably weak in those earlier times, but if outlays on marriages and ceremonies have kept pace with real wages, the pressure to enter into indentured arrangements will not have ebbed away.

Where theory is concerned, the preoccupation with perpetual bonded labor in much of the literature seems misplaced in light of these developments, especially as villagers have come to enjoy opportunities in the growing nonfarm economy. The growth of India's cities has also provided footloose rural debtors with ample, permanent hiding places beyond the reach of their rural creditors, thus introducing the real possibility of willful default at tolerable cost and hence a source of moral hazard not considered in that literature. Motivated by the accounts in chapters 2 and 3, chapter 5 emphasizes smoothing consumption when earnings from casual agricultural work are risky. A rollover or two of debt may occur, but not enduring servitude. Those accounts also revealed an important consideration that has been neglected in theoretical work. If a member of the family is engaged as an attached farm servant, then that individual becomes subservient to another man, an odious burden that is, to all intents and purposes, a private bad for the individual so engaged. This fact makes bargaining within the household highly likely, and its treatment in chapter 5 is correspondingly quite lengthy.

The second topic involves the choice of tenancy contract. Here, too, a preliminary remark is in order. Attempts to suppress tenancy are misguided, not least because landowners are adept at evading the law's provisions. Tenants' interests are best served by improvements in their outside options, and with these interests secured, tenancy—moderately regulated—is a socially useful institution.

The risk-sharing advantages of share contracts in semiarid zones emerged in what, at first sight, is a rather surprising way. Percolation wells depend on recharge from monsoonal rains. If paddy is cultivated instead of, say, sorghum, the provision of irrigation will have induced greater, not smaller, risk. Thus, if the plots were leased, sharecropping was normally chosen. At the same time, there is strong evidence that the potential drawback of Marshallian inefficiency was actually at work in Andhra Pradesh. In contrast, there is no such evidence that allocative efficiency under fixed-rent leases, which ruled on unirrigated land, was inferior to that under owner-cultivation. The twist arises from the option value of delaying the choice of crop until fairly early in the cultivation cycle. That value is virtually nil on dryland or plots under assured irrigation, but it could be significant when power supplies for pumping out of deep tube wells are erratic and the aquifers, like those in Andhra Pradesh, are shallow.

This option has a central place in chapter 6, which also addresses in detail the closely related topic of the profitability of investing in percolation wells. Farmers made heavy investments of this kind in the decades leading up to the early 1990s, and, in order to finance them, they had to borrow from public institutions. Profitability was not, however, a purely technical matter. Digging a trial pit to establish whether water is available opens the door to a potential holdup problem when official verification is required. Some classes of borrowers were also eligible for subsidies. Now, subsidizing loans, especially in the form of rebates, is strongly undesirable when greasing the wheels of bureaucracy is an established part of doing business. All manner of parties are drawn to the pot, and in dividing up the contents among themselves, they perpetuate the practice and culture of corruption.[1] Farmers had to weigh all these considerations when making their decisions.

The analysis of leasing and investment decisions in chapter 6 points to their sensitivity to the severity and probability of droughts. This analysis carries a lesson for public policy. Responding to successive droughts, the government of Andhra Pradesh declared a moratorium on debt repayments in 1981, which leads to the following idea. If a law were enacted under which a moratorium would come into force whenever some index of rainfall fell below a suitable threshold value, fixed-rent leases would become more attractive to tenants, thus promoting efficiency, so defined. Such a moratorium would also promote investment in wells, without affording officials any direct opportunities to extract bribes. Advocating such a rule as a rather crude, but simple, form of crop insurance is not at all the same thing as condoning politicians' opportunistic promises to forgive debts, egregious examples of which have occurred with dismaying regularity in the runup to elections over the past three decades. The proposed law would make the exercise of discretion more difficult.

The fourth topic deals with trade and finance, which are natural partners. Where contractual terms are concerned, decisions have to be made regarding the minimum quantity to be delivered and its timing, the levels of interest and commission rates, and the discount on the spot price. Treating all of them simultaneously poses a formidable challenge, which has not been attempted—here or elsewhere. One particular puzzle is that, in practice, some contracts call for loans at no interest. As proved in chapter 7, this will hold when the trader is risk neutral, even in the presence of the moral hazard that arises when the farmer can default. Furthermore, under fairly weak assumptions, the trader will prefer to discount the spot price rather than to charge a proportion of the total value of the delivery at that price.

As with the regulation of tenancy, the right way to deal with traders and commission agents is not to try to drive them out of the business of lending altogether but rather to weaken their hold on cultivators by improving the cultivators' outside options. The latter can be achieved not only by developing the organized financial system, but also by providing properly regulated markets in commodities. Conversely, cultivators are less at the mercy of public and bank officials when the latter are held in check by competition from traders and commission agents. The interplay of the dealings between farmers, commission agents, and a cooperative sugar mill in Chittoor District illustrates all of this quite persuasively.

It is fitting to close by returning to a broader aim of the original project—namely, to understand how agricultural development affects poverty in India. This aim should be seen in light of the general development of the Indian economy up to that time. The so-called "Hindu rate of growth," with fluctuations around a trend rate of about 3.5 percent a year, had ruled since independence in 1947, and there were no especially compelling grounds to suppose that this would change. In fact, an acceleration did occur early in the 1980s, and after some fits and starts, an underlying secular rate of 6 to 7 percent had set in by the mid-1990s and has continued to the present. As noted in chapter 1, this great improvement in aggregate productivity and the structural changes that accompanied it have provided India's rural population in the interim with opportunities that were quite out of reach 40 years ago. The outside option has become more tangible and attractive. Many have exercised it, and those who have stayed behind have been able to strike better deals in their transactions because of it. In concentrating on measures to promote agricultural development, and thus to combat rural poverty directly, Srinivasan and I proceeded on the premise that relying on an improvement in the economy's aggregate economic performance would not suffice. I do not recant this position, but it must be said that we had the "Hindu rate of growth" in mind. Macroeconomic developments matter, even when the population is heavily rural.

Moving to the other end of this economic spectrum, it is widely accepted that an individual's experience of poverty involves more than the failure to acquire, by one means or another, some given basket of goods, important though it is to have some such yardstick to measure the incidence of poverty in society at-large. Acute want will often force wrenching decisions. The attached farm servant who receives his meals and a loan does so at the price of being at another man's constant beck and call, an indignity whose burden does not appear in the official statistics. A poor household eligible for a particular subsidy must often give various officials a cut in order to get it. Compounding this violation of its right to the subsidy is the galling experience of negotiating the bureaucratic obstacle course. More egregious still are reports that, during Andhra Pradesh's second microfinance institution (MFI) crisis, field staff of at least one institution made suggestive comments about the debtors' daughters, both an outrage in itself and a clear pointer to what sometimes comes to pass. (As in life, so in literature; on such a theme, see Huq 1990 and, in nineteenth-century Normandy, de Maupassant [1881] 2010.) Nor is the experience of poverty in the present nicely confined to present events. Suffering distress this year may well awaken and sharpen the anxiety that distress will also follow in the next. Going into the field, then, can deliver a timely reminder that the condition of poverty presents more than one grim visage. Through diligent inquiry, the telling of such encounters might indicate what measures could ward them off.

NOTE

1. For a mordant assault on subsidies in the United States, especially those benefiting corporations, see Zingales (2012). Some of what he has to say applies equally well, mutatis mutandis, to humbler settings.

REFERENCES

de Maupassant, G. (1881) 2010. "La maison Tellier." In *La Maison Tellier*. Reprint, Whitefish, MT: Kessinger Publishing.

Huq, H. A. 1990. "The Daughter and the Oleander." In *Women, Outcastes, Peasants, and Rebels: A Selection of Bengali Short Stories,* edited by K. Bardhan. Berkeley, CA: University of California Press.

Zingales, L. 2012. "When Business and Government Are Bedfellows." *The Economist* (blog), August 23, 2012. http://www.economist.com/blogs/prospero/2012/08/quick-study-luigi -zingalescrony-capitalism.